OPERA AND POLITICS

Opera and Politics

From Monteverdi to Henze

JOHN BOKINA

Yale University Press   *New Haven & London*

Published with assistance from the Louis Stern Memorial Fund.

Designed by James J. Johnson and set in Monotype Van Dijck type by The Composing
Room of Michigan, Inc., Grand Rapids, Michigan.
Printed in the United States of America

Library of Congress Cataloging-in-Publication Data

Bokina, John.
Opera and politics : from Monteverdi to Henze / John Bokina.
p.   cm.
Includes bibliographical references and index.
ISBN 0–300–06935–9 (cloth)

1. Opera—Political aspects.   I. Title.
ML1700.B74   1997
782.1'09—dc21   96–53455

A catalogue record for this book is available from the British Library.

The paper in this book meets the guidelines for permanence and durability of the
Committee on Production Guidelines for Book Longevity of the Council on Library
Resources.

10 9 8 7 6 5 4 3 2 1

To Sarah

Contents

Preface

In my junior year of undergraduate studies in political science, I met the professor who has had the greatest impact on the course of my intellectual life. Richard Norton of the University of Illinois–Chicago was a musicologist, not a political scientist, and with his help I encountered what was for me a new and magnificent world of music. I experienced opera: a Chicago Symphony concert performance of *Das Rheingold* that left me literally gasping for breath; the poignancy of Wotan's farewell in a Lyric Opera *Die Walküre*. The language of addiction is appropriate here. I was hooked. My first operatic love was Richard Wagner; Claudio Monteverdi and Wolfgang Amadeus Mozart soon followed.

I suppose that I was a budding political intellectual even then. Within my new musical love, I had no interest in the cult of singers and singing. I didn't care about rivalries between tenors or sopranos. I couldn't tell whether the tenor hit or missed the high C. These things seemed fetishistic, a fixation on a part of the experience at the expense of the operatic whole. I reveled in opera as an aural and visual spectacle, but I wanted to link the sensuousness of the operatic experience to the realm of ideas. What did these splendid works tell us about the meaning of political and social life? More important, what vision did they have about what that life could and should be like? Is opera only a moment of respite in a still suffering world, or is it a source of indelible images that allow us to glimpse a possible better future? These are certainly not the concerns of all opera fans, but they were, and remain, my concerns.

Given my interest in political ideas, I found the available

literature on opera disappointing. There was, of course, the work of Theodor W. Adorno. His looming influence still inspires and constrains any late-twentieth-century attempt to decipher the political meaning of opera, including this one. Otherwise, the subject fell through the cracks in the division of labor that exists among scholars and their disciplines. Musicologists tended to treat political factors as a debasement of the intrinsic value of operatic artworks, whereas political theorists, perhaps daunted by the alleged abstractness of music, have eschewed analytical works on opera.

From the numerical mysticism of Pythagoras through romantic aestheticism to contemporary scientific musicology, the dominant Western conceptions have tended to view music as an autonomous phenomenon divorced from the other spheres of life. The notion that literature, drama, and film both reflect and shape their political environments gradually secured a niche in the other humanistic disciplines. But lacking this fundamental and indispensable notion, mainstream musicology severed the artwork from its place within culture and society. Instead of emphasizing the relation of an opera to its historical era, the autonomist approach focused on the formal and stylistic particularities of the work, especially as these revealed themselves through the technical analysis of operatic scores. In this approach, political history stopped at the boundaries of the musical artwork. The political dimensions of music were treated as anecdotes: context perhaps, but never content; the stuff for opening chapters on composers' "lives and times"; a humanistic prelude to an objective, scientific analysis of a score understood as a primal thing-in-itself. There may be vague associations between Mozart and the Enlightenment or Beethoven and the French Revolution. But these references, with their lack of any nuanced articulation of the connections, were little more than cultural shorthand for associating the icons of classical composition with the heroic eras of bourgeois politics.

In recent years, however, the situation has changed. Musicology has experienced a return of the repressed. Critical theory, semiology, poststructuralism, feminism, and ethnomusicology have punctured the vaunted autonomy of music in general and opera in particular.[1] In many contemporary musicological studies, opera has become a political text.

I watch the fate of politics within contemporary musicology with interest but no sense of urgency, for I am an outsider to the debates. I am more concerned with the state of research within my own field, the history of political theory. In order to explore the political dimensions of opera, musicology has had to overcome its traditional conception of the autonomy of music. The task for political theory is different. In order to appreciate opera as a significant embodiment of political ideas, political theory has had to recover an old insight: art and music have an intrinsic political importance.

Quentin Skinner opens his two-volume opus, *The Foundations of Modern Political Thought*, with a complaint and a plea. He bemoans political theorists' preoccupation with formal political texts and tracts. The authors of these texts discuss the "problems of political life at a level of abstraction and intelligence unmatched by any of their contemporaries." Skinner argues that it is only by going beyond the esotericism of strictly textual analysis, by surrounding the "classic texts with their appropriate ideological context," that we can begin to construct a "history of political theory with a genuinely historical character."[2] In other words, the political ideas of an age are not confined to formal texts of political theory but are embodied in a variety of cultural forms. There is some truth to Skinner's complaint, and bearing in mind that my colleagues in the political and social sciences may not be familiar with these operatic cultural forms, I have provided a plot summary and some background information for each of the twelve operas that I analyze in this book.

But to a limited extent, Skinner's plea has already been answered. There has been significant work on political ideas in some of the arts: classical Greek tragedies, Shakespeare's plays, and modern novels and films. And, in addition to the efforts of Adorno, there are important theoretical precedents for similar work on music. Plato prescribed the politically acceptable and unacceptable musical modes for his ideal Republic. Augustine performed the same task for the music of the early church. Jean-Jacques Rousseau intervened in the eighteenth-century operatic "quarrel of the buffoons," composing *Le devin du village*, a model French-language opera in his favored Italian *buffa* style. Max Weber correlated musical tonalities with the evolution of social structures. Allan Bloom's recent polemics against rock music revived the old Platonic notion that music is a crucial factor in determining the health of the polity.[3]

In this context, I have set about writing the book about opera that I always wanted to read. *Opera and Politics* is the work of a political scientist, a political theorist, who loves opera. Here I use my training in the history of political theory in order to highlight neglected aspects and meanings of works from the several periods of the history of opera: baroque, early classical, late classical, romantic, early modernist, late modernist, and postmodernist. The ideas of great political thinkers—Plato, Niccolò Machiavelli, Rousseau—reappear in this book, but in their operatic reflections and transformations.

A few words are in order about the triadic character of the political ideas that are analyzed here. The political content of these operas is partly the product of the deliberate political intentions of their creators: composers and librettists. Despite the poststructuralist declaration of the death of the author, there are no authorless operas here. It may be unfashionable, but I still believe that something of the particular vision of a Monteverdi, a Mozart and Da Ponte, and a Wagner lives on in their works. Yet I must modify this position in two ways. First, even the most distinctive personal vision has a connection to the spirit of its age. Distinctiveness lies in the particular choices and combinations made within, not beyond, the zeitgeist. And second, because I have studied works that are critically acclaimed and continue to entertain and challenge contemporary audiences, each of these operas has political implications that transcend both the artist's intentions and the zeitgeist. I have not been able, however, to construct a single formula that captures the relation between the intentional, shared, and transcendental levels of political meaning.

I am happy to acknowledge the institutions and individuals that helped to make this book possible.

My employer, the University of Texas–Pan American (UTPA), provided a year of partial released time from teaching through the Project Title III Faculty Development Program. The University also awarded a pair of Faculty Research Grants that enabled me to acquire the research and other materials that I needed.

Although this book took years to complete, a large portion of it was written during an almost miraculous five-week residency at the Rockefeller Foundation's Conference and Study Center in Bellagio, Italy. I am proud to know that my book, its spine marked with the red dot that indicates a work written by one of the center's fellows, will take its place in the library at the center's Villa Serbelloni.

Earlier versions of some chapters have been previously published. Chapters 1 and 3 appeared in *International Political Science Review*; Chapter 5, in *Vienna: The World of Yesterday, 1889–1914*, edited by Stephen Eric Bronner; and Chapter 6, in *Cultural Critique*.

Several individuals made specific contributions to this book. At Yale University Press, Harry Haskell was very supportive of a book about opera written by a political scientist; Brenda Kolb was a most perceptive manuscript editor. Patricia F. Brown, Dave Colby, Joe Friedman, Gertrude A. Fry, and Mary Roth Sharman offered helpful comments and criticisms on single chapters. I am deeply indebted to Terrell Carver, Edwin DeWindt, Timothy J. Lukes, Gary Mounce, the anonymous reviewer for Yale Univer-

sity Press, and my wife, Nancy Lashaway-Bokina, for their valu-
able critiques of the entire manuscript.

Finally, I would like to thank my students at UTPA. A number of them have had the courage to sign up for "Politics of Music
Drama," a course that I teach every three years in the Department
of Political Science. I hope that I provide them with a solid, albeit
highly politicized, introduction to the unfamiliar world of opera. I
know what they give me. Every third year, I have the pleasure of
observing what it is like to be nineteen or twenty years old and
encountering *Poppea*, *Don Giovanni*, and *Parsifal* for the first time,
and of remembering what it was like for me.

OPERA AND POLITICS

Introduction

My relationship to music is still the same: I listen to it with pleasure, with participation and with thoughtfulness, [but] chiefly I am fond of the historical viewpoint. For how can we understand any apparition unless we can observe it in its journey toward us?

—GOETHE

T the conclusion of *The Prince*, Machiavelli exhorted his sovereign, Lorenzo de' Medici, to pursue an honorable and glorious goal. The task that Machiavelli had in mind was political: gathering the several small and vulnerable Italian states into a unified nation-state. Lorenzo never accomplished this feat, nor did any other Medici, Borgia, Sforza, Visconti, or Gonzaga. Even so, these aristocratic families, through their intense concern with enhancing their own reputations, sponsored some of the Renaissance's greatest achievements in science, philosophy, technology, and the arts.

Toward the end of this period, as the late Renaissance gave way to the early baroque, Italy remained politically divided and weak, but aristocratic patronage supported a new and magnificent art form: opera. By combining music, poetry, drama, painting, costume, and stagecraft, opera became the "crowning achievement of the life of baroque man."[1] In the aristocratic principalities of Florence and Mantua, opera glorified the prince and his dynasty. In the aristocratic republic of Venice, opera commemorated the illustrious history of the regime.

From the time of its origin in the aristocratic courts of Italy, opera has been an eminently political art. It has reflected, in complex and mediated forms, the significant political personages and events that have shaped the modern Western world: kings and coups, classes and class conflict, rebels and revolutions. As it portrayed politics at this macro level, opera has addressed many of the characteristic themes of modern and contemporary political thought: monarchy and republicanism; the relations between classes, statuses, and genders; revolution and utopia; and the roles of art and the artist within an increasingly complex society.

But in this book I also explore another, more personal dimension of politics in opera. Opera has been rightly characterized as "extravagant," in part because of its tendency to portray characters in the throes of exaggerated passions and emotions.[2] Should these passions and emotions be expressed or restrained? And what are the implications of these passions and emotions for life in the state and in society? The personal dimension of politics is often characterized as a distinctly twentieth-century concern. First affirmed by the sixties' New Left and counterculture, the slogan "The personal is the political" has been adopted by feminists of the late twentieth century. But if my analyses of seventeenth-, eighteenth-, and nineteenth-century operas are sound, in opera the personal has always been the political. Far from being a strictly contemporary concern, the argument about the expression or restraint of passions and emotions is as old as the conflict between the two patron gods of music, Dionysus and Apollo.

Each of the seven chapters analyzes an opera or a cluster of operas from the periods of opera history. I have chosen works that are both critically acclaimed and still performed, but I make no claim that these operas are the typical works of their eras. Rather, like the works of the great political theorists still in the curriculum, the operas included in this book represent pinnacle achievements of their periods.

The chapters on Monteverdi, Mozart, psychoanalytic operas (Richard Strauss and Arnold Schoenberg), artist-operas (Hans

Pfitzner, Paul Hindemith, and Schoenberg), and Hans Werner Henze treat political subjects that have been ignored or neglected in scholarly literature. The chapters on Ludwig van Beethoven and Wagner adopt new perspectives on operas that have long been recognized as political. At the same time, I have had to exclude such notably political operas as Wagner's *Ring* and the works of Giuseppe Verdi, who has been aptly characterized as the most political composer; alas, I found that I had nothing new to say about these subjects.[3] And I miss, even more than the *Ring* and Verdi, something on Giacomo Meyerbeer's historical heroizing of the bourgeoisie, Modest Mussorgsky's union of pathos and nationalism, or Arrigo Boïto's portrait of the murderous artist as emperor.

Monteverdi's three extant operas encompass the political and ideological dualities of aristocratic rule in early baroque Italy. The first, *La favola d'Orfeo*, was written in absolutist Mantua. The work has long been interpreted as an operatic essay on the power of music, but I focus instead on its political dimensions, showing how it depicts the political education of a young absolutist prince. At the beginning of the opera, Orfeo is a popular, emotional, but also vulnerable young princeling. His vaunted ability to portray and provoke love, joy, and sadness with his remarkably expressive music violates the prevailing neo-Platonic model of dispassionate, rational rulership. Orfeo is rebuked by his father, Apollo, and finally learns his political lesson. By the end of the opera, he is remote, rational, and therefore invulnerable to popular and emotional threats to his rule.

Monteverdi's last two operas, *Il ritorno d'Ulisse in patria* and *L'incoronazione di Poppea*, were written for commercial theaters in the aristocratic republic of Venice. The Venetian composers who succeeded Monteverdi portrayed heroized figures and events from Venetian history. The Venetian republicanism of Monteverdi, however, was confined to a more historical, rather than neo-Platonic, view of absolute rulers.

Instead of dramatizing the neo-Platonic pieties of absolutist operas, *Ulisse* depicts the prince in more realistic terms. Like Machiavelli's *Prince*, Monteverdi's King Ulisse is a canny political animal—a political fox, cunningly learning the secrets of his opponents through deceit and disguise. The new *stile concitato* music sets Ulisse's achievements as a political lion who bests his opponents through his bravery, strength, and martial powers. A ruler of consummate *virtù*, or political skill, Ulisse achieves his goals. At the end of the opera, he is secure on his throne and reunited with his family.

Poppea broaches, but never actually completes, an aristocratic republican critique of absolute monarchy. Emperor Nerone (Nero) falls short of both the neo-Platonic and the Machiavellian models of the ideal ruler. He is a slave to his own uncontrolled passions and desires. Nerone offends his wife, his trusted advisor, the military, the senate, and the people of Rome in his pursuit of the lovely Poppea, his partner in a series of passionate duets. But 1642 was not the time for a full-blown operatic critique of absolutism, even in republican Venice. Nerone's defects do not lead to his downfall. This paradoxical opera closes with Nerone victorious over his enemies and blissfully wed to Poppea.

Nearly 150 years later, the rising middle classes were challenging the aristocracy for recognition and ascendancy. In this context, opera became a venue for an Enlightenment assessment of aristocratic absolutism. A number of studies have discussed the revolutionary meanings of Mozart's *Le nozze di Figaro* and even *Die Zauberflöte*. I have chosen instead to analyze the implications of a more politically enigmatic opera, *Don Giovanni*.

As a critique of absolutism, *Don Giovanni* inverts the Machiavellian ideal of aristocratic rulership. Like Ulisse, Giovanni exhibits the cunning of a fox and the strength of a lion. But unlike Ulisse, Giovanni has no political role to play in a modern society. This aristocratic fox and lion is a predator rather than a prince. Instead of competing with political rivals, he preys upon the upstanding members of the divinely ordained order of modern society.

All one-dimensional interpretations of *Don Giovanni* need to be modified, and this case is no exception. The opera is not only a celebration of the demise of a now parasitical and predatory aristocracy but also an operatic memorial for the end of an era. Despite his antisocial proclivities, the Don is the central and most attractive figure in the opera. Even in the grip of the avenging statue of the Commendatore, he remains true to his passions. He is allowed the principled death of a tragic hero. With the passing of aristocratic anachronisms like the Don, modern society gains security, while it loses the sensuous and ostentatious aristocratic way of life.

In 1789, two years after the premiere of *Don Giovanni*, the Bastille was stormed. Almost all the once-numerous operatic representations of the French Revolution have long vanished from the repertory. Only Beethoven's *Fidelio* remains. I agree with the scholarly opinion that *Fidelio* exemplifies the political spirit of its Revolutionary age. The Bastille-like political prison, the trumpets sounding a call to arms, the abrupt change of fortune, and the choral semblance of a concluding *populus ex machina* endow this opera with an unmistakable sense of the Revolution. But there are problems with this interpretation. The opera does not reflect the conflict between monarchy and republicanism, the political foundation of the Revolution. The oppressed prisoners are freed by the minister of a benign king. Nor does the opera reflect the struggle between the aristocracy and the popular classes, the social foundation of the Revolution. An evil aristocrat, Pizarro, persecutes Florestan, a good aristocrat.

In my analysis, *Fidelio* remains a representation of the Revolution, but one that is characterized by its political morality. From this perspective, *Fidelio*'s relation to the Revolution lies in its depiction of republican virtue, the universal ethical and moral standards of an honorable citizenry. From Cicero and Rousseau through Louis Antoine Léon de Saint-Just and Maximilien de Robespierre to Immanuel Kant and G. W. F. Hegel, one tradition maintains that these standards, even more than political institutions or social classes, are the core of republicanism.

Wagner's *Parsifal* reflects the theme of revolution in Germany. As a young man, Wagner participated in the failed Dresden uprising of 1848–49. Initially, the revolt in Dresden took up the long-delayed agenda of bourgeois political reform in Germany: national unification under a constitutional government. But during the course of the uprising, the agenda was radicalized by the self-conscious participation of part of the working class. For the first time, socialism and communism also became revolutionary battle cries. During and immediately after these years, Wagner formulated his most characteristic views. He developed his revolutionary conception of music drama as the artwork of the future. He advocated the realization of his own peculiar vision of communism.

Parsifal was Wagner's last music drama. After the Holocaust, most critics came to believe that this opera reflects the nationalistic, imperialistic, racist, and indeed proto-Nazi views of Wagner's last years. The problem with this consensus is that it ignores the persistence, under changed conditions, of the young Wagner's revolutionary views into his old age. Over the years, Wagner turned his radical program of 1848–49 into a utopian dream. The revolutionary ideals remained, but their time frame changed. The artwork no longer proclaimed the victory of the revolution, but nurtured the memory of a lost golden age. Communism was no longer the model of the revolutionary future, but the foundation of an ideal past.

In my interpretation, *Parsifal* is a utopian music drama, the projection of romantic anticapitalist ideals onto an imagined past. With *Parsifal*, the late-nineteenth- and early-twentieth-century romantic anticapitalism of thinkers like Ferdinand Tönnies and Oswald Spengler leaves the realm of prosaic cultural criticism and becomes instead the political substance of an aesthetic image of utopia. In the properly ordered grail domain of Monsalvat, daily life is governed by the music of convocations and rituals: the trombone summons to matins, the midday trumpet call, processional bells, communal prayer and singing. In Monsalvat, there is a bonded community rather than just a fragmented society: order without domination, hierarchy without exploitation, and a concern for the preservation of all forms of life. If there is a politically problematic aspect to *Parsifal*, it lies in its pointless sexual asceticism rather than its alleged proto-Nazism.

Austria, too, experienced the displacement of defeated political hopes. The Viennese intelligentsia long supported the cause of Austrian liberalism, but this liberalism enjoyed barely four decades of political prominence. By the turn of the twentieth century, Austrian liberalism was defeated by the radical forces of both the Right and the Left. The result was not another utopian projection but a psychoanalytic introjection of politics. Retaining their cultural influence yet disillusioned with politics, Viennese artists, scientists, and intellectuals turned inward, to the life of the mind and its discontents.

Freudian psychoanalysis epitomized this tendency, but this introspective examination of sickness and health pervaded opera as well. Madness had been a recurrent theme since the beginning of opera. Two works from 1909—Strauss's *Elektra* and Schoenberg's *Erwartung*—transformed the traditional operatic depiction of madness in ways that revealed a distinct kinship with the new psychoanalytic movement.

Elektra psychologizes familiar dramatic and musical materials. The opera is based on Sophocles' *Electra*. In the transition from classical tragedy to contemporary opera, however, the story is transformed from a political tale about the dynasty of Agamemnon into a Freudian "family drama" displaying the psychological imprint of early-twentieth-century Vienna. Gone are the political references in Sophocles' drama. In their stead, framed by the thunderous Agamemnon motif, is a story about a daughter's fixation on the memory of her father and about her implacable desire for the killing of her mother. Gone too is the resolution of the play—the restoration of the dynastic house of Atreus. Instead, to the frenzied rhythms of an ever-quickening waltz, Elektra dances herself to death.

Visually, *Erwartung* replicates the familiar iconography of the operatic madwoman: the distraught Woman, the only character in this brief opera, appears with disheveled hair, torn dress, and bloodied hands. Where *Erwartung* goes beyond the familiar stereotype is in its attempt to depict psychic distress through the most advanced musical techniques. Schoenberg's expressionist score is a musical replication of the stream of the Woman's consciousness. Rapid changes in tempo mirror the Woman's mood swings. Chromaticism and freed dissonance portray the depth and range of her emotions.

For Austro-German composers, psychological interiority provided little defense against the ongoing political crisis of the early twentieth century. The crisis grew out of the tensions that beset Germany in the course of its rapid development: from the militaristic empire and World War I, through the liberal Weimar Republic, to the rise of Nazism. The atmosphere of crisis engendered a number of artist-operas, operas that self-consciously explored the political roles of art and the artist. Works such as Pfitzner's *Palestrina*, Hindemith's *Mathis der Maler*, and Schoenberg's *Moses und Aron* couch contemporary conditions in allegories about the fate of art in historical periods of transition.

Pfitzner's *Palestrina* is set in the Counter Reformation. Contrary to all historical evidence, the opera depicts Palestrina, a sixteenth-century Roman composer, as a defender of Renaissance polyphony against the progressive practices of modern music, especially the new monodic style of music emanating from Florence. Pfitzner infuses *Palestrina* with a deliberately archaic tonal quality, including extensive quotations from Palestrina's polyphonic *Missa Papae Marcelli*. But polyphony here is but a symbol for the fate of German romantic music in the early twentieth century. Pfitzner understands romanticism as the last and greatest stage in the development of the hallowed tradition of German music. Like polyphony in the sixteenth century, this twentieth-century German romanticism finds itself under foreign attacks by non-German musical modernists and vulnerable to the internal

INTRODUCTION

treachery of German modernists. For Pfitzner, the defense of
musical romanticism is inherently political. Romanticism represents the uniqueness and grandeur of German culture.
As a young man, Hindemith was one of Pfitzner's German
modernist traitors. He used avant-garde compositional styles and
associated with the Weimar Left. But when the Nazis came to
power, Hindemith was anxious to cover the tracks of his youth,
and *Mathis der Maler* was the vehicle for expressing his new, mature views on music and politics. The opera sets the fictional
experiences of a real German painter, Matthias Grünewald, who is
believed to have died in 1528. Medieval chant, Protestant cho-
rales, and folk songs evoke the period within the neoclassical
score. In the libretto, Hindemith constructs a picture of art and
the artist buffeted by the crises of the Reformation and the Peasants' War. In an allegorical reference to the early stages of
Hindemith's own career, Mathis makes an ill-starred commitment
of his art to the peasant cause. The peasants are defeated, and
Mathis produces no art. Like Hindemith, an older, chastened, and
wiser Mathis gives up the exaggerated expectations of politicized
art. He now understands art as simply an apolitical craft and
thereby regains his productivity.
The action of Schoenberg's *Moses und Aron* is set in a much
earlier period of transition. The allegory takes place during the
biblical Exodus from Egypt. Politically, *Moses* examines the cognitive role of the artwork in society. Is the art image a means to
human communication and emancipation, or does it merely pro-
mote deception and manipulation? For Schoenberg, the familiar in
music, whether the romanticism of a Pfitzner or the neoclassicism
of a Hindemith, is represented by the appealing lyricism of Aron.
The musically familiar may have been progressive at one time, but
it is now compromised and manipulative, the sonic substance of
advertising, commercial mass culture, and political propaganda.
The true modernist artist, the true Moses of art, aspires to communicate the highest ideas rationally, not through crowd-pleasing
conjurer's tricks but through the most rigorous application of the

[9]

most advanced artistic techniques. Thus Schoenberg's score moves beyond the expressionist free tonality of *Erwartung* to twelve-tone serialism. But the heroic integrity of the true modernist artist is also the cause of his heroic impotence. Disdaining the popular, the pleasing, and the familiar, the aesthetically radical modernist composer has few listeners.

Twenty to twenty-five years later, in technologically advanced Western societies, the prosperity of the 1960s and early 1970s sparked a radical questioning of established values and practices and a renewed search for a revolutionary alternative. In general, the opera house was a bastion of opposition to the new radicalism, an elite haven of decorous behavior and cultural conservatism, but there were voices of dissent.

The Bassarids by Henze is one of these exceptions. The opera is based on Euripides' tragedy *Bacchae*. Although *The Bassarids* is faithful to the core of the classical play—the conflict between Pentheus, the austere young king of Thebes, and Dionysus, the sensuous young Olympian god—the opera also sets up a very contemporary conflict: the struggle between the Establishment and the countercultural New Left. The opera poses the promise and explores the limits of the sensual-sexual revolt of its own twentieth century. Like the advanced industrial societies of the late fifties and early sixties, the ancient Thebes of the opera is prosperous and orderly. But the chorus of Bassarids (followers of Dionysus) subverts the pretensions of Pentheus's Thebes. Behind the society's benign appearance is a hierarchical structure grounded in repression and state violence. As an alternative, the sensuous melodies of Dionysus lure the Thebans to Mount Cytheron, a site of sixties-style countercultural emancipation. In the cult of Dionysus, they experience the liberating possibilities of intoxication, sensuousness and sexuality, feminism and femininity, and reunion with nature.

Despite its advocacy of Dionysus, *The Bassarids* is far from an uncritical paean to the counterculture. The reign of Dionysus may be the antithesis of the old Theban order, but it, too, has its dreadful consequences. The closing scenes of the opera represent the chilling outcome of Dionysianism triumphant. The opera thus anticipates the transition from the sensuous euphoria of the sixties to the sexual diseases and drug overdoses of the later seventies and eighties.

From the perspective of the late 1990s, the radicalism of the sixties and early seventies was flawed from the outset. According to both conservatives and the fragmented remnants of the New Left, there was and is no possibility of a fundamental transformation of advanced societies. Rather, we are now in the era of the "posts": post–Soviet Union, postcommunism, post–Cold War, postideology, and postmodernism. In this new context, even political progressives must confine themselves to attempts at modest reforms within a status quo that is liberal, capitalist, self-perpetuating, and global.

The brief Postscript to this book surveys six American postmodern operas: Philip Glass's *Einstein on the Beach*, *Satyagraha*, and *Akhnaten;* John Adams's *Nixon in China* and *The Death of Klinghoffer;* and John Corigliano's *Ghosts of Versailles*. By adopting musical minimalism or reviving classical or romantic style, each of these operas tries to heal the modernist breach between composers and listeners. Whatever else it may be, the music is readily accessible. And by employing the most advanced techniques of the spoken theater, these director-driven operas attempt to overcome the conservative tastes of opera audiences and find a niche in the contemporary performing repertory.

On the surface, postmodernism represents one of the most self-consciously political periods in opera history. These operas raise crucial political issues: nuclear weapons, racism, the fate of new ideas, the Cold War, terrorism, and revolution. But the political perspective of these works is constrained by their new historical context. Limited by a seemingly inescapable liberal capitalism, unable to envision a new and better future, the operas pose political issues but take no clear and coherent position on them. Ultimately, the political subjects of postmodern operas provide these works with a false aura of seriousness and significance, and that is all.

Historical generalizations based on an analysis of twelve operas and a brief glance at six others are foolhardy at best, but I cannot resist the temptation. From Monteverdi's Orfeo to Henze's Dionysus, the personal level of politics, the politics of the expression or restraint of passions ,or emotions, is a recurrent rather than just a contemporary theme. This personal level has important implications for determining the fitness of individuals and groups for various roles within the state and society. And at the grand level of states and rulers, opera has traced the trajectory of modern Western politics: the ascendancy and demise of the aristocratic rule, the troubled reign of the commercial middle classes, the failed search for a radical alternative. Opera is and will remain many things for many people. But with this book's deliberately political focus, the operas are the media for the recording of the conscious and unconscious, explicit and implicit, "historiography of society."[4]

ONE

The Prince as Deity, Beast, and Tyrant
Monteverdi's *Orfeo*, *Ulisse*, and *Poppea*

Society recurs in great music: transfigured, criticized, and reconciled, although these aspects cannot be surgically sundered.

—THEODOR W. ADORNO

LAUDIO MONTEVERDI (1567–1643) was hailed as a "true musician of paradise" by his seventeenth-century contemporaries, and in the twentieth century he is still recognized as the "creator of modern music."[1] Three of his operas are extant—*La favola d'Orfeo* (1607), *Il ritorno d'Ulisse in patria* (1641), and *L'incoronazione di Poppea* (1642). These works were among the first examples of the new musical genre of opera, and in that genre they were the first masterpieces.

Because of Monteverdi's importance in the history of opera, many scholars have compared the musical, poetic, and dramatic qualities of his early Mantuan works and his late Venetian works.[2] But the focus here is politics. From this perspective, Monteverdi's operas represent, in sensuous and affecting form, important elements of Mantuan absolutist and Venetian republican thought in the early seventeenth century. The operas resonate with the characteristic political themes of the age: the contest between fortune and virtue, the simultaneous need to express and to restrain the passions, the rival claims of political activism and philosophic contemplation, the intoxication with power. These will be duly noted, but I will focus on Monteverdi's operatic portraits of his princely protagonists. Whereas the prince is apotheosized as a deity in the Mantuan *Orfeo*, he is brought down to earth in the Venetian *Ulisse* and *Poppea*. In these works the prince practices, more or less successfully, the historical skills of governance.

Monteverdi's early works were written during his period of service (1590–1612) at the Gonzaga court in Mantua; his later works were the products of his years (1613–1643) as Maestro di Cappella at Saint Mark's in Venice. *Orfeo*, the only one of Monteverdi's operas to survive in full score, was written for his patron, Prince Francesco Gonzaga, heir to the throne of Mantua. It was intended for performance during Carnival before the aristocratic Accademia degli Invaghiti and later received a number of performances under the sponsorship of the Mantuan court. His second and arguably most successful opera in his lifetime, *Arianna*, was also written for Francesco. It was part of the musical entertainments celebrating Francesco's marriage to Margherita of Savoy. Unfortunately, only the famous "Lamento" survives from this work.

Monteverdi chafed at the shabby treatment he received from the Gonzaga.[3] In 1612, he was dismissed from his troubled position as court composer. The following year he assumed the more congenial and lucrative post offered to him in the aristocratic republic of Venice. Sometime between 1613 and 1632, he took holy orders. His church duties were not overly taxing. While in Venice, Monteverdi continued to accept commissions from Mantua and other absolutist courts. But more important, he was able to explore the new possibilities of commercial opera in the public opera houses of Venice. Of the dozen or so operas that Monteverdi wrote after *Arianna*, only the last two, *Ulisse* and *Poppea*, survive in partial scores.

Seemingly an apolitical representation of a familiar mythological tale, Monteverdi's *Orfeo* has a latent political content. Like the Orpheus operas of his Florentine contemporaries Guilio Caccini and Jacopo Peri, Monteverdi's *Orfeo* reflects the absolutist desire for political order under the aegis of a single ruler. By force if not by argument, absolutist princes resolved the traditional Renaissance debate about the relative merits of the *vita activa civile* and the *vita contemplativa* in favor of a contemplative life for the citizenry.[4] Machiavelli's period of forced retirement from politics is emblematic of this development. Political activity became the preserve of the prince and his immediate circle of courtiers and key bureaucrats. The vast majority of the population was excluded from any meaningful form of political participation. The restless citizens of Renaissance republics were transformed into the quiescent subjects of baroque monarchs.

In this context, the artistic and intellectual pursuits of the late-sixteenth- and early-seventeenth-century academies took on added importance. Cultural achievement became a safe outlet for talented individuals who might otherwise have been attracted to political activities. At the same time, the princes grasped the propagandistic potential of the products of these academies.[5] The Medici of Florence, for example, oversaw the production of conspicuous artistic displays of their power, thus becoming pioneers in the absolutist strategy of coupling political repression with cultural propaganda. Peri's *Euridice* (1600) was just one of many works that obscured the Florentine reality of hunger, disease, poverty, violence, and brigandage behind the facade of a peaceful society in a harmonious universe.[6] Likewise, the pastoral myth of Monteverdi's *Orfeo* glorified the weakened and vulnerable Gonzaga rulers. Indeed, twenty years after the premiere of *Orfeo*, the very existence of the dynasty would be threatened by both the Monferrato War and the struggle over Mantuan succession. With Peri's and Monteverdi's musical treatments of the Orpheus story, the most advanced techniques of the most modern composers of the age were harnessed to serve absolute princes seeking to consolidate their rule in a period of crisis.

Republican Venice also sought stability and order during these uneasy times, when a series of military, economic, and political crises shook the confident complacency of the Most Serene Republic.[7] In 1606, just seven years before the arrival of

Monteverdi, Venice was subjected to a papal interdict. Armed with the arguments of another transplanted Mantuan, Fra Paolo Sarpi, Venice emerged victorious the following year. But even this victory had the effect of further weakening Venetian strength and resolve. This period of crisis forced Venice to become more self-conscious about its republican status. At a time when Renaissance republican ideals had largely been extinguished under absolutist princes in other Italian states, Venice became increasingly aware of its unique political standing in the peninsula. Belatedly, Venice recognized the key insight of such Renaissance political thinkers as Machiavelli and Francesco Guicciardini: reliable political knowledge was produced not by deduction from abstract principles (the characteristic neo-Platonic technique of absolutism, both secular and papal) but by the analysis of history. This historicism became the hallmark of the theoretical and artistic representations of Venetian republicanism.

Neither of Monteverdi's extant Venetian operas contains a direct statement of Venetian republicanism, although explicit references to the glories of Venice would pervade the operas of his successors.[8] And, unlike the republicanism of the French Revolution, that of the seventeenth century does not represent a progressive historical force in ideological conflict with a reactionary absolutism.[9] Rather, the republican tendency in Monteverdi's works lies in their concrete historical depiction of monarchs, courts, and society. Monteverdi's King Ulisse is no Orphic demigod but a Machiavellian political beast willing to use both force and guile in order to secure his kingdom. *Poppea* takes this historical approach one step further. Although stopping short of a full-blown republican critique of either monarchy or absolutism, *Poppea* depicts the actual weaknesses and abuses of Nerone in a manner that would be impermissible in an absolutist state. Mythological elements remain in both works, but it is this historical emphasis that links Monteverdi's *Ulisse* and *Poppea* to the republican politics of early-seventeenth-century Venice.

LA FAVOLA D'ORFEO: THE PRINCE AS DEITY

Monteverdi's *Orfeo* retells the legend of Orpheus, son of the muse Calliope and King Oeagrus, or Apollo.[10] Orpheus was a religious figure associated with the cult of Apollo and thus in opposition to the rival cult of Dionysus. He was also a Thracian poet-singer whose music possessed the power to move both animate and inanimate nature. Despite marked differences in tone and detail, the Orpheus poems in Virgil's *Georgics* and Ovid's *Metamorphoses* were the primary sources for Renaissance treatments of the legend. These poems tell how Orpheus's years of loneliness and sorrow were finally ended by his successful courtship of the fair Eurydice. Orpheus's happiness was short-lived, however, for his bride succumbed to a fatal snakebite. In despair, Orpheus descended into the underworld to search for her, gaining entry into the forbidden kingdom through the power of his music. Moved by the pleas of his wife, Proserpina, Pluto grants Orpheus's wish. On the condition that Orpheus not look back at Eurydice until the couple was completely outside Hades' precincts, Pluto permitted Orpheus to lead his bride back to the world of the living. But Orpheus, unable to resist looking back, lost Eurydice a second and final time. Once again in his native Thrace, the grief-stricken Orpheus vowed never to fall in love with another woman, and his amorous pursuits were thereafter all homosexual. Followers of Dionysus, enraged Thracian Bacchantes tore Orpheus to pieces. Orpheus's head was thrown into the Hebrus River, where it floated, singing and prophesying, to the island of Lesbos, until Apollo finally silenced it.

With the operatic appearance of the Orpheus legend at the courts of Florence and Mantua, a familiar subject of Renaissance art was transformed under the new conditions of baroque absolutism. Trimmed and sanitized to fit the conceptual requirements of absolutism yet infused with wonderfully expressive music, the tale of Orpheus and Eurydice became a fit entertainment for a baroque prince and an instructive representation of his power and majesty.

With the severance of political theory from popular political practice, late-sixteenth- and early-seventeenth-century Italian absolutist thought stagnated. Despite a few concessions to historical realism, the court theorists continued the early Renaissance humanist practice of writing mirror-of-princes advice books, replete with advocacy of the Platonic-*cum*-Christian monarchical virtues, for their princely patrons. Eschewing the historical realism of Machiavelli's *Prince*, these books recited familiar injunctions on the value of prudence, wisdom, temperance, fortitude, justice, and the like, all of which were embedded in texts that reflected the new position of the prince in baroque absolutism.

In his study of Florentine political thought in the late sixteenth century, Samuel Berner has identified four major themes in this absolutist literature, and three of them directly bear on the political interpretation of Monteverdi's *Orfeo*. First, Berner observes the proliferation of honorific titles. Many of these focus on the alleged antiquity of the ruling dynasty and the crucial role of the ruling family in the development of the state. Second, he notes a political distancing between the prince and his subjects. As the prince becomes increasingly associated with divine personages, both classical and Christian, a "blurred vision of a prince devoid of distinguishable characteristics" emerges.[11] Despite his well-deserved reputation for hedonism and licentiousness, the baroque prince of absolutist political theory was depicted as the epitome of reason and restraint, governing his merely sensuous subjects through innumerable sententious pronouncements. Third, Berner points to the new emphasis on the prince and his ministers as the key to understanding government operations. When compared to the earlier writings of the Florentine republicans, this literature's preoccupation with the prince represents a considerable simplification of the tasks of political theory.

The prologue to Peri's *Euridice* established a precedent for using opera as a vehicle for the flattery of the prince and his family. Peri's La Tragedia abolishes her own art by banning unhappy spectacles from the royal house and announces a work that will instead extol the beauty, honor, and glory of the new Medici queen.[12] In the rivalrous baroque courts, the Gonzaga considered themselves no less worthy of praise than the Medici. Monteverdi's 1609 dedication of the printed version of *Orfeo* is therefore abounding with servile panegyrics to Francesco. And in the prologue to *Orfeo*, it is La Musica who lauds the Gonzaga:

> Quitting my sweet Permessus' shores, to ye I come,
> Heroes renown'd, offspring of royal stock,
> Whose all-excelling worth Fame doth recount,
> Though ever falling short of high-perch'd Truth.[13]

Here, in typical absolutist fashion, honorific titles are linked to assertions of the long-standing heroism and virtue of the ruling family.

The baroque tendency toward distancing the prince from his subjects is also evident in *Orfeo*. From a political perspective, the opera depicts the *Bildung*, or the education through experience, of a beloved, accessible, and initially passionate princeling to his proper role as an admired, remote, and wise ruler. Whereas the mirror-of-princes advice books largely confined themselves to static prescriptions of the ideal monarch, *Orfeo* traces a process of becoming a reasonable and responsible prince. In the first two acts, Orfeo is surrounded by his symbolic subjects, the nymphs and shepherds. They share his joy in his bride, then his sorrow at her loss. It is clear that the young prince Orfeo is loved by his subjects. But it is also clear that Orfeo's popularity signals his tragic flaw: the prince who associates with commoners—who, by the standards of absolutist neo-Platonism, are dominated by their emotions and instincts—is also prone to being dominated by his own emotions and instincts. In order to complete his political education through experience, Orfeo must sever his intimate ties with his subjects. He therefore leaves the nymphs and shepherds behind to pursue his third- and fourth-act adventures in the underworld. But, still a slave of his passions, Orfeo loses Euridice again with his impulsive backward look. The distancing of Orfeo continues in the opening of the fifth and final act. Back in Thrace, the bereaved Orfeo shares his lamentations, no longer with the shepherds and nymphs, but with Eco, his own sonic reflection.

But the conclusion to the opera is problematic and exhibits the effect of absolutism upon the very form of opera. According to long-standing tradition, plays were classified as either comedies or tragedies. Comedies depicted the affairs of common-born characters and came to happy conclusions. Tragedies, however, depicted highborn personages meeting their unhappy fates.[14] The earliest musical plays earned their generic designation as *opera* (work) or *dramma per musica* by their failure to conform to the traditional theatrical dichotomy.[15] Peri, as we have seen, banished tragedy by resolving the threatening adventures of Orfeo and Euridice in a *lieto fine*, or happy ending. Not the slightest hint of a Euridice irrevocably lost, an inconsolable Orfeo, homosexuality, or enraged Thracians clouds the bliss of the highborn couple. With *Orfeo*, there was the possibility of a musical tragedy. The conclusion to Alessandro Striggio's original libretto depicted the Bacchantes assaulting the bereaved Orfeo, although whether this conclusion was used in the first performance of the work remains a matter of controversy.[16]

But in the published version of the score, the Bacchantes do not appear. Instead, Apollo reprimands Orfeo for becoming prey to his own emotions:

> Too much, too much didst thou rejoice
> At thy most happy chance,
> Now thou dost too much weep
> Thy hard and bitter fate. Still dost not know
> That nothing here below gives lasting joy?
> Thus, if thou wouldst enjoy immortal life,
> Come now with me to heaven as I bid thee. (53)

Accepting the rational counsel of his divine father, Orfeo is raised to eternal life in heaven, where he can contemplate the beauty of Euridice in the eternal forms of the sun and the stars. Back on earth, the chorus of shepherds returns to acclaim the apotheosis of Orfeo.

An admirer of *Orfeo*, Joseph Kerman nevertheless criticizes the concluding apotheosis as "meaningless," "disappointing," "musically and intellectually blank."[17] That Monteverdi resorted to a deus ex machina obviously violates Kerman's standards for operatic drama. And Kerman is also right to point out that a more aesthetically satisfying, tragic conclusion to *Orfeo* would have been possible. Monteverdi demonstrated this in 1608 with his tragedy *Arianna*.

But whatever the aesthetic deficiencies of this conclusion to *Orfeo*, its happy ending better served the political purposes of the prince. First, the descent of Apollo and the ascent of Apollo and Orfeo provided an opportunity for indulging the baroque taste for spectacle and exhibitions of complex stage machinery.[18] Second, with the ascension of the transfigured Orfeo, a familiar formula of baroque painting transcended the confines of two-dimensionality and became a musical tableau vivant. Although seldom present at court, Peter Paul Rubens was employed by the Gonzaga at the same time as Monteverdi. In addition to painting several versions of the Assumption of the Virgin Mary, Rubens later went on to use the image of the ascent of royalty into heaven in a series of mammoth canvases commissioned by Catherine de Médicis, the queen of France. Whether operatic or visual, the goal of such artworks was not the clarification, enlightenment, or catharsis described in classical conceptions of art but an overwhelming of critical reason through the sheer force of the spectacle. Through spectacle, the images of baroque royalty could be intermingled with images of classical and Christian divinities. Baroque opera was particularly prone to this tendency. In its printed form, complete with lieto fine, *Orfeo* became the model for opera at absolutist courts, especially Jean-Baptiste Lully's numerous mythological works for the French Bourbons.

The lieto fine not only avoids the sight of Orfeo being torn to shreds by intoxicated Bacchantes (commoners all) but also permits a lesson in Platonic rulership. By giving vent to his emotions, Orfeo allows himself to become the victim of his own base nature. But by adhering to the advice of Apollo—a mythological symbol of both reason and music, the sun and kingship—the purified Orfeo crystallizes the aspirations of the baroque prince. When he can subordinate his emotions to reason, Orfeo finally attains the neo-Platonic ideal of the prince, thus freeing himself from all contingency, be it his subjects, his own base nature, or time itself. The dream of eternal celestial rule is the aesthetic counterpart to the real life of baroque princes haunted by their own weaknesses and mortality in a period of crisis. As Arnold Hauser has observed, "Even the idea of timelessness is the product of a particular time."[19]

In addition to celebrating and apotheosizing the prince, *Orfeo* also lends aesthetic credibility to a simplified and antihistorical preoccupation with the prince as the key to understanding political and social life. By utilizing the most advanced compositional techniques—monody, the *stile rappresentativo*, and recitative— Monteverdi helped to develop the musical means for sustaining a full-length music drama and, at the same, endowed a theoretically shallow conception of the prince and society with the full force of his musical-psychological realism and intensity.

Indeed, early baroque opera as a whole was the culmination of Renaissance speculation about the rhetorical power of music. Of all the arts, music was most adept at both depicting and arousing the passions or affections. And more important, these passions or affections inclined an individual to one or another course of action. In *Orfeo*, the compositional innovations of Monteverdi's new monodic style (the *seconda prattica*) give psychological realism and affective intensity to the various turning points in the drama: Orfeo's happiness with his new bride, his sorrow at her death and resolve to enter the underworld, his pleas to Caronte at the entrance to the underworld, his despair at the final loss of Euridice, and the touching exchange between Proserpina and Pluto as they discuss Orfeo's pleas. In a curious paradox, the passionate and affective expressivity of Orfeo made him an ideal subject for early opera and at the same time made him contradict the Apollonian-Platonic political message of Monteverdi's work.

Because of this musical-psychological realism and intensity, we are willing to suspend our disbelief and accept the mythological tale with its aesthetically unsatisfactory ending. But this realism and intensity have a political effect as well: they lend plausibility to the mythical "refeudalization" portrayed in the Thracian acts.[20] Monteverdi's orchestration clearly demarcates the pastoral milieu of Thrace from the kingdom of the underworld: strings, organs, harpsichords, plucked continuo instruments, and recorders depict the agrarian fantasy world of Thrace in the first, second, and fifth acts; cornetts, trombones, and the regal depict the kingdom of Pluto in the third and fourth acts. Yet even within the first two acts, which are devoid of the usual trappings of monarchs and courts, there is an odd hint of feudalism. The urban and commercial Medici of Florence delighted in mythical depictions of their family as landed feudal overlords. Similarly, the Gonzaga, with long-standing roots in the commercial and military affairs of Mantua, fancied themselves the heirs to the medieval social order. In the first two acts of *Orfeo*, the differences in status between the noble Orfeo and Euridice and the commoner nymphs and shepherds are clearly represented. But these commoners are permitted no independent perspective on the course of events. They reflect the joy and sorrow of Orfeo much more faithfully than does his own recalcitrant Eco. Only La Messagera, Sylvia, a friend of Euridice and a member of her entourage, is allowed a small measure of autonomy and self-consciousness. Like the shepherds and nymphs, she bemoans the sad effect of her news on Orfeo, but she also reserves some of her pity for herself as the bearer of the terrible tidings.

In *Orfeo*, psychological realism is wedded to social abstraction. Text and music combine to provide compelling psychological motivations for the actions and decisions of lead characters. At the same time, these carefully constructed psychological motivations are depicted in a fantasy realm of feudal harmony. Social status has no effect on social attitudes or behavior; instead, commoners identify with their feudal overlords. In other words, *Orfeo* portrays more than one social status but only one class: the nobility. Only the nobility are depicted as having distinct goals and aspirations. In typical baroque fashion, all other social strata merely replicate the aristocratic worldview.

Flattered, deified, and mythicized, Orfeo mirrors the typical image of the prince in late-sixteenth- and early-seventeenth-century absolutist thought. Truncated and unsystematic, the operatic versions of these theories are obviously not the one-to-one equivalents found in political treatises. But in terms of effective communication, there can be little doubt that baroque opera was superior to formal political theory. Because of their heightened expressivity, novelty, and ability to move the passions, such baroque artworks as *Orfeo* "helped to prepare the mentality" for acceptance of the absolutist system.[21]

IL RITORNO D'ULISSE IN PATRIA: THE PRINCE AS POLITICAL BEAST

In 1641, Monteverdi's *Il ritorno d'Ulisse in patria* premiered at the Teatro San Cassiano in Venice. Opened in 1637, San Cassiano was the first of many public opera houses that were owned by members of the Venetian aristocracy. Like the absolutist princes who produced court operas, the various noble families regarded their opera houses as expressions of their splendor and power. But unlike the princes, individual Venetian aristocrats could not afford to underwrite the entire expense of staging opera; their financial limitations required that Venetian opera become a commercial venture. Boxes were leased to other aristocratic families, and individual tickets were sold to the public. By the end of the seventeenth century, Venice boasted sixteen public opera houses.[22] Yet the passion for the glittering world of opera can be seen as a symptom of Venetian decline and decay. Buffeted by military defeats, economic setbacks, plague, and a papal interdict, mid-seventeenth-century Venice was losing its status as a major power in international affairs. In this process, the traditional Venetian ideal of civil liberty gave way to the new Venetian reputation as a center of individual libertinage. And opera was no small part of Venice's sensual delights.

Giacomo Badaoro's libretto for *Ulisse* dramatizes the second half of Homer's *Odyssey*, which tells of the wandering hero's return to Ithaca and reunion with Penelope, his faithful wife, and Telemaco, his son. The libretto opens with Penelope bemoaning her fate and the young courtiers Melanto and Eurimaco pressing the cause of suitors who wish to take advantage of Ulisse's absence. Meanwhile, Giove successfully pleads his case for clemency with Nettuno, the father of the giant Polyphemus, who was blinded by Ulisse. Nettuno sinks the Phaeacian ship, but not before the sleeping Ulisse is placed safely on shore in Ithaca. In the guise of a shepherd, the goddess Minerva informs Ulisse about his safe return home and his wife's constancy. Ulisse exults in the favorable change in his fortunes, but he is cautious. Disguised as an old beggar, he secretly observes a quarrel between Eumete, his faithful herdsman, and Iro, the stuttering and gluttonous jester of the suitors. Ulisse's joy is compounded by the return of his exiled son Telemaco. After a miraculous metamorphosis, in which the beggar reveals himself as the glorious King Ulisse, Eumete and Telemaco are sent to the palace to inform Penelope of Ulisse's imminent return. As Penelope fends off the importunities of the now desperate suitors, Ulisse again disguises himself as a beggar and bests Iro in a wrestling match. When the suitors fail the test of the bow, the beggar, renouncing the prize of Penelope's hand in advance, requests a chance to try his strength. He strings the bow, then slaughters the suitors. Moved by the pleas of Minerva, Giunone, and Giove, Nettuno relents and grants a full pardon for Ulisse's insult. The way for the full restoration of Ulisse's happiness is now almost clear. The one remaining obstacle—Penelope's hesitation—is overcome when the old nurse Ericlea identifies

Ulisse's scar. The opera closes with Ulisse and Penelope singing a duet about their joy in their reunion.

On the surface, *Orfeo* and *Ulisse* seem remarkably similar. Both operas mine the storehouse of Greek mythology for their librettos. Both focus on the activities of an absolute prince who subordinates emotion to reason in the pursuit of his political goals. Both advance their plots at crucial moments through the use of dei ex machina. And both entrance the audience with stage effects and machinery. In these respects, *Orfeo* and *Ulisse* are both products of the baroque sensibility.

But at the same time, *Orfeo* and *Ulisse* inhabit entirely different universes of political ideas, and these differences are most apparent in their conflicting images of the prince. *Ulisse* is not a vehicle for extolling the antiquity and heroism of a ruling house but a depiction of some of the actual vicissitudes of dynastic rule. Nor is Ulisse a stereotypical symbol of monarchy, endowed with divine characteristics and prone to sententious speechifying. Instead, Monteverdi's Ulisse is a finely etched, multifaceted individual who relies on his own cunning and strength to accomplish immediate and practical tasks.

Because of its origin in Homer, *Ulisse* remains within the mythological subject matter of the earliest operas. But it is a mythological opera that presages historical opera, with its greater, if far from complete, emphasis on realism. In part, this nascent historicism can be traced to the opera's concrete depiction of human motivation and social milieu. But most of all, the historicism of *Ulisse* can be attributed to the special characteristics of its royal protagonist. Even Machiavelli, who much preferred the heroes of Roman history to the figures of Greek mythology, recognized the unique features of Ulysses-Odysseus. By combining the shrewdness of the con man with the lofty goals of the epic hero, Ulysses-Odysseus was the model prince.[23] And Monteverdi realized this model in music. Monteverdi's King Ulisse never reigns in an eternal world beyond contingency. His realm is the historical world of mutability and interdependence.

The new historical orientation is announced in the prologue. The divine forces of Il Tempo, La Fortuna, and Amore assert their dominion over human life, here personified as L'humana fragilità. L'humana fragilità may protest against the belief in "the blind and the lame" gods, but she nevertheless remains their subject.[24] Constrained by time, subjected to ever-changing fortune, and enslaved by an amorous nature, Ulisse exemplifies the Renaissance historicist conception of human nature as mortal, mutable, and imperfect. In Monteverdi's Venice, even princes are human. Unlike the princes of absolutist fantasy, such historically conceived monarchs as Ulisse may be the temporary beneficiaries of divine grace, but they never transcend their own human condition. In the prologue to *Ulisse*, mythological divinities neither ban unhappy spectacles nor praise the exploits of the ruling family. Rather, this prologue heralds the story of a dynasty whose very existence is threatened by political intrigue.

Late in the first act, Eumete apostrophizes Ulisse in terms typical of addresses to the Renaissance warrior-prince: "You undertook noble deeds, / depopulating and burning down cities" (81). Yet it was just this Machiavellian attempt to achieve noble deeds in order to enhance one's power, fame, and glory that has jeopardized the security of Ulisse's kingdom and dynasty. In Ulisse's long absence, the kingdom of Ithaca became the target of the suitors, neighboring princes desirous of expanding their domains. The suitors are abetted by Ithacan courtiers who have cast their lot with the new contenders to the throne. In the absence of the king, the twenty-year regency of Penelope is crucial. Although it is clear that the opera shares the traditional interest in Penelope as a symbol of marital fidelity, she also has political importance as an example of the Renaissance fascination with the virago.[25] In her efforts to preserve the throne of Ulisse, she exhibits considerable political skill, or virtù. Her famous dilatory tactics fend off, even if they do not actually eliminate, the dynastic threat of the suitors.

At first glance, Ulisse's successful campaign to secure his throne and dynasty seems to be the product of divine intervention. Nereids and Sirens calm the winds and waves that toss the Phaeacian ship; Nettuno's clemency spares Ulisse from sharing the fate of the Phaeacian sailors; nymphs gather and guard Ulisse's treasure on the shores of Ithaca. Minerva, the goddess of wisdom and Ulisse's protectress, plays a particularly important role. She advises Ulisse to adopt the guise of the beggar; her chariot transports Telemaco from his Spartan exile; and her power enables Ulisse to metamorphose from beggar into king at the end of the first act. These divine interventions serve as the occasions for the opera's displays of machine-driven spectacle.

Yet the overall impression is that Ulisse achieves political success because of his effective use of Machiavellian virtù. Indeed, after the early interventions of the divine forces, the opera is an artistic representation of Machiavelli's famous notion of the beastly prince: "The prince must be a fox, therefore, to recognize the traps and a lion to frighten the wolves."[26] Seventeenth-century audiences were familiar with this injunction. Despite having been banned by the Index, Machiavelli's books were commonly included in Venetian aristocratic libraries of the period.[27] Given this political overlay, the interventions of the gods do not guarantee Ulisse's success. Rather, they simply remove the extraneous obstacles blocking a direct contest between Ulisse's cunning and strength—that is, between his political virtù—and the cunning and strength of his political rivals.

From the first act, Ulisse's foxlike strategies reap benefits. Adopting the guise of a beggar, he eavesdrops on the quarrel between Eumete and Iro. He quickly learns that he has a faithful ally in Eumete, and in Iro he is given a glimpse of the character of the opposition forces. At this point, he does not immediately accede to his desire for revenge on the suitors, restoration of his throne, and reunion with Penelope. Adapting his tactics to the circumstances, he temporizes, reassuming his beggar's disguise in order to infiltrate the palace in safety. Although this subordination of desire to reason could be interpreted as the Minerva-like wisdom of a Platonic ruler, it resembles more the cunning of a Machiavellian fox evading the suitors' trap.

But the cunning of the fox is not enough. Ulisse's lionlike strength is needed to defeat the wolves. At the palace, Ulisse, still in the guise of the beggar, defeats the taunting Iro in a wrestling match. Then his strength allows him to string the bow and slay the suitors. These scenes of conflict and excitement necessitated a development in musical style. In *Orfeo*, the stile rappresentativo, or representative style, attempted a more or less naturalistic miming of the emotions and affections. In *Ulisse*, with its socially more complex external conflicts and excitations, something more than the musical representation of Orfeo's love, happiness, sadness, and despair was needed. Monteverdi first made extensive use of the stile concitato, or excited style, in his 1624 dramatic madrigal, *Il combattimento di Tancredi e Clorinda*. In *Ulisse*, the stile concitato sets every scene of martial strength and combat.[28]

Half beast but all too human, Ulisse acts within a socially diverse urban milieu that bears little resemblance to the pastoral fantasy world of *Orfeo*. Like his contemporary Shakespeare, Monteverdi is an artistic "democrat," endowing each of his characters, regardless of status, with the most distinctive and expressive examples of his musical art. Although commoners are still understood as the loyal or capricious appendages of the nobility, there can be no question that *Ulisse* represents a major step toward greater social distinctiveness and social realism in opera.

The most convention-ridden characters in *Ulisse* are the gods, who appear in their familiar roles as royal adventurers. In this opera, Nettuno is particularly regal, as he exercises the ancient monarchical rights of clemency and pardon. Even so, the human characters display more novelty and nuance.

One political faction is committed to the preservation of the dynasty. Status differences govern the manner in which this political objective is pursued. The noble Ulisse and Penelope, as we have seen, seek this goal according to their gender-determined capacities for political virtù. Their commoner allies, the old servants Eumete and Ericlea, are unshakable in their loyalty to the ruling family. In their devotion to Ulisse and Penelope, Eumete and Ericlea come closest to the mythically refeudalized shepherds and nymphs of *Orfeo*. Yet even here, the historicism of *Ulisse* keeps the servants from becoming exactly like the anonymous commoners of the earlier opera. As individuals, Eumete and Ericlea have proper names. Their actions advance the plot. And, most important, their reactions do not reflexively imitate those of the nobility. Although their views are ultimately congruent with the aspirations of the dynasty, they are not automatically so. Both Eumete and Ericlea need to be persuaded by their noble betters, and they can persuade in return.

The suitors, of course, are the core of the dynastic opposition. Although Monteverdi's music invests Antinoo, Anfinomo, and Pisandro with their own indelible personalities, the plausibility of their political actions is never given a fair hearing. Ulisse has been absent for twenty years and can reasonably be presumed to be dead. Certainly desirous of increasing the power and wealth of their respective kingdoms, the suitors seek to marry his presumptive widow. If the positions were reversed, we can easily envision that the wily Ulisse would be doing at least this much. But the opera, following Homer, never concedes the reasonableness of the suitors' position. Instead, we are presented with an ad hominem contest. On one side are the dynastic forces of conventional virtue (Penelope's fidelity, Eumete's and Ericlea's faithfulness) and Renaissance virtù (Penelope's dilatory tactics, Ulisse's cunning and strength). On the other side are the antidynastic forces of personal appetite and political incompetence, represented by the likes of Iro, Antinoo, Anfinomo, and Pisandro. In the political milieu of *Ulisse*, potentially dangerous aristocratic rivals are not persuaded from their perfidy, but conquered.

The character flaws of the suitors infect their supporters. In Monteverdi's musical sketches of Iro, on one hand, and Melanto and Eurimaco, on the other, we have some of his most influential pieces of historical realism. By the theatrical conventions of the age, all common-born characters, including the loyal Eumete and Ericlea, are comedic. But in Iro, a jester, the overtly humorous aspect of comedy is emphasized. Like his masters, Iro is a slave to his passions and appetites. But unlike his masters, who figuratively hunger for the wealth and power of Ithaca, Iro's hunger is literal and base: he always wants to eat. His defeat in the wrestling match demonstrates his deficiencies in the manly skills. Upon the deaths of the suitors, his aristocratic patrons and meal tickets, Iro commits suicide rather than face the prospect of an uncertain food supply. His aria, marked "parte ridicula" in the score, parodies the noble lament, a form that Monteverdi developed to great effect in *Orfeo* and *Arianna*. If *Orfeo* reprises an often copied mythological image of art and the artist, Iro revives a stereotype of classical Roman comedy: the parasite with an insatiable appetite.[29]

The courtiers and young lovers Melanto and Eurimaco also reflect and reinvigorate a theatrical convention: the commoner couple as the comedic counterpart to an aristocratic pair.[30] Unlike Ulisse and Penelope, who delay their conjugal satisfaction until the end of the opera, after they have successfully completed their political tasks, Melanto and Eurimaco cannot restrain their desire for each other. (Their passionate duet, which Monteverdi places in the first act, foreshadows the love music he created for Nerone and Poppea the next year.) Fearing that Penelope's constancy will jeopardize their secret liaison, Melanto and Eurimaco try to sway Penelope to give in to the suitors. Their private peccadilloes force them to become a political liability to the dynasty. The fate of Melanto and Eurimaco is not detailed in the opera. Because their commitment to the suitors is based entirely on their weakness for each other, it seems likely that their political loyalty could be controlled once Ulisse regains the Ithacan throne.

An array of nobles, servants, courtiers, and jesters fill the stage of Monteverdi's *Ulisse*. All of them, whether noble or base, are subject to the frailty of the human condition, but social status determines how this frailty is expressed. The best representatives of the aristocracy are able to restrain their passions and emotions, thereby gaining a measure of political virtù. Commoners, however, are prone to giving in to their appetites, and their loyalty to their noble overlords can never be entirely trusted. Although the commoners inherit the greatest realism and complexity in the comedic theatrical tradition, they remain the appendages of the aristocracy. In *Ulisse,* as in *Orfeo,* only the nobility constitutes a class in the modern sense of the word.

L'INCORONAZIONE DI POPPEA: THE PRINCE AS TYRANT

Monteverdi's *Ulisse* is not a protohistorical opera, a way station between the absolutist opera of Florence and Mantua and the historical opera of Venice. In its particular combination of mythology and history, *Ulisse* is a masterpiece that stands on its own merits. Yet, when it is placed between *Orfeo* and *Poppea,* the transitional character of *Ulisse* is striking. Musically, *Ulisse* marks the transition from *Orfeo*'s emotionally charged recitative to *Poppea*'s mixture of recitative and relatively self-contained set pieces. In *Poppea,* recitative takes on its traditional operatic function of advancing the plot, whereas arias and ensembles become the vehicles for the emotion-laden reflections of the characters. Even the poetic vocabulary for the expression of these emotions changes. *Orfeo* follows the Renaissance-Petrarchan ideal of attempting to portray the inner conflicts and passions of the characters. But in *Poppea,* inner passion is replaced by a superficial and supremely sensual desire that was consonant with the baroque enthusiasm for the sensuous poetry of Giambattista Marino. Indeed, Francesco Busenello's libretto for *Poppea,* which premiered in 1642 at Venice's Teatro di Santi Giovanni e Paolo, luxuriates in the sensuous description of external objects of desire.[31]

In its almost complete dedication to a historical perspective on the prince and society, *Poppea* fulfills the historicist tendency of *Ulisse.* In *Poppea,* mythology is confined to the prologue and to a few, obviously dispensable interventions in the plot. If *Ulisse* advances a historical image of the prince by replacing encomiums to the ruling house with descriptions of some of the real problems of dynastic rule, *Poppea* goes one step further. *Poppea*'s thoroughly unheroic Nerone plunges his own throne into a web of opposition and conspiracy. Similarly, if *Ulisse* does not endow the prince with the remote, absolutist attributes of divinity, *Poppea* depicts a ruler who is so far from divinity that he is a slave to his own base, emotional nature. Nerone's character weaknesses in turn corrupt the morality and civic virtue of his subjects. In addition to its aristocratic leading characters, *Poppea* presents an array of soldiers, nurses, servants, students, and artists, each of whom are affected and frequently compromised by the amorous adventures of their intemperate emperor.

If *Poppea* is the first thoroughly historical opera, one naturally inquires into the character of its history. It clearly is not a slavish recounting of the factual details of Nero's reign. The opera represents, for example, the forced suicide of Seneca as the central event of Nerone's liaison with and marriage to Poppea. But Nero's affair with Poppea began in A.D. 59 and culminated in marriage in A.D. 62. Nero did not order the death of Seneca until A.D. 65, and he did so probably because he had wearied of Seneca's tutelage and was suspicious of Seneca's participation in the Piso Conspiracy.[32] *Poppea* both edits and conflates the historical events on which it is based.

The true historical character of *Poppea* lies in its relation to the Venice of the 1640s. The opera's treatment of Nerone reveals both the achievement and the limitation of the Venetian republican ideal. On one hand, the simple fact that a prince could be depicted in a realistic and indeed critical way testifies to the persistence of Venetian republicanism. But on the other hand, the edge of this republicanism is blunted, and the opera's last scenes portray the absolutist tyrant as happy and triumphant. Like the republicanism of Machiavelli, the Venetian preference for a republic did not require an antipathy for monarchy.[33] The result is an opera that abounds in sensuality and brutality but lacks the practical and republican didacticism of the Renaissance historical consciousness. Thus divorced from any practical political intent, the story of Nerone and Poppea remains at the level of an exquisitely realized historical anecdote—a masterpiece of baroque musical-historical entertainment fit for a Venetian audience thirsting for hedonistic delights that posed no challenge to the precarious status quo.

Poppea broaches a number of themes of Renaissance political thought: the conflict between ideas of fortune and of virtue, the merits of the vita activa versus the vita contemplativa, the proper relationship of the prince to his subjects. Yet none of these themes is pursued to a definitive resolution. The result is an opera marked more by ambiguities than by a prescriptive vision of a properly ordered moral and political life.

As usual, the prologue foreshadows the political message of the opera. It opens with a debate between the mythological gods Fortuna and Virtù. Fortuna, typically, is a capricious woman who claims responsibility for human wealth and fame. But Virtù is no Machiavellian symbol of masculine strength, cunning, and dexterity in politics. Rather, Virtù is also a woman, and she represents the traditional, pre-Machiavellian notion of virtue as rationally guided moral constancy. In any case, the debate of the prologue, like the political themes of the opera itself, is not resolved. It is interrupted by the appearance of Amore, who asserts his dominion over human hearts and empires alike.

This ambiguity carries over into the rest of the opera. The complex plot of *Poppea* centers on Nerone's resolve to divorce the empress Ottavia, the daughter of the emperor Claudius and thus a key to the legitimacy of Nerone's accession to the throne, so that he can marry Poppea. The first act opens with Ottone, Poppea's lover, finding Nerone's guards in front of her house. The grumblings of the awakening soldiers are interrupted by the appearance of Nerone and Poppea. After Nerone leaves, Arnalta, Poppea's old nurse, cautions Poppea about her hopes for marriage with the emperor. Meanwhile, in her palace, a sorrowful Ottavia is consoled by her nurse, Nutrice. Seneca, the philosopher, statesman, and former tutor of the emperor, enters and urges the empress to endure her grief, but Valletto, the empress's page, wants Seneca to provide more tangible assistance. Alone in his garden, Seneca is met first by Pallade (Athena), who warns of the fatal consequences of his intervention, and then by Nerone, who is enraged by Seneca's advice against divorce. Returning to Poppea, Nerone pledges Seneca's speedy death. Later, Ottone enters, but Poppea rejects his attempt at reconciliation. Ottone finds consolation in the arms of Drusilla, Ottavia's lady-in-waiting.

In the second act, Seneca's death sentence is heralded by the god Mercurio, then confirmed by the reluctant Liberto, the captain of Nerone's guard. Although his students urge him to defy the sentence, Seneca nevertheless retires to his bath to take his life. In an interlude, Valletto woos Damigella, a pretty maid, and Nerone celebrates Seneca's death with his friend, the poet Lucano. Meanwhile, Ottavia incites Ottone to kill Poppea, who disguises himself in Drusilla's clothes. Calmed by Arnalta's lullaby, Poppea falls asleep, but she is awakened by Amore and alerted to the approaching assassination attempt.

Nerone deals with the conspirators in the third act. He has Drusilla tortured. She later volunteers to share Ottone's sentence of exile, and Nerone announces his intention to not only divorce but also exile Ottavia. Arnalta looks forward to her status as servant to an empress, while Ottavia bids farewell to Rome. Acclaimed by the consuls and tribunes, Poppea is crowned. The opera closes with Nerone and Poppea declaring their love in a passionate duet.

For diverse reasons, three aristocrats—Ottavia, Ottone, and Seneca—provide the core of the opposition to the marriage of Nerone and Poppea. Although each of these figures is morally and politically justified in her or his opposition to the marriage, each is also depicted as being somehow compromised. Ottavia is presented as a paragon of aristocratic virtue, long-suffering at the hands of her wayward husband. Her moving lament to her Roman fatherland at the time of her banishment is reminiscent of Monteverdi's best work in this genre. But the noble Ottavia is not above a little blackmail of unwilling accomplices (Ottone) and a little murder for a good cause. Nerone's correct suspicion of Ottavia's responsibility for the attempt on Poppea's life justifies her exile. Likewise, the noble Ottone rightly believes that Poppea's love for Nerone is as much a product of ambition for the throne as it is of genuine affection. Yet Ottone has trouble maintaining a pose of righteous indignation. Spurned by Poppea, he readily accepts the proffered charms of Drusilla. And despite some hesitation, he ultimately agrees to Ottavia's assassination plan. This last incident provides not only a moment of dramatic tension but also, via Ottone's disguise, an element of sexual ambiguity. Gender travesty pervades *Poppea* and would run rampant in the Italian baroque operas of Monteverdi's successors.

The true antagonist of the opera is Seneca. Curiously, Seneca, not Nerone, is invested with some of the characteristics of the baroque absolutist prince. It is Seneca, the "true friend of heaven," who is twice visited by gods during moments of blissful solitude and repose.[34] It is Seneca who is given to sententious Stoic pronouncements about reason, virtue, and self-restraint, citing both their intrinsic value and their effectiveness in creating sound governments. And it is Seneca who, although never advocating a return to the republic, reminds Nerone that the imperial system should respect law, morality, the senate, and the wishes of the people. Indeed, Busenello's libretto contained a scene depicting Seneca enthroned in heaven, but Monteverdi did not set the scene to music.[35]

But even Seneca, the chief spokesman for good imperial government, is a compromised figure.[36] There are ambiguities and ambivalences in his own pronouncements. His commitment to morality and virtue in political life leaves room for Machiavellian crimes to, as he says, "extend the empire" (116). And in echoing contemporary Venetian doubts about the vita activa, he realizes that his long years of service to Nerone and Rome seem to contradict his espoused values of solitude, contemplation, and philosophy. Seneca's dilemmas may resemble those faced by many people who are committed to both the life of the mind and the life of practical political action, but minor characters delight in pointing out Seneca's other flaws. Valletto demands that Seneca dispense with his usual series of pious pronouncements. Nerone's soldiers complain about Seneca's pedantry, sycophantism, and financial opportunism. Even Seneca's suicide does not pass without critical comment. His Stoic hymn about the transitoriness of human life and the joys of eternal life after death is answered by his young disciples, who praise the sweetness of life in this world. This Epicurean affirmation of sensuous life is later underscored in Nerone and Lucano's orgy of poetry and song, which is often performed as a scene of drunken revelry.

Ruled by passion and impulse rather than reason, motivated by self-interest rather than the good of the state, Nerone fulfills both the Platonic and the Aristotelian conceptions of the tyrant. But in the ambiguous moral universe of *Poppea*, the most incisive criticisms of Nerone's rule have a more modern and practical, a more Machiavellian, foundation. In his impulsive and self-interested actions, particularly his pursuit of another man's lover, Nerone needlessly risks the security of his throne and dynasty.[37]

The first time Nerone appears on stage, he is singing a passionate love duet. Whereas the cunning Ulisse postpones his tender love duet with Penelope until after his political tasks are completed, the lovesick emperor causes his guards to grouse that he is ignoring the military threats in the provinces. And unlike Melanto and Eurimaco, the commoner lovers in *Ulisse*, Valletto and Damigella, a maid, provide no clear counterpart to the aristocratic pair in *Poppea*. Only the more ribald and comedic language of Valletto and Damigella separates them from Nerone and Poppea, who have lost all sense of aristocratic dignity or political responsibility.

Consistent with Machiavelli's advice to avoid the hatred of the people and dominant social groups, Seneca informs Nerone that the pillars of the imperial order—reason, law, the senate, the people, and even the gods—oppose Nerone's divorce from Ottavia. But Nerone expresses his contempt for all these. For this impulsive tyrant, "Force is the law in peace and the sword in war, / and does not need to be in the right" (115). Nerone's force is not the judicious use of Machiavellian, lionlike strength. Rather, like Thrasymachus in Plato's *Republic*, Nerone foolishly relies on force as the sole foundation for his rule. Later in the opera, Nerone reveals his impetuousness as a judge. When the assassination attempt on Poppea is thwarted, he precipitously condemns the conspirators with ingenious and brutal punishments, but he does so with no regard for Roman law, proper procedure, or the security of his throne and dynasty. Characteristically, the opera does not depict the well-known historical consequences of Nero's tyrannical incompetence. Although the identities of the composer and librettist of "Pur ti miro," the closing duet, are unknown,[38] the love and passion between the now-crowned Poppea and Nerone have the last words in the opera.

Nerone's slavery to his own passions determines his relationship to his subjects. In characterizations that are compatible with Renaissance republican critiques of tyranny, the Roman people are reduced to the status of bondsmen, and the attendants at court are corrupted.[39] Invoked by Seneca and Ottavia but despised by Nerone, *il popolo* are an abstract and ultimately ineffectual factor in *Poppea*. No chorus offers the perspective of the citizenry on the palace intrigues. By implication, the people are passive spectators of events that they cannot control. Venetian commercial opera houses frequently held down expenses by reducing or eliminating the chorus, and in this case fiscal frugality coincided with political realism. Popular political activism was not characteristic of imperial Rome, nor was it encouraged in a republican Venice concerned more with the stability of its ruling aristocracy than with popular extensions of the vita activa civile.

The common people who are actually depicted in *Poppea* are all attendants at court, and each is infected with the moral and political decay of their tyrannous master. We have already encountered derelict and malcontent soldiers, besotted artists, libidinous servants, and recalcitrant student-disciples. Originally stock characters derived from commedia dell'arte, fairs, and other popular entertainments, Nutrice and Arnalta, the elderly nurses, are excellent examples of how the opera endows commoners with characteristics that not only are particularizing and realistic but are also sheer negations of those possessed by an uncorrupted aristocratic order. In response to Ottavia's complaints about Nerone's infidelity, Nutrice recommends sexual revenge: Ottavia should take a lover of her own. Likewise, early in the opera, Arnalta, *en travesti*, has some advice for her mistress. She cautions Poppea about her affair with Nerone, not so much for its adulterous immorality but for the danger that could come from a vengeful Ottavia. Later Arnalta exults in her elevated status.

Also writing in the middle of the seventeenth century, Algernon Sidney, a radical republican, would have attributed the decayed moral atmosphere of *Poppea* to monarchy itself. He speculated "whether bawds, whores, thieves, buffoons, parasites, and such vile wretches as are naturally mercenary, have not more power at Whitehall, Versailles, the Vatican, and the Escurial, than in Venice, Amsterdam, and Switzerland."[40] But in *Poppea*, the inability of commoners to find a firm foothold for virtuous moral or political action is the product of not so much monarchy per se but the corrupted monarchy of a tyrannous prince. In *Poppea*, the critique of one-person rule is foreshortened. The spectacle of courtly corruption serves not as the occasion for a disquisition on republican virtue but as an excuse for voyeuristic titillation at the expense of a monarchy gone sour.

Despite their many differences, *Orfeo, Ulisse,* and *Poppea* share an unremittingly aristocratic social outlook. Individual princes and aristocrats may or may not have the noble character that is expected of them. Individual commoners are depicted with distinctive dress, occupations, language, and mannerisms but without independent perspectives on the central dilemmas of the operas. Instead, the commoners mirror or distort the views of their overlords. Like the plays of Shakespeare, Monteverdi's operas regard society as "just a conditioning background" for the adventures of princes and aristocrats.[41] Roughly a century later, Giovanni Battista Pergolesi's miniature operatic masterpiece, *La serva padrona* (1733), heralded society's emergence from the background. And by the late eighteenth century, in Mozart's late comedies, status differences became nascent class conflict, and society, not the personal strengths and weaknesses of nobles, became the causal force of historical change.

TWO

The Dialectic of Operatic Civilization
Mozart's *Don Giovanni*

Aristotle's proposition on the aesthetic effect of art epitomizes the dual function of art: both to oppose and to reconcile; both to indict and to acquit; both to recall the repressed and to repress it again—"purified."

—HERBERT MARCUSE

PERA was the most distinctive cultural achievement of the baroque era, equally at home in the seventeenth-century courts of absolute monarchs and in commercial theaters of aristocratic republics. But in the eighteenth century, opera was transformed by the new spirit of the Enlightenment. No opera captures the essential contradiction of this new spirit more profoundly than *Don Giovanni*, by Wolfgang Amadeus Mozart (1756–91).

In an attempt to follow up on their successful Prague production of *Le nozze di Figaro* (1786), Mozart and librettist Lorenzo Da Ponte, the poet to the Imperial Theater in Vienna, wrote *Il dissoluto punito ossia il Don Giovanni* (1787), to be performed in the same city. *Così fan tutte* (1790) would be the final collaboration between Mozart and his most talented librettist.

From the time of its premiere in Prague, *Don Giovanni* has been attended, or plagued, by an arid formal controversy: whether it is the "perfect" opera.[1] Yet even its admirers admit that it is not a seamless synthesis of music and text, à la *Così fan tutte*, but rather a mélange of ambivalences and chance encounters culminating in an anachronistic deus ex machina. One commentator condemns Da Ponte for his failure to "rationalize the action" of the libretto.[2] Another is gentler, merely acknowledging the "untidiness" of the opera.[3] The core of the *Giovanni* problem is its central character, who manages to be at once a comic villain and a tragic hero.

In this chapter I shall not criticize *Don Giovanni* for its lack of rationalization. Nor shall I resolve its untidiness in some higher synthesis. My task here is to take the apparent slips of a consummate librettist and a consummate music dramatist out of the realm of individual artistic contingency and to interpret them, instead, as aesthetic manifestations of political conflicts. From this perspective, the unrationalized untidiness of *Don Giovanni* articulates a central contradiction of its age: the conflict between the individual's desire for sensual freedom and the containment of this desire by an increasingly complex and intrusive modern (that is, postfeudal) society. In other words, along with its many other qualities, *Don Giovanni* is also a political text.

The opera does not address the most visible political debate of the prerevolutionary period: whether a monarchy, aristocratic parliament, or republic is the most appropriate form for the state of an enlightened society.[4] Indeed, it is one of the intriguing curiosities of this opera that the state, which is provided numerous points of possible intervention by the action of the plot, is instead manifested in only a few brief references to ineffectual "authorities."

But *Don Giovanni* is a political text to the extent that it is a disquisition on the character and limits of those introjected values, ideals, and traditions that are the indispensable foundation of life in an enlightened state. G. W. F. Hegel called these internalized behavioral dispositions "custom," "second nature," and "ethical life."[5] Alexis de Tocqueville was more elegant, referring simply to the "habits of the heart."[6] Whatever the terminology, the recognition that a significant portion of human conduct was apparently self-regulated represented a decisive restriction on the coercive claims of the absolute state and church.[7]

The most characteristic and problematic of these enlightened habits was the pursuit of individual self-interest. Enlightenment thinkers legitimized political and economic self-interest as the foundation for just and prosperous political societies. In social contract theory, political justice was predicated on the self-interested political consent of the people. Economic prosperity was likewise based on the hedonism of laissez-faire capitalism, the successful practice of which depends upon resourceful cunning and improvisation.[8] Yet when this legitimation of rational political and economic self-interest threatened to spill over into sexual relations, many of these same Enlightenment thinkers scrambled to put the genie back in the bottle. Here the limits of self-interest were drawn tight. Despite the enlightened constriction of the absolute state, at the end of the eighteenth century "sex became a matter that required the social body as a whole, and virtually all of its individuals, to place themselves under surveillance."[9]

From this viewpoint, which enables one to find the imprint of society in the apparent lacunae of an artwork, *Don Giovanni* can be interpreted as a representation of two incompletely reconciled tendencies in Enlightenment political thought, two interpretations of the fate of the individual in the transition to the thoroughly modern social order. On one hand, the opera reflects the dominant Enlightenment view of historical change as progress. As a comedic exhibition and condemnation of Don Giovanni's anachronistic "style of baroque living,"[10] the opera aligns itself with the era's familiar advocacy of reason over fear, industriousness over self-indulgence, reconciliation over force, and stability over caprice. Far from wanting to overturn all forms of social hierarchy, advocates of Enlightenment progress merely stripped class-, status-, and gender-based relationships of their feudal dross and refitted them according to the requirements of the modern social order. From Francis Bacon and John Locke through Gottfried

Wilhelm Leibniz to Voltaire and the Marquis de Condorcet, the tendency was to extol modern society for its commitment to reason and science in guiding human affairs. This belief in progress has often been one-sidedly identified as *the* Enlightenment view of history.

But the Don Giovanni of Mozart's opera is more than a comic villain who disrupts modern and progressive society with his obsolete adventurism. Despite his violence, deceit, and attempted seductions, he remains the tragic hero of the opera: a symbol of what is lost in the transition to modernity, perhaps a sign of fulfillment in some better mode of life still to come. The intellectual context for Don Giovanni's tragic heroism is also deeply rooted in late-eighteenth-century Enlightenment thought.

The view of history as progress produced its own antithesis: a focus on the preservation and cultivation of the nonrational dimensions of human life. Herein lies the source of the complexity of *Don Giovanni* and its central character. The reversal was announced by Rousseau, refined in the aesthetic writings of Kant and Friedrich von Schiller, and intensified in the novels of Pierre Choderlos de Laclos and the Marquis de Sade. Despite his Enlightenment belief in Providence and his optimism about the possibility of social and political reform,[11] Rousseau's *Discourse on the Arts and Sciences* (1750) pilloried the dominant view of history for its excessive faith in reason, science, and progress and for its insensitivity to the still-valid legacy of the past and to matters of the heart. In his *Discourse on the Origin of Inequality* (1755) and other writings, Rousseau regarded each step into modern civilized society as, not an advance of reason and science over traditionalism and superstition, but an additional step into inequality, falsehood, and the frustration of the passions and instincts. Later, in the theories of German Idealism, aesthetics, broadly conceived as the science of human sensuousness, became the refuge of those aspects of human nature that were denied or devalued by the dominant Enlightenment view of history. Kant's

Critique of Judgment (1790) argued for an aesthetic faculty—at once intuitive and rational, subjective and universal—which mediated between the scientific pronouncements of pure reason and the moral lawfulness of practical reason. In Schiller's *Letters on the Aesthetic Education of Man* (1795), aesthetics shed its Kantian formalism and abstraction, and became the means by which a sensuous wholeness could be restored to the fractured lives of modern human beings.[12]

For the aesthetic philosophers who were attentive to the nonrational aspects of human nature, passion and instinct became the benign foundations for the indispensable sensuousness of an integrated human personality. But the artists of the age identified this passion and instinct with a cutting edge. Laclos's *Les liaisons dangereuses* (1793) and Sade's fiction (from *Les 120 journées de sodome* [1784] through *Justine* [1791]) saw a compulsive, ineradicable, and socially disruptive sexual drive as basic to human nature.

This artistic preoccupation with sexuality permeated spoken and musical theater. The story of Don Juan, the libertine nobleman of Seville, became a favored vehicle for theatrical disquisitions on the problems of passion, instinct, and sexuality. Don Juan was the subject of innumerable popular entertainments. In literary culture, the theme first appeared in Tirso de Molina's *El burlador de Sevilla* (1630). It was later taken up in Molière's *Don Juan, ou le festin de pierre* (1665), Thomas Shadwell's *Libertine* (1676), and Carlo Goldoni's *Don Giovanni Tenorio, ossia il dissoluto* (1736). Sexual conflicts propel Mozart's *Figaro* and *Così*. And of course they pervade *Don Giovanni*, which was no less than the eighth operatic account of Don Juan to appear between 1776 and 1787.[13] Although Søren Kierkegaard was certainly right in claiming that it is the Mozart–Da Ponte opera which has become the model of the subject, *Don Giovanni* was hardly the final word on the theme.[14] The figure of Don Juan appears in many later works, including Lord Byron's unfinished epic *Don Juan*, Aleksandr Pushkin's tragedy *The Stone Guest* (1830), Richard Strauss's tone poem

Don Juan (1888), and George Bernard Shaw's play *Man and Superman* (1905), to mention only a few.

HISTORY AND FORM

Both baroque and early classical opera were preoccupied with representations of the state and its rulers. But in such later classical works as *Don Giovanni*, society is no longer just the background for the actions of powerful figures on a grand political stage; instead, it emerges as the increasingly differentiated and self-conscious basis for the determination of an individual's fate. Although this society lends regularity, security, and a measure of fairness to human life, it also poses the ultimate and insurmountable obstacle to the fulfillment of human desire.

The new awareness of the importance of society was incorporated into the evolution of operatic art. In the 150 years between the early baroque masterpieces of Monteverdi and the later classical comedies of Mozart, opera underwent a complex development. Formally, the increasing awareness of the importance of society led first to the differentiation, then to the remixing, of operatic subgenres. Thematically, the recognition of society led opera to the incorporation of the Enlightenment interest in didactic art, that is, in art as a vehicle for the communication of moral and political precepts.

By the early eighteenth century, operatic subgenres had acquired a class content. In the preceding century, commoner characters had freely intermingled with aristocrats in Monteverdi's *Ulisse* and *Poppea*. These commoners were not fully conscious rivals to the aristocracy, who were pursuing their own class interests; rather, they were colorful additions who provided relief and contrast to the political intrigues of the noble protagonists. But in the eighteenth century, the "stuttering servants and lecherous tenor nurses and transvestite *castrati*" of baroque opera found their way into their own subgenre, opera buffa.[15] These characters no longer intervened in affairs of state but confined their actions to the social sphere. The conventions of opera buffa as a comedy of manners required a lieto fine, or happy ending. Through disclosure, compassion, or a change of heart, the conflicts between the characters were reconciled.[16] These didactic happy endings also prescribed standards of moral behavior within society.

Matters of state, usually set in classical mythology or history, became the preserve of aristocrats. Opera seria, the operatic equivalent of tragedy, was more rigid and formalistic than opera buffa: it usually adhered to the unities of time and place, retained the baroque penchant for spectacular dei ex machina, and clearly distinguished between plot-advancing recitatives and reflective arias. But the sheer display of princely power, so characteristic of baroque opera, no longer sufficed, because these displays lacked enlightened didacticism. In opera seria, the aristocratic hero experienced some form of a tragic fate that was no less prescriptive than the happy ending of opera buffa. Classical opera seria defined the parameters of eighteenth-century enlightened rulership.

Long before the collaborations between Mozart and Da Ponte sounded the death knell of the buffa-seria distinction, the subgenres began to mix. Comic opera was the vehicle of change. The configuration of characters in comic opera was socially differentiated. Serious characters, usually but not always portrayed as aristocrats, embodied the traditional virtues of constancy, bravery, honor, and love. Comic characters, usually portrayed as lower-class types, were fickle, cowardly, base, and lewd. A middle character either lacked the clearly defined personalities of the serious or comic types or possessed aspects of both.[17] There was also greater musical continuity in the new mixed comedies. The traditional aria-recitative dichotomy fractured dramatic unity. But in Mozart's comic operas and especially in his late works, the incorporation of symphonic technique and the construction of extended finales through the integration of aria, recitative, and ensemble devices gave comic opera more continuity and a greater sense of dramatic plausibility.[18]

As a mixture of comic and serious elements, *Don Giovanni*

draws on familiar components of the Don Juan story. The first act opens with Don Giovanni's valet, Leporello, impatiently waiting. The Don has entered the bedroom of a young noblewoman, Donna Anna, whom he attempts to seduce or rape. Her father, the Commendatore, responds to her cries for help. In the ensuing duel, Don Giovanni kills the old man. The Don escapes. Donna Anna's betrothed, Don Ottavio, promises to help capture and punish her father's unidentified killer. Meanwhile, Don Giovanni has an unwelcome encounter with an abandoned former lover, Donna Elvira. While Leporello distracts Elvira with an account of the Don's amorous conquests, the Don makes another quick exit. Near Don Giovanni's villa, the Don and Leporello meet up with the wedding party of a peasant couple, Zerlina and Masetto. Don Giovanni is attracted to Zerlina, and he invites the party to visit his estate, thereby managing to separate Zerlina from her companions. As he is attempting to seduce Zerlina, Elvira makes another untimely appearance. When Anna and Ottavio also happen on the scene, Giovanni characterizes Elvira's accusations as the ravings of a madwoman, and Anna realizes that the Don, although he prevaricates, is in fact her father's murderer. Inside his villa, Giovanni stages a wedding banquet for Zerlina and Masetto. Disguised by masks, the three avenging nobles—Elvira, Anna, and Ottavio—are invited to join the festivities. Giovanni again attempts to seduce Zerlina, but her cries for help alert the others. Giovanni tries to blame Leporello for Zerlina's distress, but the avenging aristocrats see through his ruse. In most stagings, the act ends with Giovanni and Leporello making an improbable escape.

The second act finds Don Giovanni and Leporello exchanging their garb. Leporello, in the guise of the Don, is to distract Donna Elvira, while the Don, in the guise of Leporello, is to seduce Elvira's maid. Masetto enters with a band of armed peasants who are searching for Giovanni, whom they are determined to kill. Disguised as Leporello, the Don expresses his sympathy for their cause and then splits the peasant forces in two, sending them in opposite directions. Left alone with Masetto, Giovanni disarms him and beats him with his sword. Zerlina comes by and comforts Masetto. Leporello, still dressed as Giovanni and still in the company of Elvira, is confronted by an infuriated Anna, Ottavio, Zerlina, Masetto, and assorted servants. In order to save his own life, Leporello reveals his true identity, then makes his escape. Ottavio resolves to summon the authorities. Leporello and Giovanni reunite in a moonlit graveyard, where a statue of the slain Commendatore accuses the Don. Giovanni responds by inviting the statue to dinner at his villa. Later, Giovanni is enjoying a late supper at his villa when Elvira bursts into the room, pleading with him to repent and accept her love. Much to the surprise of the terrified Leporello, the statue of the Commendatore comes to the door. Accepting the statue's proffered hand, the Don is pulled down to eternal damnation, rejecting his last opportunity to repent his sins. In the denouement, the surviving principal characters, joined by the authorities (nonsinging ministers of justice), are assembled to acclaim the justness of Don Giovanni's punishment and to disclose their plans for their respective futures.

THE SOCIAL ORDER OF OPERATIC SEVILLE

Before assessing the social and political meaning of the Don Giovanni's character, I shall sketch the mise-en-scène of his activities. The setting of the opera's action is much more than a mere backdrop. Whether Giovanni is viewed as a comic villain or a tragic hero, his antagonist is not a single character but a society: the mobilized social forces of operatic Seville.

The Seville of *Don Giovanni* is a contradictory conceit, a construct of the eighteenth-century aesthetic imagination. On one hand, it clearly evokes a pre-Enlightenment historical backwardness. Its iconic associations with the Inquisition, superstition, and unreconstructed absolutism flatter the self-proclaimed Enlightenment of more progressive European metropolises. For Mozart's audiences in Prague, Paris, or Vienna, Spanish Seville was a plausible venue for the adventures of anachronistic noblemen and perambulating statues. But on the other hand, the seventeenth-century Seville of *Don Giovanni* is stripped of its historical particularity. Instead, it is invested with a post-Enlightenment society's expectations regarding proper class, status, and gender behaviors.

In his analysis of the prehistory of the historical novel, Georg Lukács noted the tendency of Enlightenment writers to project eighteenth-century assumptions about behavior and belief back onto earlier ages.[19] *Don Giovanni* is similarly cavalier about historical accuracy. The music contains no elements of local Spanish color but only the eighteenth-century cosmopolitan tonality and forms of Italian opera. The stage band accompaniment to the Don's last supper—three excerpts from late-eighteenth-century operas, including Mozart's own *Figaro*—confirms the score's proleptic version of events. The libretto also eschews historical realism in favor of a selected depiction of society according to eighteenth-century assumptions. One would never know from the opera that, by the seventeenth century, Seville was a city in decay: a century past its heyday as a center for international trade, it was then plagued by beggars, thieves, and gangs as well as a formidable array of local, royal, and church authorities (including the Inquisition) who vainly tried to reimpose order amid the squalor.[20]

Without any overt sanctions by the state or the church, the two prescribers of lawful and moral behavior, the opera assumes a Seville with a complex but self-regulating system of modern class, status, and gender relations. On several occasions, Leporello envisions positions of servile employment (certainly not feudal service) where his master would treat him fairly. The Commendatore and Donna Anna share familial love and respect. The cases of Donna Anna and Don Ottavio, Zerlina and Masetto, and even Donna Elvira and Don Giovanni suggest an expectation that current and prospective marital partners will be faithful to each other. Masetto and his peasant allies look for decent treatment from aristocrats, who will then receive well-deserved deference. And throughout the social order of operatic Seville, there is the assumption that people will identify themselves honestly and speak the truth.

Apparently without reference to the criminal codes of the state or the moral codes of institutional religion, this orderly operatic Seville is nevertheless suffused by certain social regulations that are clearly understood and consensually observed. In its depiction of "lawful" behavior without an institutional foundation, the opera incorporates elements of social contract theory, particularly elements of the second of Locke's *Two Treatises of Government* (1690). With its complex social system, Seville is not an example of Locke's "state of nature." But it does lack any sign of an effective government. Seville is depicted as a Lockean, prepolitical society subject to the requirements of an unwritten body of natural law "that is plain and intelligible to all rational Creatures."[21]

But Don Giovanni destabilizes Seville's system of social relations. His relationship with his valet abuses and corrupts a member of the lower classes. His duel deprives a dutiful daughter of her loving father. His attempts at seduction disrupt established conjugal relations. His adventures substitute unenlightened aristocratic deception and opaqueness for the emerging Enlightenment ideal of honesty and transparency in social relations. The Don ruptures the opera's presumption of regularity and order in modern society.

The sexual reputation of the Don (to which I shall return) is scrupulously documented in Leporello's famous "catalogue" aria, which details Giovanni's disruptive influence on conjugal relations. Throughout the twenty-four hours or so dramatized in the opera, the Don vainly tries to add to the "mille e tre" of his Spanish sexual conquests, completely contemptuous of the effects—including possible offspring—that may devolve from his encroachments on established relationships.

And Don Giovanni has a no less disruptive effect on the class structure. According to late-eighteenth-century operatic conventions, the Don is a middle character, exhibiting some of the serious character traits associated with the aristocracy but also some of the comic character traits of the lower classes. The Don retains his aristocratic wealth and courage, but otherwise he behaves in a declassed manner. His noble status is no more than a means for his own pleasure: a token by which he can bully Masetto and dazzle Zerlina; a source of wealth for personal servants, impromptu wedding feasts, liveried musicians, and midnight banquets. To be sure, the Don has the traditional aristocratic virtue of courage under duress, but his sense of honor has been stripped of all political and social responsibility.

Operatic Seville is a distinctly postfeudal society. The opera is rife with references to the then modern conception of the proper behavior for aristocrats and servants. These class distinctions not only pervade the libretto but also structure the musical forms. The noble avengers—Anna, Ottavio, and Elvira—are given the *da capo* arias of traditional eighteenth-century opera seria, whose repeat sections are the musical embodiment of aristocratic reason and balance. The commoner characters—Leporello, Zerlina, and Masetto—sing looser forms more closely related to popular songs. But the Don, the disrupter of Seville's class structure, lacks a formal, extended aria of his own. Tactically adapting his musical language to the situation at hand,[22] the Don musically invades his milieu through recitatives, ensembles, and fleeting ariettas.

The Don's destabilizing effect on the class structure is most clearly represented in the wedding banquet scene at the end of the first act. Three stage bands play simultaneously. Donna Anna and Don Ottavio dance a courtly minuet, while Leporello forces the unwilling peasant Masetto to dance a popular waltz. The Don leads Zerlina in a contredanse, a dance without clear class associations. Although these dances have different rhythms, Mozart synchronizes them through intricate counterpoint. But the Don's attempt to seduce Zerlina destroys the musical representation of social harmony, as he turns the class structure into social cacophony. In the sphere of Don Giovanni's activities, Seville is no longer a model of social stability based on class status.

If there is little doubt that the Don disrupts the social order of
Seville, the crucial question remains as to the character and evaluation of his disruptions. It is clear that the Don is an anachronistic remnant within a fictional representation of Enlightenment
social order. But the opera's normative evaluation of this disruptive remnant is far from clear. Is the Don a mere comic anachronism? Or is he a tragic martyr for the principles of the old order?
Here emerges the essential contradiction of the opera—its simultaneous representation of two Enlightenment attitudes toward
historical progress. In the realm of formal political theory, the
representation of related yet distinct ideas is usually the task of
rival theorists, schools, or texts. But the association of music with
these ideas is different, is more synthetic. According to Hegel,
"Only if music becomes a spiritually adequate expression [of an
age] in the sensuous medium of sounds and their varied counterpoint does music rise to being genuine art."[23] Like the operatic
ensemble, that simultaneous expression of varied viewpoints that
is the bane of dramatic purists, *Don Giovanni* contains the "varied
counterpoint" of a "spiritually adequate expression" by fusing the
progressive and regressive, the rational and aesthetic, perspectives of the Enlightenment in a single work—indeed, in the persona of a single character.

THE COMIC GIOVANNI: OPERA AS ENLIGHTENED
CRITIQUE OF THE BAROQUE

The Don is a mixed character in a mixed work. The ambivalence of
Don Giovanni extends to the opera's conclusion. The final sextet
suggests a buffa reaffirmation of the status quo. But already in the
second production of the work—in Vienna in 1788, a production
overseen by Mozart—this scene may have been dropped. Object-
ing to the "repressive morality" of this sextet, Gustav Mahler
dropped from it his stagings, a practice followed by a number of
directors and conductors.[24] In these productions, the opera ends
as a tragedy, with the Don descending into the underworld.

From a political viewpoint, the two possible endings of *Don Giovanni* imply two different views of historical progress and two different views of the fate of the individual within historical progress. From the dominant and rationalistic Enlightenment view of history as progress, Don Giovanni is a comic figure, a caricature of an outmoded princely type, whose lifestyle is exhibited and condemned from the standpoint of progressive social forces. Seen through the eyes of modern society, the Don's aristocratic manner of life receives a withering critique. His principled pursuit of a variety of sexual experiences is mere fickleness, his martial skill mere force, his proclamations of honor mere rationalizations, and his love mere lasciviousness. A Machiavellian prince without a state, Don Giovanni's adventures introduce capriciousness and violence into the natural, divinely ordained order of Enlightenment society.

The primary means of turning Don Giovanni into a subject of ridicule is the depoliticization of the seventeenth-century setting of the opera. *Figaro* encased its depictions of characters' sexual adventures within a distinctly eighteenth-century social, economic, and political context. *Don Giovanni* meticulously represents society's expectations of class, status, and gender behaviors, and economic considerations are at least implied. Instead of using his gifts of cunning and improvisation within the newly legitimized capitalist economy, the Don is an idle aristocrat financing his life of pleasure with the wealth of his inherited estate. But in this opera the state is evanescent. *Figaro* represented the political decline of the eighteenth-century aristocracy, a diminution epitomized by Count Almaviva's belated assertion of the old seignorial right. The Count, however, retained important roles in the state, appearing at various points as ambassador to London, commander of an army regiment, and judicial magistrate. But *Don Giovanni* illustrates the growing irrelevance and parasitism of the traditional aristocracy, and it does so in the starkest possible terms. The Don's sexual exploits are not the perquisites of political power. Rather, the noble Don is anachronistically excluded from any position in the seventeenth-century political order.

Eschewing neo-Platonic pieties about the virtuous, remote, and austere prince, Machiavelli described his ideal prince as a political beast engaged in the rough-and-tumble politics of the emerging absolutist state. He extolled a ruler who possessed fox-like cunning in his intrigues against his rivals and lionlike courage when force was the necessary alternative. Despite Machiavelli's reputation for realism, his vision of the prince retains a normative element. What elevated the prince's cunning and force above those of the common con man or thug was the loftiness of his sphere of activity: the prince exhibited his cunning and force in the affairs of state.[25]

Don Giovanni is no less cunning and forceful than the Machia-vellian King Ulisse in Monteverdi's *Ulisse*. But in *Don Giovanni*, the Renaissance-baroque prince is marginalized from the state, the proper and epic sphere for noble intrigue and force. He thus is no model of absolutist realpolitik; rather, he is represented as a political anachronism and a social parasite, a peculiarly dangerous Don Quixote who perpetuates an outworn capriciousness, vio-lence, and uncertainty without any grand political goal. The victims of the Don's exhibitions of cunning and force are not rival princes but members of a modern society who are adhering to their appropriate social roles.

If the absence of the state diminishes Don Giovanni from a Machiavellian prince to an anachronistic parasite, it also deter-mines the terms of his pursuit and punishment. From the Don's forced entry into Donna Anna's room through his duel with the Commendatore to his assault of Masetto and Masetto's mobiliza-tion of a peasant vigilante force, the opportunities for interven-tion by state authorities are numerous and serious. Except for the belated and adventitious appearance of the ministers of justice in the denouement, the local police authorities of Seville are curi-ously absent. Other agencies would also have had an interest in such events as those depicted in the opera. Where, for example, are the representatives of the Hapsburg monarchy, who presumably would have mediated this dispute between local nobles? Where are the agents of the Inquisition, who would have delved into the activities of a nobleman known to be as blasphemous as he was profligate?

Despite Don Giovanni's alleged crimes, he is pursued not by agents of the state or the church but by representatives of the very social order that he has offended. The opera thus becomes a representation of the character and limits of social control in a prepolitical condition of civilization. First the Commendatore, then Donna Anna and Don Ottavio, and finally Zerlina, Masetto, the peasants, and the still reluctant Donna Elvira each exercise what Locke called the natural executive powers of revenge and deterrence.[26]

The avenging characters repeatedly assert the righteousness of their campaign against Don Giovanni. Without referring to the criminal codes of the state or the moral codes of institutional religion, they are firm in their conviction that the Don is guilty of violating the clearly known and consensually observed natural laws of society. And like the natural laws of contract theory, the social ordinances of *Don Giovanni* have a transcendental foundation. In terms recalling eighteenth-century Deism more than seventeenth-century Catholicism,[27] the avengers continually invoke the assistance of God and heaven in their attempts to bring about Don Giovanni's repentance for his crimes against the natural order of society.

The use of natural executive powers against the Don displays the familiar liabilities of this means of social control. The absence of state authorities acting as impartial judges of the events in the opera casts some doubt on the avengers' grievances. The circumstances surrounding Don Giovanni's entry into and actions within Donna Anna's bedchamber are unclear. In any case, his attempts at seduction are singularly unsuccessful, at least during the period of time depicted in the opera. Because his slaying of the Commendatore occurs during the course of a duel between the two noblemen, it is not an outright murder. His assault on Masetto takes place only after the peasant has openly declared his intention to kill the Don. An impartial judge might have convicted Don Giovanni, but only after considering circumstances that were at least mitigating.

Despite the existence of natural executive powers, the enforcement of natural law is problematic. Devoid of state authority, society's campaign against the Don is not only ambiguous but also ineffective. Supernatural force, represented by the ghostly statue of the Commendatore, becomes the avenger of the existing social order, whose violators are then condemned to perdition. The conditions of punishment are not determined by the state. Nor is the Don sent to the hell of Roman Catholic tradition. Rather, the violator of the natural laws of society is condemned to "remain below" in the ancient realm of "Proserpine and Pluto."[28]

The deus ex machina of the statue and the Don's horrible punishment recall the tragic practices of opera seria. Moreover, Don Giovanni's refusal to repent, his refusal to reflect on his actions, contradicts not only the buffa tradition but also the most cherished Enlightenment assumptions about an individual's ability to use reason to learn from his mistakes. But in the closing sextet, the surviving characters make a belated and only half-convincing attempt to deprive the Don of tragic status: to recall the comic element and restore this opera to a semblance of opera buffa. Thus, "in accordance with convention," the opera concludes with Zerlina, Masetto, and Leporello—the buffa types—stepping out of character to announce to the "good people" of the audience the moral of the work. Then the surviving characters sing:

> This is the evil-doer's end!
> The death of sinners
> Will always match their life! (260)

Don Giovanni, the degraded prince become social parasite, has been condemned by the transcendental force of natural law for his refusal to give up his life as an anachronistic adventurer and to accommodate himself to the mores of a modern, progressive society. Considered as a comic figure in a buffa opera, Don Giovanni has only one viable choice, and that is an accommodation to this society.[29] When the Don refuses to make this choice, the executive powers of society metamorphose into an "unconquerable cosmic force," which excises the social danger and effects a restoration of the social status quo.[30]

THE TRAGIC GIOVANNI: OPERA AS ENLIGHTENED CRITIQUE OF MODERN SOCIETY

From the rationalistic standpoint of the eighteenth-century Enlightenment, the character of Don Giovanni is a comic subject of ridicule. Because the Don has no role in the modern state, his exhibitions of cunning and force do not serve the epic goals of the heroic prince; instead, his exploits victimize members of society. And because the Don has no sense of enlightened social responsibility, his anachronistic adventures introduce an element of instability into an otherwise coherent modern social order.

But this comedic perspective on the Don illustrates only part of his enigmatic character. If an advocate of modern social progress could see the Don as a dangerous clown, a critic of social progress could see him as the tragic victim of social repression. From the time of their youths, both Mozart and Da Ponte had had contact with this Rousseauesque reversal of the dominant Enlightenment view of history. In 1768, when Mozart was twelve years old, he composed the music for the opera *Bastien und Bastienne*, an adaptation of Rousseau's opera *Le devin du village* (1752). The politics of Rousseau's opera lay in its simplicity and apparent naïveté. *Le devin* was Rousseau's artistic contribution to the raging "war of the buffoons" and a conscious assault on the complexity and artificiality of contemporary French court opera. In 1766, when he was seventeen years old, Da Ponte wrote poems on two Rousseauesque themes: "Whether the happiness of mankind is increased within the social system, or whether he would be happier in a simple state of nature," and "Man, by nature free, through laws becomes enslaved."[31] (These poems provoked a censure from the Venetian senate, an early instance of Da Ponte's series of scrapes with the censorial arm of the law.) While writing not only the libretto for *Don Giovanni* but also the texts for two other composers, Da Ponte described his working conditions in such a way as to suggest his sympathy for a sensuous philosophy of life and even a type of kinship with the Don: "I shall write evenings for Mozart, imagining I am reading the *Inferno*, . . . a bottle of Tokay to my right, the ink-well in the middle and a box of Seville snuff on my left. A beautiful young girl of sixteen (whom I would have liked to love simply as a daughter, but . . .) lived in the house with her mother, who looked after the family, and she came into the room whenever I rang the bell, which in fact I did pretty often."[32]

I do not believe that either Mozart or Da Ponte self-consciously set out to overlay the character of Don Giovanni with elements of Rousseau's philosophy. Nor do I believe that Don Giovanni is an example of Rousseau's natural man. The point is rather that both the composer and the librettist were familiar with the reversal of the dominant, rationalistic Enlightenment view of history and that elements of this reversal endow the Don with the heroic-tragic aspects of his character. From this perspective, the Don is still an anachronism, but one who defends an aesthetic existence endangered by the repressive logic of modern society. The specificity of the Don's aesthetic character can be derived by comparing it to the unmediated sensuousness of Leporello and the repressive social responsibility of Don Ottavio. The heroic stature of the Don is manifested in the encasement of his character within the structures of classical tragedy.

Contemporary productions are fond of emphasizing the kinship between Giovanni and Leporello. Some productions have even switched the performers back and forth between the two roles, taking advantage of similarities in the parts' vocal ranges.

Peter Sellars's celebrated 1989 production went beyond vocal similarities to characterological ones: Sellars cast the two parts with twin brothers. To be sure, both Giovanni and Leporello are devoted to sensual gratification. But unlike contemporary productions, the opera as written takes pains to distinguish between the sensuousness of the two characters. Unlike Leporello's, the Don's sensuousness is aesthetic—a fusion of reason and sensibility.

Leporello is a stock lower-class character of a type common in opera buffa. His sensuousness is merely part of the unreflected immediacy of his social existence, an example of what Marx called mere need and greed. Early in the opera, he complains about the bodily discomforts of his station in life: of being overworked, exposed to the elements, ill-fed, and deprived of sleep. When threatened, he cravenly fears for his life. Although he vows to quit the employ of the Don, his loyalty is quickly repurchased with a small bag of gold. And throughout the opera he desires the Don's leftovers, whether wine, food, or women. His sensuousness is not a matter of conscious choice or philosophical principle but one of economic necessity. Although his sensuousness represents a genuinely emancipatory example of lower-class hedonism, it is no model of natural human existence. Leporello is, rather, the victim of the limited and deformed possibilities of his class and status.

If Leporello satisfies his sensuous need and greed according to the possibilities of his social station, Don Ottavio is the epitome of sense-denying social reason. The object of his desire, his marriage to Donna Anna, is constantly thwarted by his curious and ineffective conception of feudal-modern social duty. Sensing the bloodlessness of Ottavio's feudal pledge to defend her honor and avenge her father's death, Anna's aria, "Or sai chi l'onore," tries to instill the "wrath of a just fury" in Ottavio's feeble efforts (106). Later, when Leporello escapes and the avengers are convinced that Giovanni is in the area, Ottavio drops the pretense of reaching for his sword and goes off to summon the authorities instead. The would-be executor of feudal blood revenge becomes the modern and reasonable member of a neighborhood crime-watch association. It is little wonder that, in the denouement, Anna delays the marriage for another year and that Ottavio, still bound by the repressive logic of his status and class, meekly accepts this postponement.

Don Giovanni is not necessarily more complicated than are Leporello or Ottavio. Indeed, partly because he has no extended, self-reflective aria, the Don seems to be, from a psychological point of view, the simplest character in the opera. We cannot develop a sense of his inner conflicts and doubts, nor are we sure that he has any. True to the martial traditions of his class (unlike both Leporello and Ottavio), he exhibits courage and skill under duress. But the decisive difference between the characters is a matter of self-conscious principle. The Don's aesthetic existence synthesizes reason and sensuousness.

Privileged by birth, wealth, and status, the Don has chosen, from among many other options, a life of sensuous pleasure. Avoiding the tedium of representing an extended Hugh Hefnerish outlook, the opera makes only a few brief but crucial references to the Don's philosophy. Giovanni's allusions to the principles of his worldview occur in the form of toasts. The first-act arietta "Fin ch'han del vino" extols wine, women, dancing, and music within the buffa form of a patter song. The theme returns toward the end of the second act. Rejecting Elvira's pleas for his repentance, the Don toasts women and wine, "the support and glory of mankind!" (240). Between these two episodes lies the toast of misunderstanding—sung first in harmony, then in unison—between Giovanni and the disguised noble avengers at the wedding banquet. Singing "Viva la libertà!" the Don salutes the freedom of his premodern life of pleasure and privilege. The avengers, however, praise the freedom of a modern social order cleansed of the caprices of anachronistic predators.

The Don's aesthetic nature is not a conquest of the mind over the body. The foundation of the Don's sensuousness is as corporeal as Leporello's. Early in the opera, Giovanni detects Elvira's presence by sense of smell and then visually perceives her beauty. The two sense perceptions mingling, the Don is powerfully attracted to her; as Leporello observes, "He's on fire already!" (54).

But the Don's sensuousness goes beyond mere need and greed to the pinnacle of human existence in what Marx called species-being. Overcoming the old operatic and philosophic dichotomies of mind and body, idealism and materialism, the Don is devoted to the development of "all physical and intellectual senses," to the "open revelation of human faculties."[33] Unlike Ottavio's reason, which denies him sensual gratification, Giovanni's reason is the culmination and fulfillment of his sensuousness. The Don is a connoisseur. Eating heartily, the Don takes the time to observe the tastiness of his last supper. He admires the vintage of his last wine. As he dines, his musicians play excerpts from the latest operas. And Leporello's catalogue aria makes it clear that the Don's desire for many types of women, including apparently unattractive ones, is the product not of indiscriminate lust but of his refined taste for variety.

But like Leporello's sensuousness and Don Ottavio's social responsibility, the Don's aesthetic existence is deformed by status and class, by a society based on domination. His aesthetic existence is the prerogative of only a few men, each of them privileged by birth and supported by the unseen labor of countless others. His threats and violence are unsublimated. And, although there is no reason to doubt his sincerity when he claims that he loved every one of the women he seduced,[34] his love is tainted by domination. He refers to his lovers as "conquests." With his peculiar penchant for amorous bookkeeping, he strips his lovers of their individuality, reducing them to anonymous, interchangeable ciphers in a ledger.

Despite its faults, the Don's aesthetic existence is heroized by the opera's embedding of his activities within a semblance of classical tragedy. From Giovanni's entry into Anna's bedchamber through the Don's last supper, the opera observes the classical unity of time. And by depicting these events in and around an area of Seville, the opera retains a classical unity of place.

DON GIOVANNI

What the opera seems to lack is the classical unity of action. Instead of an inevitable series of events, the opera appears to be episodic and disjointed. But even here there are suggestions of tragedy, or at least of a tragedy transformed by the modern Enlightenment recognition of the power of society. According to Leo Lowenthal, in drama the idea of fate has undergone a distinct historical development. In classical tragedy, fate was foreordained by the gods. In baroque drama, fate was determined by personal qualities, admirable or despicable. But in the drama of the Enlightenment, with its heightened awareness of society, fate becomes the product of chance encounters in society.[35] Accidental encounters and opportune escapes pervade *Don Giovanni*. The Don's tragic fate is sealed when the last of these chance meetings is with the statue of the Commendatore, the supernatural avenger of the social order.

Giovanni may lack the political stature of many heroes in classical tragedy. But the penultimate scene does depict him as a tragic martyr for an idea: the tradition of his premodern aesthetic existence. He welcomes his social fate, the statue of the Commendatore, into his home. He bravely accepts the statue's proffered hand. A man of refined sensibility during his lifetime, he feels intensely the agony of his last moments. He is chilled by the statue's stony grip, then seared by the leaping flames of hell.

Given one last chance to repent, to repudiate his aesthetic existence as sin and error before the supernatural incarnation of social modernity, Don Giovanni steadfastly refuses. Faced with a choice between his aesthetic life and the new world of sober bourgeois normality, the Don in his last words utters his monosyllabic credo of unvarnished truth. He cries, repeatedly, "No!" The heroism of the Don's death is opera's paramount example, in Herbert Marcuse's famous phrase, of the "Great Refusal": "To live one's love and hatred, to live that which one *is* means defeat, resignation, and death. The crimes of society, the hell that man has made for man become unconquerable cosmic forces."[36]

As we have seen, the political meaning of *Don Giovanni* lies in

its simultaneous, and unresolved, articulation of two Enlightenment views of historical progress, two views of the fate of the
individual within a stable but intrusive modern social order. From
the dominant Enlightenment view of history as reason and progress, the Don is a reactionary anachronism whose violence, deceit, indolence, and licentiousness are condemned by the modern
social values of order, honesty, industry, and self-control. But from
the alternative Enlightenment view of history as antisensual re-
gress, the Don is a tragic figure, a principled defender of an
aesthetic life of play, indulgence, and fulfillment who is victimized
by the representatives of a toiling, repressive, and frustrating
social order. In this interpretation, where no one-dimensional
account of the Don can capture his historically grounded duality,
the alleged failure of Mozart and Da Ponte to reconcile these
conflicting tendencies is no failure at all. Rather, the simultaneous
and unresolved coexistence of both tendencies testifies to the
depth with which *Don Giovanni* articulates a central contradiction
of its age.

Two years after the premiere of *Don Giovanni*, the Bastille was
attacked. With the outbreak of the French Revolution, political
morality lost its pre-Revolutionary ambivalence, and such works
as Beethoven's *Fidelio* rejected all nostalgia for the aristocratic way
of life. The aristocracy's self-indulgences and abuses of power were
universally condemned, by both effective state authorities and the
court of public opinion.

THREE

Opera and Revolutionary Virtue
Beethoven's *Fidelio*

Monarchy is not a king, it is crime. The republic is not a senate, it is virtue.

—LOUIS ANTOINE LÉON DE SAINT-JUST

N spite of a number of details that do not quite fit, Ludwig van Beethoven's opera *Fidelio* is a sensuous representation of a crucial shift in the history of political ideas: the virtuous republicanism of the later Enlightenment and the French Revolution. From the time of the ancient Roman republic, republicanism has been compatible with a number of nonmonarchical constitutional arrangements that provide for citizen participation in government. Historians and theorists had long viewed a republican form of government as particularly desirable but also fragile and vulnerable, because it depended on both a proper configuration of political institutions and the population's civic virtue, or patriotic habits, attitudes, and practices.

In Machiavelli's *Prince*, as we have seen, virtù was conceived in terms of a ruler's self-possession, strength, and cunning in political combat. Monteverdi's late operas, *Ulisse* and *Poppea*, are permeated with this conception of virtù, and Mozart's Don Giovanni demonstrates his anachronism by untimely exhibitions of his virtù-osity. But in *The Discourses*, Machiavelli's other great theoretical work of the same period, virtù described not the characteristics of princes but the political morals and ethics of the

[65]

citizens of republics. It was this conception of political virtue that was transmitted by Rousseau and appropriated by the republican thinkers of the French Revolution. By the late eighteenth century, virtue was a protean political concept prescribing a regimen of patriotism, sincerity, frugality, and military service for male citizens and a life of domesticity, modesty, childbearing, and breastfeeding for women.[1]

Indeed, during the French Revolution, there was a tendency to emphasize civic virtue over the institutional arrangements of republicanism. In *The Social Contract*, Rousseau maintained that a virtuous state was compatible with a monarchical government.[2] And during the National Convention phase of the Revolution, virtue was seen no longer as the correlate of republican institutions but as the chief characteristic of republicanism. According to Robespierre, "Immorality is the basis of despotism, . . . as virtue is the essence of the Republic."[3]

Likewise, in Beethoven's *Fidelio*, Revolutionary republicanism is not primarily a concern about governmental institutions. The opera's happy conclusion, for example, is presided over by the enlightened minister of an enlightened king. Nor does the opera depict the characteristic class conflict—aristocracy versus the popular classes—of the French Revolution. Indeed, among the opera's characters, the principal victim of aristocratic tyranny is an aristocrat. Instead, as an opera abounding with symbols of the Revolution, *Fidelio* derives its political character through its pervasive concern with republican virtue, both male virtue (fidelity to the state) and female virtue (fidelity to the husband).[4]

BEETHOVEN, MOZART, AND THE RESCUE OPERA

We are accustomed to associating Mozart and Beethoven. The reasons are obvious. In many respects, their lives, ideas, and achievements were remarkably similar. Only fourteen years separate the births of Mozart (1756–91) and Beethoven (1770–1827).

Both were born into plebeian families with a history of music making in the service of court and church. Both began their musical careers as keyboard virtuosi. Both struggled to make a living in Vienna during the period when aristocratic patronage was declining and the capitalist market for music was still underdeveloped. Both espoused many progressive political and social ideas. And both achieved enduring fame as composers who were masters of sonata form.[5]

And yet, as Adorno once suggested, the short span of years that separates the births of Mozart and Beethoven in fact also separates two radically different "social climates." What divides the two composers are the French Revolution and its transformation of Enlightenment political ideas. The Bastille was stormed two years before Mozart's early death, yet we have no record of him referring to the Revolution. Beethoven, however, was nineteen years old when the Bastille fell, and in spite of his later objections to Napoleon's imperial title and military campaigns, he retained the "fever of the Revolution" throughout his life.[6] Whereas Mozart's social climate was attuned to Montesquieu, Voltaire, and other writers of the early Enlightenment, Beethoven's social climate was influenced by Rousseau, Kant, Fichte, and Hegel, and reflects Enlightenment thought in its later, Revolutionary phase.[7]

This political difference had enormous consequences for the two composers' political and social values, and thus also for the operas that expressed these values in sensuous form. Beethoven undertook a lifelong, "fastidious" search for suitable opera librettos.[8] Although Beethoven was an ardent admirer of Mozart's compositions in general, Beethoven's ambivalence toward Mozart's late comic masterpieces set the parameters of this search. On one hand, Beethoven decried the corruption of the Mozart–Da Ponte collaborations for courts and their aristocratic audiences. Just as Rousseau set a moral tone in his polemics against the theories of Voltaire and the early Enlightenment, Beethoven declared the moral bankruptcy of the Mozart–Da Ponte operas. Like many of his contemporaries, he considered *Così fan tutte* to be beneath contempt. And although he admired the music of *Figaro* and *Don Giovanni*, he declared his "aversion" for the "frivolous" subjects of these works, claiming that the latter was so "scandalous" that it "debased" art. On the other hand, he detected a new moral value in *Die Zauberflöte*, the Mozart–Emanuel Schikaneder singspiel for a Viennese suburban theater and its bourgeois audience. Beneath the numerous absurdities and magical interventions in *Die Zauberflöte* Beethoven saw and extolled the German character of the opera, proclaiming it "Mozart's greatest work."[9]

For the libretto of his only opera, Beethoven set a German-language text, but he did not follow Mozart into the tradition of singspiel and magic opera. Rather, the immediate models for *Fidelio* were the "rescue operas" of Mozart's French contemporaries. Written in the homeland of the Revolution, the rescue operas of such composers as Luigi Cherubini, Etienne-Nicolas Méhul, and Jean François Lesueur have long vanished from the performing repertory. Yet in their time they embodied the new moral seriousness of the Revolution.

Curiously enough, the rescue opera was the aesthetic outgrowth of developments in French comic opera. The opéra comique was an alternative to the traditional and aristocratic opera seria. In the opéra comique, recitatives were spoken rather than sung. The traditional opera-seria stereotypes of plot and character were replaced with situations and personages based on real life. Indeed, in some rescue operas the characters and plots were obviously drawn from current events. There were limits, of course, to this new realism. The didactic intent could be achieved only if the characters and plots were both accurate reflections of life and typifications of their historical epochs.[10] Some common-born characters continued to be stereotypical buffoons, but others were depicted as real people whose travails were worthy of serious consideration on the stage. Imperiled by natural or political dangers, the virtuous lead characters were, at the last possible moment, delivered from their ominous fates. By the time of the rescue operas (the late eighteenth and early nineteenth centuries), realism and drama had been heightened, but much of the humorous content had been excised from the opéra comique.[11]

The rescue opera displayed a new understanding of the political efficacy of individuals and groups. In the comic operas of the early Enlightenment, the resolution of social problems was merely a matter of adjustments within the existing social system. Indeed, the genre's conventions prescribed a strengthening of the status quo, however improbable the plot twists required to achieve it.[12] But in the rescue opera, the resolution of political problems frequently entailed a fundamental and abrupt alteration in the existing relations of political power. The resolution of these political problems was the outcome of real actions by virtuous people. Gone were the old happy endings effected by supernatural dei ex machina or singspiel magic; the rescue opera had no need for avenging statues of commendatores. In their place was the populus ex machina: deliberate actions by the hero or heroine with the assistance or acclaim of the chorus of virtuous citizens.

With the disappearance of the French rescue opera from the performing repertory, much of the distinctive political spirit of this age has been lost. Several later operas—from Umberto Giordano's *Andrea Chénier* (1896) and Jules Massenet's *Thérèse* (1907) to Gottfried von Einem's *Dantons Tod* (1947), Francis Poulenc's *Dialogues des Carmélites* (1957), and John Corigliano's *Ghosts of Versailles* (1991)—have set historical or fictional incidents from the Revolution, but all are pervaded by greater or lesser degrees of estrangement from the politics of the great event. By default, it has fallen to an Austro-German work, Beethoven's *Fidelio*, the only opera from the first decade of the nineteenth century to remain in the performing repertory, to represent in opera the republican spirit of the French Revolution.[13]

LEONORE AND FIDELIO

Fidelio is an adaptation of John Nicolas Bouilly's drama *Léonore, ou L'amour conjugale.* The play was based on an actual incident from the Reign of Terror, although the action was transferred from France to Spain. The opera libretto went through a number of revisions, but it remained faithful to the essential outlines of the rescue narrative of the play. The hero Florestan knows damaging information about Pizarro, a political rival and governor of a prison, and Pizarro illegally holds Florestan in the prison's dungeon. Leonore, Florestan's wife, impersonates a young man named Fidelio and begins working as a turnkey at the prison. By assisting Rocco, the jailer, Leonore hopes to find a way of freeing her husband. But Leonore's disguise leads to unwanted complications. Rocco's daughter, Marzelline, falls in love with Fidelio, much to the chagrin of Jaquino, the prison doorkeeper who wants to marry Marzelline. Meanwhile, Pizarro is warned that Fernando, minister of the king, will soon inspect the prison, and Pizarro resolves to kill Florestan before the inspection. Armed with a pistol, Leonore stops the attempted murder, just as trumpets announce the arrival of the king's minister. Florestan is set free and reunited with Leonore.

Although Beethoven always preferred the title *Leonore*, the opera was staged under the name *Fidelio*. Theater managers wanted to distinguish Beethoven's work from no fewer than three other operatic settings of Bouilly's Leonore—one each by Pierre Gavaux (1798), Ferdinand Paër (1804), and Simon Mayr (1805). By critical convention, *Leonore* is now the designation for Beethoven's 1805 and 1806 versions of his opera, with the title *Fidelio* being reserved for the 1814 rendering that has remained in the performing repertory.

In November 1805, when Beethoven's *Leonore*, with the libretto by Joseph Sonnleithner, premiered in Vienna, the city was occupied by French troops. Many of Vienna's aristocratic and bourgeois opera patrons had fled. The performances were sparsely attended, and what small audiences there were included a number of French officers. The opera was quickly withdrawn. Stephan von Breuning made a few cuts in the libretto for a planned revival in 1806, but Beethoven withdrew the score after only one performance in a dispute with the director of the theater. In 1814, running concurrently with the meetings of the reactionary Congress of Vienna, the opera in its definitive form as *Fidelio* finally achieved success. The 1806 cuts from the original version were restored, but otherwise Georg Friedrich Treitschke, the third librettist to work on the piece, subjected the opera to a severe pruning. The domestic disputes between Marzelline and Jaquino were trimmed, as were the misunderstandings between Fidelio and Marzelline. The concluding scene, Florestan's liberation, was rearranged. In spite of these revisions, *Fidelio* remains an uneven work. It contains magnificent scenes that could have been written only by the master of late classical dramatic symphony, but these gems exist alongside scenes that can only be described as banal.

It is not my intention to resolve the critical problems of *Fidelio*. Nor shall I explore these problems in terms of the predilections and deficiencies of the composer and his librettists. Instead, I shall reconceive the opera in political terms as an aesthetic representation of Revolutionary republican virtue. From this perspective, it is clear, the opera contrasts three pairs of moral and political values: self-interest and patriotism, inconstancy and fidelity, and tyranny and republicanism.

FROM SELF-INTEREST TO PATRIOTISM: ROCCO AND FLORESTAN

One of the gnawing critical problems in the interpretation of *Fidelio* is the disjunction between the comedic scenes of domesticity in the first act and the heroic events of the second act. To be sure, the mise-en-scène provides a measure of continuity. The courtyard squabbles and misunderstandings of Rocco's family take place within the ominous confines of the prison walls, a striking symbol of the power of the oppressive state. Yet, unlike the efforts of Figaro and Susanna in Mozart's *Figaro*, the heroic actions depicted in *Fidelio*'s second act do not seem to grow out of earlier expressions of private self-interest. In *Fidelio*, heroic patriotism requires the ability to transcend self-interest. The division between self-interest and heroic virtue crippled *Leonore*, and it lingers in *Fidelio*'s abbreviated account of the affairs of Rocco and his household.

This disjunction can be attributed to the persistence of old comic opera conventions in a work that had taken on a new political sobriety. The central characters in the domestic scenes— the jailer, Rocco, and his daughter, Marzelline—are descendants of eighteenth-century comic opera's most hackneyed stereotypes: the basso buffo and the soubrette. In early opera, the character of the basso buffo, or comic bass, provided a contrast to the usually aristocratic hero. Essentially benign, the comic bass's attachment to immediate gratification and physical pleasures obstructs his attempts at heroic action; Mozart's Papageno in *Die Zauberflöte* is a late and incomparable realization of the type. The soubrette was a frivolous, fickle soprano who furnished a contrast to the constancy of her noble better.

In *Fidelio*, Beethoven invests these characters and their needs, particularly Rocco, with a new seriousness and legitimacy, but he still depicts them as mired in an egoism that obstructs virtuous action. As theater, Beethoven's innovation is disastrous. As comic characters Rocco and Marzelline are not very humorous, and as serious characters they are not very effectual. One commentator describes Rocco, with his interminable homilies on fiscal prudence as the foundation of domestic happiness, as not so much a buffoon as a bore.[14] But when one considers the opera as a political text, one begins to see that the ambivalences and ambiguities of Rocco and Marzelline reveal much about the relation between egoism and republican virtue.

Rocco combines the familial, political, and economic themes of the opera: he is at once a loving and loquacious paterfamilias, a dutiful functionary of the state, and a fervent advocate of economic self-interest. Yet, within the universe of *Fidelio*, it is the last aspect, epitomized in Rocco's signature first-act "Gold" aria, that defines his personality and colors his conceptions of fatherhood and state service. His character may be tedious, but it is not without complexity.

Rocco's economic pragmatism does not preclude genuine affection for the members of his small circle. He tries to facilitate the marriage plans of Marzelline and Fidelio. He is firm but sympathetic in disabusing Jaquino of his hopes for marrying Marzelline. But never far from Rocco's mind is the economic well-being of his family. Welcoming the weary Leonore back from her trip to the blacksmith's, where she had had prison chains repaired, Rocco is impressed by the favorable deal struck by his young assistant. He hints that his daughter's hand will be a fine reward for such an enterprising young man. After a quartet, within which Marzelline expresses her love for Fidelio and her joy at their imminent marriage, Rocco begins his "Gold" aria. He cautions the young couple that love alone will not lead to a happy household, repeating a refrain about the beauty and power of gold.

Rocco's paean to gold is the key to understanding both the dignity and mendacity of his character. Unlike Mozart's Papageno, whose desire for the pleasures of domesticity is unmediated, Rocco advocates a thoroughly bourgeois conception of the family and its happiness: domestic pleasure is predicated on economic success.

Rocco's preoccupation with bourgeois self-interest also pervades his conception of the relation between citizen and state. In its expectation of patriotic duty and military service, the idea of republican virtue requires the citizen to overcome self-interest and to act for the greater good. Rocco tries to be virtuous. He repeatedly justifies his sometimes distasteful actions as being required by his state "duties," subordinating his personal preferences to the transcendent requirements of the state. But here again Rocco's ability to achieve a degree of patriotic virtue is enhanced when virtue is linked to economic self-interest. When Pizarro asks Rocco to murder the prisoner in the dungeon, Pizarro appeals first to the jailer's sense of duty: "You have acquired a cool head / and a steady nerve / through long years of service."[15] But whatever the deficiencies in Pizarro's own character, he is at least a shrewd judge of the weaknesses of his subordinates: he enhances his request for the jailer's help by offering a pouch of gold.

I shall return later to Pizarro's ethical corruption and how it affects the state. But here I wish to note how it affects a benign but essentially selfish character like Rocco. On one hand, neither duty nor self-interest are inconsistent with occasional acts of courage on behalf of others. Rocco defies Pizarro's orders by agreeing to Leonore's appeal that the prisoners be allowed to exercise in the prison courtyard. Later, when faced with Pizarro's anger, he displays some Figaro-like ingenuity by justifying the prisoners' exercise as a commemoration of the king's name day. In spite of the pouch of gold, Rocco refuses to act as an executioner, agreeing only to dig the doomed prisoner's grave. Fraught with misgivings, Rocco also allows Leonore to offer the Florestan a crust of bread and some wine.

But on the other hand, Rocco is hardly a paragon of republican virtue. The combination of his own bourgeois mentality and a corrupted state prevents him from taking the kind of decisive, self-sacrificing, heroic action that would prevent Florestan's unjust fate. In the first act, when Rocco tells Leonore about the prisoner in the dungeon, he acknowledges that the prisoner could either be a great criminal "or have great enemies, / which comes to much / the same thing" (75). Bound to his job by economic necessity, Rocco never questions whether Florestan's case transgresses proper judicial practice. Indeed, although Rocco later refuses to murder Florestan outright, he admits to collaborating in the prisoner's slow death by following Pizarro's orders to cut his rations; the jailer weakly rationalizes that this slow death is somehow merciful, delivering the prisoner from his wretched condition. Later, in the dungeon, Rocco denies the prisoner's request that Leonore, whom he thinks is in Seville, be informed of his imprisonment. Again Rocco rationalizes: "I would bring ruin / on myself, and it would be no help to you" (139).

Although he is a descendant of the traditional basso buffo, Rocco's ability to overcome the desire for immediate creature comforts and pursue a more mediated, economic conception of self-interest clearly separates him from his appetitive predecessors. Yet this preoccupation with economic self-interest is also the limiting factor in Rocco's character. It pervades his understanding of the family and conjugal love, and it also perverts his virtue by forcing him to serve a corrupted state. Anticipating Marx's critique of the role of the individual within the modern state, *Fidelio* depicts *Homo oeconomicus* as a consummate bourgeois incapable of the self-sacrificing virtue of the true *citoyen*.[16] Within the aesthetic universe of *Fidelio*, Rocco and Marzelline are neither villains nor virtuous heroes. Rather, they establish a set of expectations about nonheroic, morally and politically ambivalent human behavior.

Fidelio is an allegory of the French Revolution, the supreme example of bourgeois republican virtue. Yet one of this opera's paradoxes is that truly virtuous actions are reserved for the heroic tenor Florestan and the heroic soprano Leonore, two nominal members of the aristocracy. For Florestan and Leonore, love and family are not fetters binding them to private self-interest but the foundations of their honorable conduct.

Florestan is never able to act as a true hero. Having been shackled to a rock for two years in the prison's deepest dungeon and more recently weakened by the cuts in his rations, he can merely recount the heroic action which brought him to his fate and invoke the memory of his devoted wife as solace. Florestan's plight evokes that fear of being buried alive, a theme that permeated the French prison literature of the 1780s.[17]

The opening of the second act foreshadows the linkage of conjugal love with republican virtue. In his recitative "Gott, welch' Dunkel hier," Florestan faces his unjust fate with the fortitude traditionally displayed by aristocrats of opera seria. But in his famous aria "In des Lebens Frühlingstagen," which follows, he breaks new republican ground. Whereas Rocco is an example of economically induced political ambivalence, Florestan is a paragon of republican virtue. Unlike Rocco's verbal discretion, Florestan's honest political speech was his "crime": "I boldly dared to speak the truth." Whereas Rocco's motives are mendacious, Florestan's are patriotic: "My duty I have done!" (125). Unlike Rocco's narrow protectiveness of his family, Florestan's consolation is his undiminished love for Leonore. In a burst of religious-mystical ecstasy (a mode completely alien to the courtly and worldly spirit of the Mozart–Da Ponte operas), Florestan sees an apparition: "An angel just like Leonore / just like Leonore, my wife, / who is leading me to Freedom / in Paradise!" (127).

Unlike both early baroque operas and late romantic operas, which juxtapose the demands of reason to the inclinations of the passions, *Fidelio* reflects the spirit of Revolutionary republicanism, where emotion gives fervor to rational political action. In the late Enlightenment, there "was the acceptance of the heart as the legitimate consort of the head."[18] The Revolution itself "was both the daughter of reason and the daughter of enthusiasm."[19] Florestan is bound by chains that are very real, and the conjugal love that sustains his republican virtue is idealized and mystical, an impotent fantasy born of his delirium and suffering. But unbeknown to Florestan, his beloved Leonore, in the guise of Fidelio, actively plots his rescue.

FROM INCONSTANCY TO FIDELITY:
MARZELLINE AND LEONORE

In spite of Marzelline's reduced role in the final version of *Fidelio*, her egoism and inconstancy provide an effective foil for Leonore's display of the virtues of republican womanhood. In Marzelline's preoccupation with economic security, she is truly her father's daughter. Even before Rocco offers the counsel of his "Gold" aria, Marzelline's first-act aria, wherein she fantasizes about the pleasures of married life with Fidelio, recognizes that this life will also be one of shared labor. In *Leonore*, Marzelline's bourgeois prudence is even more pronounced. Her romantic preference for the newcomer Fidelio acknowledges his favorable career prospects, which are contrasted with the unspecified career liabilities of Jaquino.

But it is conjugal fidelity, rather than economic self-interest, that most tellingly separates the profane Marzelline from the virtuous Leonore. Marzelline severs her long relationship with Jaquino when she becomes infatuated with Fidelio. When Fidelio is finally unmasked as Leonore, there are clear indications that Marzelline will return to her first love. In operatic tradition, fickleness is a typical trait of the soubrette. In *Fidelio*, however, Marzelline's inconstancy sets off Leonore's realization of the ideal of Revolutionary republican womanhood. In its stereotyping of moral relations, Revolutionary republicanism viewed citizenship as the "public expression of an idealized family."[20]

Although Leonore and Florestan have long been separated, the structural parallelism between each character's recitative and aria in the first act illustrates their unbroken kinship. In the recitative "Abscheulicher!" Leonore excoriates the evil Pizarro and reminisces about bygone days of wedded bliss with her husband. In the aria "Komm, Hoffnung," it is hope—the emblematic emotion of the French Revolution, the "Great Hope of 1789"— that sustains her resolve to free Florestan.[21]

Initially, Leonore's love has merely the particularistic aim of freeing Florestan, but this particularism is overcome during the course of her mission. A foretaste of this transcendence occurs in the prisoners' scene of the first act. At first, Leonore's request that the prisoners be allowed to exercise in the courtyard is merely a ploy for giving her an opportunity to search for Florestan. When she realizes that her husband is not among the group of prisoners, she sympathizes with their plight: "Anguish courses through my body" (123). But on Pizarro's orders, she must return the prisoners to their cells. In the first act, the movement from conjugal to republican duty, the emergence from the darkness of tyranny to the freedom of light, is anticipated but still dormant.

The culmination of this transformation of conjugal love to republican duty takes place in the dungeon scene of the second act. Still unsure whether the condemned prisoner is Florestan, Leonore resolves to free the man regardless. "Whoever you may be," she avows, "I'll save you" (133).

The pinnacle of Leonore's physical heroism—indeed, the climax of the opera itself—comes when, pistol in hand, Leonore blocks Pizarro's attempt to kill her husband. Yet it is clear that Leonore's status as a heroine is based not only on her courage but also on the loftiness of her motives. She has traversed a course leading from the pursuit of conjugal duty to the fulfillment of the Kantian categorical imperative to treat *all* human beings as ends in themselves, not as means to effecting one's own purposes. To phrase it more politically, Leonore's conjugal fidelity leads her to pursue public duty and self-sacrifice for the good of the community. The music commemorates the levels of her achievement. At the conjugal level, Leonore's and Florestan's separate but parallel recitatives and arias give way to their rapturous duet when they are reunited. At the political level, the chorus of citizens at the opera's conclusion proclaims Leonore as the exemplar of the communal ideal of womanhood.

In its heroizing of Leonore, *Fidelio* mines the stock of familiar cultural symbols. Leonore's provision of bread and wine for the condemned prisoner alludes to eucharistic rites and meanings. Within the history of opera, Leonore both evokes and transmutes a familiar iconography of heroism. Reversing the gender roles of Monteverdi's Orfeo and Euridice, the female Leonore descends into the underworld of death to restore the male Florestan to the world of the living. Reversing the gender roles of Mozart's Sarastro and the Queen of the Night in *Die Zauberflöte*, the female Leonore defends light, virtue, and freedom against the male Pizarro, a symbol of darkness, corruption, and tyranny.

Leonore treads a line separating the bourgeois republican conception of proper female domesticity from two highly improper forms of female political activism, which was both a manifestation of the decay of the ancien régime and an unintended consequence of the Revolution. In the first case, from the standpoint of the theorists and practitioners of republican virtue, the essential goodness of womanhood had been perverted by the artifice and intrigues of influential women in aristocratic courts and salons.[22] (The scheming female characters in the Mozart–Da Ponte operas may have prompted Beethoven's moralistic distaste for these works; conversely, the subordination of the scheming, aristocratic Queen of the Night in *Die Zauberflöte* may have contributed to his enthusiasm for that work.)[23] As a disguised aristocratic woman who intervenes in a political situation of capital importance, Leonore can be conceived as a personification of female deception and the moral decay of the old order.

The second, more intriguing type of improper female political activism was a by-product of the Revolution itself. Leonore resembles a Revolutionary republican woman: "mounted on horseback, in male costume, a scarf fluttering at her neck, a pistol in each hand."[24] This image appealed to some supporters of the Revolution who believed that liberty, equality, and fraternity applied to women as well as men. But for the theorists and practitioners of republican virtue, such trouser-clad militant women were aberrations, *femmes-hommes* blurring the proper distinctiveness of the sexes and neglecting their "natural" domestic duties as wives and mothers for "unnatural" political roles.

The opera avoids any implication that Leonore is one of these viragos of the Revolution. Her departures from the republican conception of female domesticity are forced upon her by the tyranny of Pizarro. In several scenes, she is physically discomforted by the labors of her male alter ego: she is fatigued by carrying the prison chains; she suffers from the cold of the dungeon; she loses her breath trying to help Rocco lift the stone of the cistern that is to serve as Florestan's tomb. She feels remorse about causing the rift between Marzelline and Jaquino. She breaks into tears at the prospect of accompanying Rocco into the dungeon. She nourishes the still unrecognized prisoner with bread and wine. Throughout, she draws the spiritual strength for her actions from love, specifically wedded love. When she succeeds in her quest, she reveals no enduring interest in politics, nor does she claim such an interest on behalf of other women. She desires only the restoration of her domestic happiness. Leonore's travesty and activism are thus neither symptoms of aristocratic decadence nor assertions of female political equality. Rather, Leonore's forced departures from female domesticity are but examples of the execrable effects of aristocratic tyranny.

The gender politics represented by Leonore mark a milestone in the history of opera. Leonore is the transition figure between the profane, activist female protagonists of Mozart and Da Ponte and the ethereal heroines of late-nineteenth-century romanticism. Physically weak, emotional, and nurturing, Leonore is nevertheless capable of more than an operatic love-death. The love that motivates her is conjugal love, a primary form of human association which is acclaimed by the choral community, and not romantic love, which severs lovers from social and political bonds. The fulfillment of Leonore's love requires the accomplishment of real and difficult goals in an aesthetic representation of the real world, not an abnegation of the real world for some imagined other world. Poised between operatic classicism and romanticism, Leonore has tears in her eyes, but a pistol in her hand.

FROM TYRANNY TO THE VIRTUOUS STATE: PIZARRO AND FERNANDO

As mentioned earlier, Bouilly's drama *Léonore* was based on an actual incident from the Reign of Terror. By following Bouilly's example and changing the *Fidelio*'s setting from France to Spain, Beethoven was able to preserve his loyalty to the republican spirit of the Revolution. If *Fidelio* had adhered to its historical model, its political character would have been, not that of an emblem of the Revolution, but that of an aesthetic critique of the excesses of the Revolutionary republic. Transposed to eighteenth-century Spain, an actual abuse from the Terror becomes an opportunity to excoriate the tyranny of the ancien régime.[25]

Yet the change in setting does vitiate *Fidelio*'s ability to represent the historical parameters of Revolutionary republicanism. Socially, as we have seen, the transference to Spain transforms the struggle of the bourgeoisie and popular classes against the aristocracy into a struggle of at least nominal aristocrats against the tyranny of another aristocrat. Republican politics are also distorted. The closing scenes of the opera are heavily laden with the symbols of Revolutionary republicanism: trumpets recalling the storming of the Bastille; the movement from the darkness of oppression through hope to the light of emancipation; the identification of this emancipation with both the slogans of the Revolution and popular aspirations. But the political content of the opera mixes the symbols of Revolutionary republicanism with the restoration of a properly constituted monarchy.

In *Fidelio*, Leonore's love for Florestan transcends its strictly conjugal character and becomes the spiritual foundation for the performance of patriotic duty. But Leonore's growth will remain merely subjective and personal unless her patriotism finds its objective basis in lawful and just state institutions. Thus the opera does not end with the rescue of Florestan and some entirely possible individual escape from the prison. It concludes, rather, with the popularly acclaimed affirmation of Leonore's virtue in a properly reconstituted state.

The characters who embody the standards of the properly constituted state and the improperly constituted one are Don Fernando and Don Pizarro. But from the aesthetic standpoint of effective theater, they are the most problematic. Lacking the roundedness of finely drawn characters, they seem to be little more than mouthpieces for their respective political positions. Pizarro is the simplest of the two. He is a raging personification of aristocratic tyranny: obsessed with personal honor, personalistic in the performance of his state functions, as corrupt as he is corrupting. Fernando is only slightly more complex. At once a magnanimous representative of a benign monarch and a dutiful member of the monarch's civil service, he also serves as the spokesman for the principles of Revolutionary republican virtue. Beethoven's music endows these characters with a credibility that they would not have had in a play whose lines are spoken.

Pizarro is the symbol of the tyrannical state. The cause of his tyranny predates the events of the opera, in the unspecified crimes that Florestan reported. In "Ha, welch ein Augenblick!" his famous aria of revenge, Pizarro gloats over his ability to use his position as prison governor to first imprison, then murder, his rival:

> Once I was nearly humbled,
> a prey to open scorn,
> laid low, yes, about to be laid low.
> Now I have my chance
> to slay the would-be slayer! (89)

Pizarro thus perverts the state into an instrument of personal force.

By punishing Florestan for speaking the truth, Pizarro establishes himself as the enemy of freedom and reason. But Florestan is only Pizarro's most obvious victim. Denied its telos in a properly constituted state, the civic virtue of all who come under Pizarro's power is compromised. Rocco's good nature is hardened by years of service to a tyrant; his weakness for gold is manipulated to force him into actions that go against his conscience. During their brief moment of relative freedom in the prison courtyard, the prisoners must guard their tongues for fear of Pizarro's spies. The soldiers dread the rages of their commander. Marzelline's affection for Jaquino is alienated. Leonore is forced to abandon her beloved domesticity and risk her life in the guise of a man. If Pizarro's plan to murder Florestan had been successful, the witnesses Rocco and Leonore would have been the next victims in his never-ending cycle of crime and cover-up. In the tyrannous state of Pizarro, virtue is at best a subjective quality, never an objective condition of political life.

When Leonore, pistol in hand, steps between Florestan and the charging Pizarro, the force of the tyrannous state is temporarily checked by a counterforce. Then the trumpet is sounded. Acting on the instructions of Pizarro, the trumpeter is the unconscious harbinger of political progress, the vehicle of the cunning of history. This age-old clarion of royalty and nobility announces the arrival of the king's minister, Don Fernando. But in *Fidelio* the trumpet call takes on new connotations as well. It is the tocsin for the operatic storming of the Bastille, for victory over the old forces of tyranny and capriciousness.[26] Acting in the name of the king, Fernando will absolve Leonore's use of counterforce and affirm her virtue as the ethical foundation of the state.

Fernando symbolizes both the constitutional monarch and the dutiful public servant. Although he does not appear in the opera, the king is present through Fernando, his representative.[27] In the closing scene of the opera, the principals emerge from the dungeon into the sunlight of the prison parade grounds; beneath a statue of the king, the sun imagery of the monarchy mixes with the sun imagery of the Revolution.[28] This absent-yet-present king is represented as a figure of altruistic concern for all his subjects. In the first act, when Pizarro discovers the prisoners exercising in the courtyard, the invocation of the king's name day spares Rocco from Pizarro's wrath. In the finale, Fernando proclaims the king as the guarantor of justice and magnanimity:

> At our good king's express wish
> have I come to you, poor people,
> to dissipate the night of evil
> which has long enshrouded you. (169)

But Fernando is not simply the representative of the king. He takes pleasure at the sight of Leonore and especially Florestan, "my friend, my friend whom I thought dead" (173). He charges the wife of his old friend with the happy task of removing Florestan's chains. The opera then takes pains to demonstrate that this is not merely the victory of personalistic magnanimity over personalistic malice. Fernando's actions are the duties of a public servant in a properly constituted state. Rocco reports that Fernando has come to the prison with a list of all the prisoners, whose cases Fernando promises to review. Pizarro's malfeasance is initially established by the absence of Florestan's name on the list. In *Leonore*, Fernando calms the crowd's call for harsh punishment of Pizarro by promising due process: he will take the miscreant's case to the king.

Fernando's magnanimity recalls the examples of countless enlightened monarchs and nobles of opera seria. But the figures of his speech and the context of his actions suggest the properly constituted Revolutionary state as much as they do an Enlightenment monarchy. As the assembled chorus of prisoners and people hail his arrival at the prison, Fernando reproaches their servile petition for justice in a speech radiant with the Revolutionary ideals of liberty, equality, and fraternity:

> Kneel no longer slavishly,
> harsh tyranny's far from my mind.
> I come as a brother to my brothers,
> and gladly help if I can. (169)

To music extracted from his own *Cantata on the Death of Joseph II* (1790), Beethoven then combines the chorus and principals in a paean to Leonore, giving the resolution of the plot the semblance, if not the actuality, of a Revolutionary populus ex machina.[29]

With the reconstitution of the properly ordered state, the virtuous political life of the community is restored. Florestan is released from his unjust punishment. In *Leonore*, Rocco hurls the purse of gold back at Pizarro. Although this scene was cut in *Fidelio*, Rocco is still given the opportunity to delight in the fact that he no longer has to serve a tyrant. The prisoners will have their cases reviewed. Marzelline will once again discover the charms of Jaquino. But most important of all, Leonore's heroic virtue will become the ethical model for the political community.

In his only known interpolation in the libretto, Beethoven inserted lines from Schiller's "Ode to Joy": "Let all who have won fair wives / join in our celebration" (177). The lines are repeated by both Florestan and the chorus, as they will be by Beethoven himself, nineteen years after the premiere of *Leonore*, in the choral movement of the *Ninth Symphony*.

I have argued that *Fidelio*'s emphasis on republican virtue makes the opera an enduring emblem of the French Revolution. On the other hand, I have tried not to ignore the social and political ambiguities in the opera which do not quite fit the typical image of the Revolution. One contemporary interpreter has gone a step further. For Peter Conrad, the ambiguities of *Fidelio* indicate the restorative-reactionary character of the work.[30]

Because of *Fidelio*'s ambiguities, a definitive political interpretation of the opera is probably impossible. And although knowing the composer's intentions would not resolve these ambiguities, one cannot help but be intrigued by the meaning of an incident that occurred in the last weeks of Beethoven's life. From his rooms—which, as usual, were strewn with the manuscript scores of many of his compositions—Beethoven removed one score, *Leonore*, and entrusted its safekeeping with his friend Anton Schindler.[31] A gesture of affection for this lone essay into his admired art of opera? An honor to Leonore, the ideal of faithful married love that Beethoven was never able to experience? Both motives may indeed have guided him, but perhaps there was a third one. By singling out this opera, the composer—long deaf and now fifty-six years old, sick, and near death—also affirmed the persistence of the Revolutionary spirit of his youth.

FOUR

The Utopian Vision of Romantic Anticapitalism Wagner's *Parsifal*

In all of us is the wish to return to the has-been and to repeat it, that if it were once unblest it may now be blessed.

—THOMAS MANN

POLITICIZED Richard Wagner (1813–83) was and is inescapable. In Wagner's lifetime, commentators most often characterized him as either Wagner the young rebel or Wagner the middle-aged protégé of King Ludwig II of Bavaria. The first persona recalled the Wagner of the Dresden uprising in 1848–49: formulating his revolutionary conception of music drama, proclaiming the coming victory of his own unique vision of communism. The second persona evoked the Wagner of the 1860s. Political revolution may have been on hold, but Wagner still scandalized Germany with his romantic escapades and untimely interventions into Bavarian politics.

The Holocaust provoked a reexamination of the historical and cultural factors that prepared the path to Nazism. In this reevaluation, critics and biographers began to change their political views of Wagner, emphasizing the last ten to fifteen years of life: the Wagner of a brief but strident enthusiasm for the new German Empire, the Wagner of intensifying racism. Within the genealogies of Nazi ideas, Wagner's explorations of medieval myths, his rabid nationalism and anti-Semitism, and even his vegetarianism and antivivisectionism took on a fateful significance.[1] The older Wagner came to be seen as an important ideologist of nationalism and imperialism and as a precursor of twentieth-century German racism.

According to advocates of this perspective, the older Wagner's views pervaded not only his increasingly dogmatic essays and pronouncements but also his music dramas. And *Parsifal*, his last music drama, struck many critics as an especially important vehicle for the representation of his political ideas.

In spite of the fact that Wagner wrote both music and text for *Parsifal* (as he did for all his music dramas, each of which he conceived as a *Gesamtkunstwerk*, or total work of art), a dichotomy has characterized many evaluations of *Parsifal*. The music received near universal praise. For friends and foes alike, the score was no flawed product of an aged and infirm composer but the supreme achievement of an artist at the peak of his powers. Indeed, for many critics, the very brilliance of *Parsifal*'s music rendered its socially and politically unhealthy libretto particularly dangerous. A luminous score sugarcoated a nasty textual pill.

The focus on the problematic relation between text and music dates back to *Parsifal*'s first performances.[2] In the late nineteenth and early twentieth centuries, the discussion centered on religious issues. To take the most famous example, Friedrich Nietzsche hailed the music of *Parsifal* as "sublime and extraordinary."[3] His assessment of the text was another matter. For Nietzsche, the Christian aspects of the work symbolized the apostasy and decay of his former hero and the model for his superman: "Richard Wagner, seemingly the all-conquering, actually a decaying, despairing romantic, suddenly sank down helpless and shattered before the Christian cross."[4] With *Parsifal*, Wagner abandoned his political and aesthetic ideals and crawled back to Christianity.

Later criticism shifted the scene of *Parsifal*'s textual mischief from religion to political ideology. As ideology, *Parsifal* reflected, in mystical form, an idealized image of existing and emerging political forces. Adorno's *In Search of Wagner*, written in 1937–38, restated the music-text problem. Adorno lauded *Parsifal*'s skillful orchestration and advanced tonality, but these musical achievements cloaked the dangerous political ideology of the work. He characterized *Parsifal* as endorsing asceticism and syphilophobia, with the racially elitist brotherhood of the grail knights serving as the "prototype of the sworn confraternities of the secret societies and *Führer*-orders of later years." Adorno even criticized *Parsifal*'s "sentimental" opposition to cruelty to animals.[5]

After the Holocaust, Adorno's scattered criticisms were stitched into a full-blown identification of *Parsifal* with German imperialism and Nazi racism and genocide. Karl Marx once called Wagner a "neo-German-Prussian State-musician."[6] John Zerzan renewed this national-imperial line of thought by characterizing "*Parsifal*'s pseudo-erotic religiosity" as the "authoritarian and mystical justification" of the political, industrial, and military order of Wilhelmian Germany.[7] This time, the knights of the grail were idealized Prussian politicians, industrial barons, and Junker warlords.

Other critics moved the ideological locus of *Parsifal* from the Second to the Third Reich. As usual, the music was praised: "incredible beauty," a "monumental masterpiece."[8] As usual, this music was deemed to have rendered toxic ideas palatable. The music drama's theme of sexual purity was understood as a plea for Aryan racial purity. Interpreted in light of Wagner's most racist and anti-Semitic prose works and viewed retrospectively from the standpoint of history after Auschwitz, *Parsifal* came to be seen, in the words of Paul Lawrence Rose, as the "most profoundly anti-Jewish Wagnerian opera" and the "triumph of the Aryans."[9] Robert Gutman epitomized this trend when he declared that *Parsifal* was nothing less than the "gospel of National Socialism."[10]

From Nietzsche's jeremiad through Adorno's social criticism to the recent polemics, the worst fears of musical "autonomists," or those who view music as an apolitical creation detached from its social and political context, appear to have been fulfilled. To date, political approaches to *Parsifal* have not illuminated a masterpiece but have withered it. The tragedy of the Holocaust has inclined the political critics to an interpretation that belies the experience of this serene and moving work, while the autonomists offer still more apolitical exegeses of *Parsifal*'s musical structure, religious pedigree, and medieval sources. These autonomist studies may restore a sense of the aesthetic achievement of the artwork, but they obscure the element of truth found in even the most one-sided and defaming political interpretations of *Parsifal*'s ideology: this music drama does present a discernible and significant vision of social and political life.

Instead of reviewing the existing political and apolitical interpretations of Wagner's last music drama, I shall offer a new political view: *Parsifal* as a utopian work, as a projection of Wagner's revolutionary ideals onto an imagined past. Three differences distinguish my interpretation from its predecessors.

The first involves a different understanding of the relation of artistic ideas and images to their historical context. Political interpretations of *Parsifal* have emphasized the work's ideological content: the way that its ideas and images reflect a falsified picture of existing and emerging political forces. Except for noting the music drama's ideology of sexual repression, I shall emphasize instead the extent to which *Parsifal* abandons ideology and instead constructs a utopia.[11] The work does reveal a relation to its nineteenth-century historical context. But as a vision of utopia, *Parsifal* does not garb the modern present of the Second or emerging Third Reich in the heroic attire of medieval grail knighthood. Instead, *Parsifal* negates its historical context. In its negation of nineteenth-century conditions, the work constructs an imaginary utopia that rejects and transcends those conditions.

In addition to shifting from an ideological to a utopian perspective, I shall analyze the content of *Parsifal*'s utopian vision. Wagner once declared that he was "neither a republican, nor a democrat, nor a socialist, nor a communist."[12] He could have extended the list. Wagner was also not an anarchist, a monarchist, or a nationalist, although he advocated aspects of all three systems. In this context, where Wagner's ideas overlap the traditional categories of political theory, a broader cultural concept is more useful. There is one categorization that is elastic enough to embrace Wagner's protean ideas and images, yet structured enough to retain a measure of historical specificity and conceptual clarity. Long a staple in aesthetic and intellectual studies by Georg Lukács, the term "romantic anticapitalism" refers to the tendency to oppose and criticize capitalism on the basis of its destruction of certain values from the past. Since romantic anticapitalism may be leftist or rightist, revolutionary or reactionary, interpreting *Parsifal* in this context will restore a sense of the music drama's open political possibilities.

Finally, I shall emphasize the continuities rather than the discontinuities between the political views of the young, revolutionary Wagner and the old, allegedly reactionary Wagner. To be sure, whereas the young Wagner talked about the future, revolution, and a Feuerbachian advocacy of free love, the older man focused on the past, the possibilities of regeneration, and a Schopenhauerian sexual renunciation. But otherwise, in both their young and old manifestations, Wagner's simultaneous support for monarchy and republicanism, his hostility to commerce and money, his interest in socialism and community, and his vision of music drama as a component of fundamental political change are remarkably persistent.

ROMANTIC ANTICAPITALISM

Romantic anticapitalism is the critique of the capitalist present in the name of certain lost or endangered values from a real or imagined past. For some artists and thinkers, the image of the lost golden age is sheer escapism: an imaginary flight from a drab present to a meaningful but hopelessly extinct past. For others, however, the cherished eras of the past have continued significance as models for possible social and political change. As a vision of change, the historical worldview of romantic anticapitalism usually exhibits three stages: the nostalgia for a precapitalist past, the experience of loss, and the quest for recovery.[13] Romantic anticapitalism has been particularly strong in Germany.

In the early nineteenth century, when capitalism in Germany was merely a matter of relatively small-scale enterprises scattered among the country's states, Johann Fichte established the moral tone of romantic anticapitalism by characterizing the capitalist present as the "epoch of absolute sinfulness."[14] For Fichte, the present age was afflicted with a tragic flaw: the gulf between what is and what ought to be, the gap between the materialistic busyness of everyday life and the neglected call to higher ethical duty. Fichte acknowledged the economic productivity of capitalism, but he condemned its deleterious effects on political and spiritual values.

The peculiarities of capitalist development in Germany reinvigorated and intensified German romantic anticapitalism. Whereas modern industrial capitalism had long been underway elsewhere, particularly in Britain and to a lesser extent France, it did not come to Germany until the second half of the nineteenth century, accelerating after German unification in 1871. When it finally did come, German industrialization was rapid, large-scale, state supported—and thoroughly disruptive to traditional German values.[15] The new manifestations of German romantic anticapitalism appeared to be more scientific than Fichte's, but they still focused on the disparity between present reality and lost moral rectitude. In *Community and Society*, Ferdinand Tönnies distinguished between the authentic individuality and interpersonal bonds of a precapitalist community (*Gemeinschaft*) and the self-interest, social fragmentation, and social conflict of a capitalist society (*Gesellschaft*). Later, Oswald Spengler's *Decline of the West* rued the decay of a precapitalist culture (*Kultur*) and its replacement by a capitalist civilization (*Zivilisation*). The unique spiritual values of a community-culture may have been free of the economic materialism of a society-civilization, but these values were not therefore free from all determination. For both Tönnies and Spengler, rather, a genuine community-culture retained its biological and organic relation to nature.

In the sensuous realm of art, *Parsifal* is part of this romantic critique of the capitalist present, part of this yearning for a utopian haven in the past. Contrary to the view that *Parsifal* is a compendium of the old Wagner's ominous notions, the idea for the music drama dates to the early stages of Wagner's career as a composer, when he first read Wolfram von Eschenbach's medieval epic *Parzival* in 1845. His later reading of Chrétien de Troyes's *Perceval* suggested the close identification of the grail and spear, the two central symbols of the music drama, with Christian iconography. But here as elsewhere in his music dramas, Wagner did not merely set the mythological material to music. Rather, the medieval legends suggested characters, settings, incidents, and symbols that Wagner adopted and transformed according to his own aesthetic needs.

Full-time work on *Parsifal* did not begin until after the first Bayreuth Festival in the summer of 1876, but the subject intruded into Wagner's earlier life and work. "Parsifal" was King Ludwig's nom de plume in his correspondence with Wagner. In addition to the sketches and fragments Wagner wrote in the 1850s and 1860s, aspects of the Parsifal subject turned up in a number of his sketches, fragments, and music dramas.[16] *Tannhäuser* features the author of *Parzival*, Wolfram von Eschenbach, and his patron, Landgrave Hermann of Thuringia, as central characters. The original *Parzival* was unabashed in its treatment of sensuousness and sexuality, but Wagner anticipated the asceticism of his own version by contrasting his fictional Wolfram's advocacy of nonsexual courtly love with Tannhäuser's championship of physical sexuality. A similar contrast nearly occurred in *Tristan und Isolde*. At one point, Wagner planned to have Parsifal appear in the third act. As the knight of sexual self-restraint, Parsifal was to pass through Kareol and reprove the mortally wounded Tristan for his incontinence.

The title character of *Lohengrin* is Parsifal's son. In the third-act climax to the drama, Lohengrin reveals his name and noble lineage, and describes the grail realm of Monsalvat and its order of knights. The relation of *Lohengrin* to *Parsifal*, however, goes beyond the kinship of the title characters. The grail music of *Lohengrin*'s prelude and Lohengrin's third-act narrative are the models for the later grail music of *Parsifal*.

Although lacking specific references to the characters or music of *Parsifal*, *Die Meistersinger von Nürnberg* shares that opera's political perspective. Coloristic evocations of the past are indispensable parts of Wagner's music dramas, yet the social orders of the Norway of *Der fliegende Holländer*, the Thuringia of *Tannhäuser*, the Brabant of *Lohengrin*, the Cornwall of *Tristan und Isolde*, and the realm of the Gibichungs of *Die Götterdämmerung* are all hostile to his heroes and heroines. But like *Parsifal*, *Meistersinger* is also an exercise in romantic anticapitalist utopianism. *Meistersinger* takes a more realistic and comedic path to utopia. Set in sixteenth-century Nuremberg, the music drama relates a story about Hans Sachs, a cobbler and also the most renowned poet-singer of his era. *Meistersinger* portrays a communal order of artisans and apprentices, Christian piety and civic pageantry, all governed by the practical wisdom of the mastersingers' guild. As in *Parsifal*, the internal threat to the utopian order of fictionalized Nuremberg comes from the potentially disruptive force of human passion and sexuality. Again as in *Parsifal*, this internal threat is exacerbated by ominous external forces.

But Wagner always considered history, even fictionalized history, as a constraint upon his artistic imagination.[17] Moreover, Wagner maintained that it was myth and legend, rather than history, that revealed a nation's character in its purest form. In *Parsifal*, his second musical essay on romantic anticapitalism, Wagner turned from the fictionalized history of *Meistersinger* to myth and legend. He characterized *Parsifal* as a *Bühnenweihfestspiel*, a consecration stage play. It was first performed in Wagner's Bayreuth Festspielhaus in July 1882, just seven months before his death.

Parsifal tells the tales of Monsalvat's three grail kings: the reign of the virtuous founder king, Titurel; the travails of his son and successor, Amfortas; and the accession of the new virtuous king, Parsifal. From a moral perspective, the reigns of the three grail kings represent the Christian salvation scenario of innocence, sin, and redemption. But from the standpoint of the history of political ideas, the three reigns correspond to the three stages of romantic anticapitalism: Titurel's golden age, Amfortas's loss of utopia, and Parsifal's quest for recovery.

The music drama is divided into three acts. In the first act, the opening scene takes place in a forest on the outskirts of the realm of the grail knights. After Gurnemanz, an elderly but vigorous knight and comrade of Titurel, and two squires finish their morning prayers, the vanguard of a train bearing King Amfortas arrives. Amfortas hopes to get some relief from the pain of his unhealing wound by bathing in the forest lake. Meanwhile, Kundry appears. A wild woman who is cursed with eternal life, she serves the knights as a messenger. She offers a flask of balsam to assuage the king's wound. The king is borne to the lake, and some youths who have remained behind berate Kundry for her failure to recover the sacred spear. Gurnemanz explains that the spear is held by Klingsor, a sorcerer and enemy of the grail brotherhood. Klingsor snatched the spear while Amfortas was in the embrace of a beautiful seductress, and the king was wounded by it in the ensuing struggle. According to the prophecy given to Amfortas, the spear can be recovered only by an innocent fool who is enlightened by compassion. The story is disrupted by the commotion caused by the shooting of a swan. The proud young archer, Parsifal, enters, and Gurnemanz scolds him for killing an animal within the sacred precinct of the grail. Questioned by Gurnemanz about his parentage, Parsifal knows very little, but Kundry provides some details. Hearing the summons to the grail ceremony in the castle called Monsalvat, Gurnemanz invites Parsifal to join him, in hopes that the young man is the innocent fool of the prophecy.

The second scene is in the great hall of Monsalvat. The

knights enter, and then Amfortas is carried in on his litter. Titurel's voice enjoins Amfortas to perform his sacred duty of uncovering the grail. At first Amfortas refuses because the ceremony exacerbates the pain of his wound, but eventually he complies with his father's wish. As the uncovered grail glows, the knights partake in the ritual feast. At the end of the service, only Gurnemanz and Parsifal remain in the hall. The old knight asks Parsifal if he has understood what he has just seen, but Parsifal only shakes his head. Believing that Parsifal is just a fool, Gurnemanz orders the young man to leave.

The second act is set in Klingsor's magic castle and garden. Unlike Gurnemanz, Klingsor realizes that Parsifal is the prophetic fool. Through his magic mirror, he sees Parsifal approach his domain. He summons the unwilling Kundry, whom he holds in thrall. She appears in her second guise as a beautiful seductress, and he commands her to use her wiles on Parsifal. When Parsifal easily defeats Klingsor's knights in combat, Klingsor causes his castle to disappear and be replaced by a magic garden. Flower maidens try to seduce Parsifal, but their playful efforts end when Kundry arrives. She finally succeeds in kissing Parsifal, but the kiss has an unintended effect: Parsifal is enlightened rather than seduced. Through compassion, he finally understands the events that transpired in the hall of Monsalvat, particularly the plight of Amfortas. Kundry calls for Klingsor's help, and wielding the spear, Klingsor appears on the castle wall. He hurls the spear at Parsifal, who seizes it out of the air. When Parsifal makes the sign of the cross with the spear, Klingsor's castle crumbles, and his garden shrivels into wilderness.

The third act takes place on Good Friday and is in two scenes. Once again at the edge of the grail domain, a now very old Gurnemanz is joined by Kundry, who once again offers to serve the grail brotherhood. Dressed in full armor, a knight approaches. When he removes his helmet and kneels in prayer before the spear, Gurnemanz and Kundry recognize Parsifal and the sacred relic. Kundry anoints his feet with oil, and then Gurnemanz anoints his head and proclaims him as the new king of the grail. As his first official act, Parsifal baptizes Kundry. Parsifal and Gurnemanz discuss the magical effect of Good Friday on nature. Again hearing the summons from Monsalvat, Gurnemanz leads Parsifal and Kundry to the castle, where Amfortas has promised to perform the grail ceremony one last time in honor of Titurel's death.

Within the great hall, one group of knights carries Amfortas on his litter, while another bears Titurel's bier. Despite the threats of the knights, the anguished Amfortas refuses to honor his promise and uncover the grail. He pleads for the welcome relief of death instead. Parsifal enters and heals Amfortas's wound with a touch of the spear. As Parsifal elevates the glowing grail, Amfortas and the knights kneel in homage, and Kundry is released into death.

UTOPIA: THE REIGN OF TITUREL

The story is taken up in medias res, during the kingship of Amfortas. But important elements of the music drama disrupt the present time of the plot to recall an earlier era on Monsalvat—the golden age of Titurel's reign. Part of this tugging backward, away from the forward motion of the plot, is embedded in the tales of Gurnemanz. This recollection is also evoked by the sights and sounds of the old rituals which continue to exist, albeit precariously, under Amfortas.

During the reign of Titurel, the grail brotherhood on Monsalvat is the negation of nineteenth-century life, particularly its German variant. Gone are a materialistic industrial capitalism, the authoritarian state, militarism, and urbanization. Instead, in its portrayal of Monsalvat during its heyday, *Parsifal* juxtaposes utopian images of society, politics, time, and nature to a tawdry nineteenth-century reality.

The key to this utopia is the multilayered symbol of the grail. Following Chrétien de Troyes, Wagner identifies the grail with the Christian tradition. It is both the chalice of the Last Supper and the cup with which Joseph of Arimethea caught Jesus' blood on Calvary. This Christian dimension establishes the preciousness of the grail, which along with the spear is entrusted to Titurel's care.

But the grail is more than this. Wagner also follows Wolfram von Eschenbach in retaining the grail's much older, pre-Christian power of sustenance and fertility.[18] When the community of the grail is moral, as it is under Titurel, there is no need for an economy on Monsalvat in any of the conventional senses of the term. Productive labor is not needed to sustain life. Neither money nor private property is desired. In this miraculous communism (or, even better, "communialism"),[19] the only need of the brotherhood, the need for nourishment and sustenance, is satisfied by the grail at the midday eucharistic feasts.

Freed by the grail from the yoke of material scarcity, the reign of Titurel is also free from many of scarcity's repressive institutions and practices. In his depiction of the interpersonal life of the grail brotherhood, Wagner echoes the romantic dichotomy of a modern and strife-ridden society-Gesellschaft versus a premodern and harmonious community-Gemeinschaft. Under Titurel, the grail brotherhood is not a society in the usual sense—an apparently random association of disparate individuals who just happen to be pursuing their rationally calculated but antagonistic personal and class interests in close geographical proximity to each other. Instead, the grail brotherhood is an exclusive community. The grail knights do not choose their membership in the community according to their own preferences. Rather, only morally pure males who combine sexual continence with Christian piety are "called to its service by paths denied to sinners."[20] In spite of the importance of the knights, their individual identities are subordinated to the community. Only Gurnemanz and the absent Gawan are named. As members of the community, the knights keep themselves ready for their only purposive and obligatory activity. Instead of advancing their own self-interests, they have a duty to answer calls for the defense of the virtuous against the forces of evil.

Within the grail community, there is a status hierarchy but no economic classes. The members are divided into pages, squires, and knights. In the absence of any form of private property, feudal or capitalistic, these communal status differences bear none of the exploitative marks of a class system. The interests of the statuses are not economically antagonistic. Pagehood and squirehood are merely stages in the apprenticeship of young knights.

Similarly, the political forms of Monsalvat are hierarchical and martial, but devoid of authoritarianism and militarism. The grail knights and the grail king represent the uncanny persistence of the young, revolutionary Wagner's unusual political views. For both the young and the old Wagner, a proper political order is a mixture of what might be loosely called republicanism and monarchy.[21]

Republicanism is the collective element in Wagner's ideal political order. For Wagner, republicanism was not so much a matter of constitutions or institutions, still less of squabbling parliamentary parties and interests. It was, rather, a feeling of fraternity and love, freedom and common purpose, among members of the same community. From his 1843 choral work *Das Liebesmahl der Apostel* (*The Love Feast of the Apostles*) through his 1849 prose sketch *Jesus von Nazareth* to *Parsifal*, a recurrent image captures Wagner's unique republicanism: the fraternity of the apostles, the members of the new religious community of Christianity, at the eucharistic feast of the Last Supper.[22] In *Parsifal*, this image finds its definitive artistic statement in the first- and third-act eucharistic meals of the knights, the members of the grail brotherhood.

If Wagner's republicanism defies the standard interpretations of the term, his views on monarchy are even more surprising. For Wagner, monarchy was not the antithesis of republicanism, but rather its pinnacle.[23] Wagner's republican king is no remote and authoritarian kaiser issuing restrictive commands to docile subjects. Instead, he is primarily a religious and sacerdotal figure, the

spiritual guide of the republican band of brothers. Wagner's republican king is epitomized by the gentle King Jesus presiding
over the communalist-republican gathering of the Last Supper.
The authority of Wagner's republican king is based on the performance of his duties, and not necessarily inheritance. The good
republican king, like King Titurel in *Parsifal*, is the guide and
teacher who protects the general will and general good of the
state. In close association with the brotherhood, Titurel has a
military function: he assigns the knights to their military missions. But he also guards the relics and performs the grail ceremony.

In spite of their martial duties as defenders of virtue, the
brothers of Monsalvat are remarkably free of aggression and militarism. The missions of the knights are strictly defensive and
therefore free of political or territorial aggrandizement. Inspired
by the cathedral of Siena, the grail castle looks more like a church
than a military fortress, and its great hall resembles a sanctuary.[24]
Unlike the militarism of the Second Reich—indeed, unlike the
chivalric pomp and circumstance of Wagner's *Lohengrin*—the defense of the virtuous via combat is an intermittent and necessary
duty, not something that is continually cultivated, relished, and
displayed. When they are not on a mission, the grail knights have
the appearance and demeanor of a religious order. When the ar-
mored Parsifal returns to Monsalvat in the third act, Gurnemanz
reprimands him for wearing the "sombre apparel of war" in the
sacred territory (160).

The social and political order of the grail brotherhood is
subject to deeply binding conceptions of historical and daily time.
Within a society, history is a chronicle of the numerous and varied
events of the past. But within the grail community, history is a
fateful tradition: a living legacy of those few morally defining
experiences that determine the collective purpose and dilemmas
of the community. From this perspective, the long narratives of
the garrulous Gurnemanz are more than an efficient means of

presenting plot background to the audience. Within the grail community, Gurnemanz's simple act of retelling tales defines and renews the collective identity of the brotherhood.

Elements of the music create an illusory phantasmagoria of daily time in Monsalvat during its golden age. The first act opens with trombones calling the brotherhood to morning prayers. Later, midday bells summon the brotherhood to the castle. The knights enter the hall of the castle in a choral procession. Hymns accompany the eucharistic feast. The sounds of *Parsifal* recall a romantic life of piety and contemplation. Except for the times when they are called away on missions, the days of the brotherhood are marked by frequently repeated convocations and rituals, rather than the alarms, commuter schedules, factory whistles, time clocks, and beepers of industrial societies.

These trombones, bells, and hymns are more than markers in imaginary theatrical time. They also create an audible illusion of a utopian place. Far from what Wagner called the "smoke and pestilential business odour of our town civilization,"[25] the edenic territory of Monsalvat is hallowed, the home of a community that combines spirituality with a deep appreciation of nature. At the beginning of the music drama, before Gurnemanz and the squires are awakened for prayers by the trombones of the distant castle, the men sleep unsheltered at the forested edge of the sacred realm. In addition to being intensely religious, the grail community remains close to nature. In the forest lake, Amfortas seeks temporary solace from the torments of his wound. And on Monsalvat, all animate life is sacred. Gurnemanz describes Parsifal's shooting of the swan as nothing less than murder (90). Indeed, subscribing to a notion shared by the French utopian Charles Fourier, Wagner portrays even inanimate nature as a reflection of the health or sickness of the human spirit.[26] The Good Friday Magic (*Karfreitagszauber*) music describes the exaltation of Monsalvat's grasses and flowers on the holiest day of the Christian liturgical calendar.

Freed by the grail from the shackles of material scarcity,

Titurel's Monsalvat is a romantic utopia. The brotherhood leads a premodern, communal life of piety, fraternity, and duty in harmony with animate and inanimate nature. The brotherhood has something else as well: immortality, the ultimate sign of what Ernst Bloch called the "unfettered life" of utopia.[27] Sustained by the grail, the brotherhood is free from the tyranny of death.

LOSS: THE REIGN OF AMFORTAS

In *Parsifal*, the reign of Amfortas represents the second stage of romantic anticapitalism: the loss of utopia. In the first act, during Parsifal's initial and unsuccessful visit to Monsalvat, Titurel lives but has ceded the kingship to his son, Amfortas. In this act, the romantic utopia is already imperiled. In the third act, before Parsifal's second and successful visit to Monsalvat, Titurel is dead. Only the promise of one last grail ceremony at Titurel's funeral remains from the old utopian order.

Elements of an alien modernity disrupt and then nearly extinguish the utopian community of Monsalvat. Into the communal and anonymous order enters a new, assertive, and self-interested spirit of individual ambition and sexual desire. To be sure, in themselves ambition and sexual desire are certainly not new. Indeed, they have been the bane of many utopian schemes at least since the time of Plato's Republic. But they are new to the self-abnegating and continent universe of Titurel's Monsalvat. With the introduction of ambition and sexual desire, the old, passive predicates of utopia—the brothers "are called" to membership in the community, the knights "are called" on missions to save the virtuous—give way to the purposive actions of calculating and self-assertive individuals.

The sorcerer Klingsor is the external threat to Monsalvat. Long ago, this (presumably) sexually impure man's eager attempt to join the grail brotherhood had been rejected by Titurel. But even this rebuff did not quell Klingsor's ambition. Wishing to demonstrate the permanent suppression of his sexual desire, he castrated himself. Rejected once again, Klingsor quite understandably became the implacable enemy of the grail brotherhood.

In his conflict with Monsalvat, Klingsor cultivates the knowledge of evil magic. The contest between the Christian faith of the brotherhood and the black magic of Klingsor may replicate the central conflict of *Lohengrin:* Christianity is the new religion that must fight against the remnants of the old faith. But in *Parsifal,* there are hints of a reversed chronology. The simple and primitive Christian faith of Titurel must struggle against a newer, more modern spirit of human knowledge, artifice, and contrivance. Surrounded by "implements of witchcraft and necromantic apparatus" (110)—that is, surrounded by the medieval symbols of protomodern science and technology—Klingsor looks forward to the day when he gains control of the grail as well as the spear. One of Klingsor's major achievements, the creation of a magic garden in the desert, is the luxurious but unnatural product of human contrivance. It withers before the primeval power of the spear restored to the control of the righteous.

Kundry mediates between the realms of Klingsor and Amfortas. As an undying penitent for her ancient sin, she willingly serves the grail brotherhood. But as a woman who experiences sexual desire, she is involuntarily subject to the spells of Klingsor. Klingsor used Kundry to seduce Amfortas and gain the spear. He is unsuccessful in his attempt to use Kundry to seduce Parsifal.

The internal threat to the old order comes from King Amfortas himself. He is gripped by personal ambition. Upon acceding to the throne, the "all too daring Amfortas" abandons Monsalvat's passive and defensive concept of being called to military duty (80). Instead, "he could not wait" to initiate military action against Klingsor (84). While on this mission, Amfortas compounds ambition with sexual desire. He succumbs to Kundry, loses the spear, and receives his wound.

With Amfortas's loss of the spear and his subsequent refusal to nourish the brotherhood through the grail ceremony, the old utopian order of Monsalvat is nearly destroyed. When Parsifal returns to Monsalvat in the third act, he observes that "every-thing seems changed" (162). The premodern community based on the miraculous communism of the grail is gone. In its stead Parsifal finds the fractured, anticommunal disorder of a society once again subjected to economic scarcity.

Accompanied by neither knights nor squires, Gurnemanz lives alone. Nature may have grown less hospitable, for he no longer sleeps exposed to the elements but lives in his hermit's hut in a corner of the forest. No longer nourished by the collective feasts of the grail, the knights must engage in primitive, economically productive labor. They are reduced to individual foraging for subsistence: "Herbs and roots / each finds for himself" (158). In spite of Wagner's advocacy of vegetarianism in his prose writings, the new herbivorous diet proves to be no substitute for the old miraculous fare. The Gurnemanz of the third act is visibly aged and weakened.

The political life of the grail community is similarly debased. The brotherhood is spiritually and physically exhausted. The old harmony between the republican and monarchical elements is broken. However well intentioned, Gawan goes off on his own quests without the permission of his king. In both the first- and third-act grail feasts, an element of fraternity remains among the knights: they sing together in chorus. But this fraternity is now primarily a solidarity of opposition. There is a fundamental antagonism of interests between the brotherly republic of knights and their king. The needful knights demand that the unwilling Amfortas perform the grail ceremony.

Amfortas calls his own kingship a "woeful inheritance" (102). Indeed, compared to his father, Amfortas bungles every function of the grail king. By losing the spear, he fails as a custodian of the precious relics, the essential symbols of the community. As long as the spear is in Klingsor's hostile hands, the custodianship of the grail itself is in jeopardy. Likewise, Amfortas fails as a sacerdotal high priest. As the only morally defiled member of the brotherhood, he is unwilling to officiate at the grail ceremony. Finally,

Amfortas is a failure as a military commander. The knights no longer receive calls for help. With the cessation of the knights' duty, the very purpose of the Monsalvat community has been lost.

With the loss of utopia, the pallor of death pervades Monsalvat. Denied the vision of the grail, Titurel dies. Instead of fulfilling its traditional role as a daily celebration of immortal life, Amfortas's last grail ceremony commemorates the death of his father. The two sinners, Amfortas and Kundry, long for death as a release from their curses. In the third act, Gurnemanz waits for death. In the Wagnerian vision of *Parsifal*, spirituality and nature are the grounds for an immortal life in community. In contrast, the individual ambition and sexual desire of modern life lead to death in society.

RECOVERY: THE REIGN OF PARSIFAL

The reign of Parsifal represents the third stage of romantic anti-capitalism: the quest for recovery. This quest is partly constituted by Parsifal's heroic deeds, including his acts of heroic sexual renunciation. But the quest is also an account of the Bildung, or experiential education, of the title character. In order to fulfill the prophecy given to Amfortas and recover romantic utopia, Parsifal must attain compassion. His compassion in turn brings a new epistemology and a new ethic to Monsalvat. For Parsifal, knowing is not a matter of Titurel's simple Christian faith nor Amfortas's and Klingsor's more modern calculations. Rather, Parsifal knows through compassion, an empathetic insight into and identification with the plight of others. Likewise, the deep but uncompassionate piety of Titurel was unable to withstand the modern, self-interested spirit of ambition and sexual desire. In contrast, the Monsalvat of Parsifal will be suffused with the new, dearly won ethic of compassion.

In his naive first-act visit to Monsalvat, Parsifal fulfills part of the prophecy. His ignorant responses to Gurnemanz's questions establish his innocence and foolishness. He also makes strides in becoming a compassionate being. Once boasting of his ability to hit "whatever flies" (88), Parsifal first learns to feel sorrow when he shoots the swan. Later he clutches at his heart in a sympathetic reaction to the pain of Amfortas during the grail ceremony. But the embryonic compassion of the first act is not yet an emotional enlightenment. Parsifal's compassion has not yet reached full consciousness and articulation. Once again questioned by Gurnemanz at the end of the ceremony, he can only mutely shake his head.

By his achievements in the second act, Parsifal establishes his identity as the rescuer of the grail community. Early in the act, he defeats Klingsor's knights, then resists the flower maidens. Parsifal's education in compassion is fulfilled in his encounter with Kundry. Reminded by Kundry about his mother, he accepts responsibility for causing her death. Kissed by Kundry, he now understands what he could only feel during the first-act grail ceremony. He comes to a full empathetic understanding of the downfall and plight of Amfortas. Unlike Amfortas, however, Parsifal resists Kundry's attempt at seduction. Defending himself against Klingsor's attack, the sexually continent Parsifal recovers the spear.

A consciously compassionate Parsifal returns to Monsalvat in the third act. As the new grail king, Parsifal rectifies the pernicious effects of modern ambition and sexual desire. The sacred relics are restored and secure. Parsifal returns the spear, unsullied by use in any of his battles on the way to Monsalvat, to the grail community. Inspired by his compassion, Parsifal touches Amfortas's side with the spear and thereby heals his wound. The grail is no longer threatened by the ambitions of a Klingsor or the impetuous and desire-filled actions of an unworthy grail king.

Compassion likewise marks Parsifal's sacerdotal duties. His "first office" is the cleansing baptism of Kundry, which frees her from her curse (170). Before he unveils the grail, he absolves

Amfortas of his sins. Sympathetic to the plight of the "pale and woeful" knights, Parsifal officiates at the grail ceremony (166). The breach between the brotherhood and their king is healed.

From external evidence, we know about Parsifal's success as a military commander. According to *Lohengrin*, the grail community recovered its purpose under its new, compassionate king. Once again the knights are sent on missions to defend the virtuous.

The drama ends with what must be the most exquisitely set epigram in the history of musical theater. The line is first sung by the chorus of low-voiced knights at the base of the castle hall and is then taken up by the youths and boys at the middle and top of the dome: "Erlösung dem Erlöser!" (Redemption to the redeemer!) (180). Thus the last line of *Parsifal*, the last line of Wagner's last music drama, sums up the irony of the story. Parsifal, the foretold redeemer, must redeem himself for his failed first visit to Monsalvat before he can redeem others.

WAGNER CONTRA NIETZSCHE

Parsifal's last line has a significance that goes beyond the boundaries of the artwork. Early and late in his career, Wagner, the self-anointed redeemer, also sought the redemption of a fallen political and artistic reality. "Redemption" was the term that Wagner used to refer to a fundamental and saving transformation of the human heart, although as the years passed he revised his vision of how it was achieved. For the young Wagner, redemption meant political revolution. But in his later years, Wagner lost his confidence in politics. For the old Wagner, redemption entailed a regeneration of the human spirit through art.

In the typically moralistic manner of romantic anticapitalists, the young Wagner condemned modern society. The modern capitalist economy was based on egoism and greed. Rather than satisfying genuine human needs, it served the interests of the owners of capital and property. The working class, the only truly productive class, was exploited and impoverished. While the workers did the work, the aristocracy alternated between a dissipated idleness and a pernicious meddling in the affairs of the state. Capitalism had disastrous consequences for art in general and Wagnerian art in particular. All art was corrupted by privatization, commercialization, and commodification. And the Wagnerian reform of musical theater was further inhibited by the hidebound conventionalism that plagued the modern opera house.

With ideas derived from Hegel, Pierre Joseph Proudhon, Ludwig Feuerbach, and Mikhail Bakunin, the young Wagner sought redemption through political means: through the "lofty goddess *Revolution.*"[28] On the rubble of the present, the revolution would create the just socialist future of brotherhood and freedom, equality, and communal love. Once freed from the evils of capitalism, a new humanity would be born. In this context, the arts would recover the popular foundation and essential unity that they enjoyed during the golden age of the ancient Greeks. The young Wagner envisioned, as a paean to the success of the revolution, a new Wagnerian total work of art (which would eventually become *Der Ring des Nibelungen*) that would have its festival performance in a temporary theater on the banks of the Rhine.

As he grew older, Wagner became more pessimistic about the prospects of redemption through political means. This pessimism was the result not only of the failure of his first attempt at redemption via revolution but also of his disappointment with the insufficiently Wagnerian course of Ludwig's kingship and the new Second Reich. Going against the prevalent nineteenth-century belief in progress, including progress through revolution, Wagner now understood politics as merely part of the pervasive and ongoing degeneration of humanity in the historical era. The primordial goodness of human nature had been suffocated by the decadence of civilized society.

A faint hope for redemption still remained. In his later years, Wagner believed that political changes were pointless unless they were preceded by a regeneration of human nature. He reconceived this quest for the recovery of utopia, this redemption through regeneration, as partly a biological issue. Confirmed by his reading of the French racist thinker, Arthur de Gobineau, the young Wagner's social and religious anti-Semitism now took on a racial cast. But Wagner also saw redemption through regeneration as partly a program for the recovery of lost spiritual health, and it is in this sense that his late prose works connect with the themes of *Parsifal*.

Wagner believed that, just as Parsifal restored the utopia of Monsalvat by infusing it with compassion, an ethic of compassion or sympathy is the "only true foundation" for spiritual regeneration in modern society.[29] Motivated by compassion, we no longer treat other human beings as alien creatures to be used, manipulated, and vanquished. When our sense of sympathy is not corrupted by utilitarian concerns, we realize that other human beings suffer just like we do. Indeed, Wagner extended the renewed ethic of compassion beyond human affairs to our relations with animals. True compassion means an intuitive identification with the suffering of all living creatures.

As we have seen, Adorno disparaged this compassion as mere sentiment. Compared to the materialistic, individualistic self-interest of liberal capitalism and the materialistic, collective self-interest of Marxism, compassion appears to be a hopelessly fuzzy and idealistic foundation for a renewed political and social order. But thirty years later Max Horkheimer, Adorno's friend and colleague, followed Schopenhauer and Wagner in condemning reason, the source of rationalizations "in the struggle with nature and with men," and lauding compassion as the alternative: "As long as there are hunger and misery on earth, he who can see will have no peace."[30]

Along with much patent nonsense, including ruminations about fruit-eating panthers and tigers living on the margins of Canadian lakes, Wagner's 1880 essay "Religion and Art" lays out the practical guidelines for realizing the ethic of compassion in the late nineteenth century. He proposes a four-point program. No longer the sensuous Dionysian of his youth, he recommends temperance unions to mitigate against the destructive effects of alcohol. Pursuant to his goal of extending sympathy to animals, Wagner champions both vegetarianism and societies for the prevention of cruelty to animals. And finally, reviving an idea from his revolutionary youth, he advocates socialism. Still using the moralistic terms of a romantic anticapitalist, the old Wagner argues that the abject condition of the working class exhibits the "profound immorality of our civilization."[31]

At first glance, religion would appear to be the agency for Wagnerian spiritual redemption and regeneration. But for Wagner religion, like politics, has not escaped the general decay of the human condition. In the modern era, religion has become "artificial," a collection of ideas, images, rituals, and symbols that have lost their ability to transform and elevate the human spirit.[32] Contra Nietzsche, who believed that *Parsifal* represented Wagner's reversion to Christianity, the Christian aspects of the music drama exemplify Wagner's opportunistic, almost cynical exploitation of the Christian tradition. Instead of Nietzsche's Christian Wagner, Maurice Boucher's portrait of Wagner as religious manipulator is closer to the mark. According to Boucher, for Wagner the various aspects of Christianity were "somewhat like the properties found in the storage room of a bankrupt theatre, waiting for a good play to put them to use."[33]

As Wagner's confidence in both politics and religion waned, however, his belief in the transformational efficacy of art soared. Art understands the still valid essence of religion, and art actualizes this legacy in works that can still move the spirit. Of course, as agencies of Wagnerian redemption through spiritual regeneration, all arts are not created equal. According to Wagner, it is music that is the "world-redeeming incarnation of the divine dogma" and that saves the "noblest heritage of the Christian idea in its purity of over-worldly reformation."[34] Again contra Nietzsche, who misinterpreted the libretto of *Parsifal* as a symptom of the aged artist's spiritual weakness, the old Wagner's aspirations for his art were never more ambitious. The *Ring* as Gesamtkunstwerk merely commemorated the achievement of political revolution. But *Parsifal* as Bühnenweihfestspiel is the actual agency of possible change. By preserving the compassionate essence of spiritual regeneration in an effective form, *Parsifal* is the hope for redemption in a fallen world.

In the writings of his later years, Wagner's vision of redemption through regeneration was a mélange of odiousness, eccentricity, and insight. But in his music dramas, Wagner attained greater clarity. With *Parsifal*, late-nineteenth-century romantic anticapitalism was no longer a matter of conservative cultural criticism, but rather the political substance of a sonic and visual image of utopia.

The romantic anticapitalism of *Parsifal* is in part the product of Wagner's pessimism about the prospects for real political change. In comparison to many twentieth-century operas, however, *Parsifal* is a document of unbridled political optimism. Freudian psychoanalytic theory is arguably the most distinctive and pervasive tendency within twentieth-century political thought. Conceived under the influence of Freudian theory, operas like *Elektra* and *Erwartung* deepen our understanding of their characters' motivations but abandon the heroic quest for political change and improvement. Indeed, in many Freudian works, there are no longer true operatic heroes and heroines; instead, there are central characters who are either victims or victimizers. Rather than portraying grand, heroic acts, operas search, regressively and reductively, for psychological motives.[35] This psychological sensibility also pervades our understanding of earlier works. It was perhaps inevitable that, late in the twentieth century, a critic should interpret *Parsifal* not in terms of the concepts of Christianity, nationalism, anti-Semitism, or romantic anticapitalism but in terms of the central character's troubled childhood and dysfunctional family.[36]

FIVE

The Politics of Psychological Interiorization
Strauss's *Elektra* and Schoenberg's *Erwartung*

Men, even madmen, do not simply invent their world. The materials they employ for its construction are, by and large, public property.

—PETER GAY

TRAUSS *and* Schoenberg? *Elektra* and *Erwartung*? Contemporary composers, contemporary operas, yet their linkage belies the traditional interpretations of these composers and works as antipodes.

As the preeminent German composer of the late nineteenth and early twentieth centuries, Richard Strauss (1864–1949) was the central figure in the mainstream of Austro-German art music. He enjoyed associations with the most illustrious musical institutions, including the Dresden, Berlin, Munich, and Vienna operas, the Berlin Philharmonic, and the Bayreuth and Salzburg festivals. In spite of some tonal experimentation, he was the putative heir to Wagnerism and was regarded as the leader of a neoromantic musical orthodoxy. Along with Giacomo Puccini, Strauss was the last opera composer to see his works regularly enter the performing repertory. During the Nazi era, he was named honorary president of the Reichsmusik-kammer.

[111]

Arnold Schoenberg (1874–1951), on the other hand, was the most outstanding representative of musical modernism. His works were championed by the institutions of the Viennese and international musical avant-garde, including the Wiener Tonkünstlerverein, Ansorge Verein, Vereinigung Schaffender Tonkünstler, the Rosé Quartet, the International Society for Contemporary Music, and, most important, the Verein für Musikalische Privataufführungen (Society for Private Musical Performances). Although Schoenberg had success with early works in a Wagnerian vein, his infrequently performed modernist operas retain critical and theoretical significance today. During the Third Reich, he was the chief representative of what the Nazis called "degeneracy" in music.

In spite of their contemporaneity, *Elektra* and *Erwartung* are frequently contrasted. Strauss's *Elektra* (1909) was the first of his successful collaborations with Viennese librettist Hugo von Hofmannsthal. The opera premiered in Dresden in 1909, with performances in Vienna later that year and in most of the major opera venues within the next few years. This one-act opera employs several principal singers, large orchestral forces, and Wagnerian leitmotifs.

Schoenberg's *Erwartung* (composed 1909, published 1916) set a libretto by Marie Pappenheim, a poet married to a Viennese psychiatrist.[1] The opera premiered in Prague in 1924, with infrequent performances thereafter. This one-act monodrama is set to the free tonality of musical expressionism.

The facts of the Strauss-Schoenberg, *Elektra-Erwartung* contrasts cannot be denied. Yet the continued emphasis on these contrasts undervalues their points of continuity. Despite their differences, the operas share the deep "psychological sensitivity permeating Viennese cultural life at the turn of the century."[2]

This psychological sensitivity was a product of the political defeat of the Viennese intelligentsia. Viennese artists, scientists, and intellectuals had long identified with the cause of Austrian liberalism, but this liberalism enjoyed barely four decades of political ascendancy. By the turn of the century, Austrian liberalism was routed by the forces of aristocratic-clerical reaction, anti-Semitic populism, ethnic nationalism, and working-class radicalism. Retaining their cultural influence yet disillusioned with the overt politics of parties and the court, the Viennese intelligentsia turned inward, to the life of the mind and its discontents.

Freudian psychoanalytic theory was the epitome of this politically motivated inward turn. Sigmund Freud's late work, particularly *Civilization and Its Discontents*, offered a grand theory about the fate of human happiness and satisfaction in civilized life. (Echoes of this late psychoanalytic theory reverberate in Henze's *Bassarids*, the subject of Chapter 7.) But early in the century, it was the more individually focused and therapy-based research on hysteria, dreams, and sexuality that invaded the opera house. Although madness had been a recurrent theme since the beginning of opera, *Elektra* and *Erwartung* transformed the traditional operatic depiction of madness in ways that reveal a distinct indebtedness to the new psychological sensitivity. The new focal points were the conflicts in mental life: the relations between consciousness and the unconscious, sexual instinct and social repression, infantile experience and adult distress.

As befits an opera based on a classical play by Sophocles, *Elektra* psychologizes familiar dramatic and musical materials. *Erwartung* goes beyond the familiar in its musical-dramatic attempt to replicate psychic suffering.

MADNESS IN OPERA

Elektra and *Erwartung* enter into an ongoing operatic preoccupation with the emotions, passions, and affections: that is, with the musical-dramatic representation of the nonrational and irrational aspects of human behavior. But if many opera characters are motivated by varying degrees and combinations of love, despair, and rage rather than by reason, there was a musical-dramatic need to distinguish between characters who were temporarily in the throes of some nonrational or irrational passion and "mad" characters who were somehow beyond the socially accepted extremes of passion. The "mad scenes" of nineteenth-century romantic opera are only the most notorious examples of this distinction. Already in the early seventeenth century, Monteverdi and his contemporaries devised effective—and remarkably enduring—techniques for representing the differences between madness and extreme passion.[3]

Dramatically, textually, and musically, mad characters violate the conventions of opera. The mad character appears infrequently, thereby establishing a vivid contrast to the "normal" behavior of the other characters. Before these infrequent appearances, other characters may alert the audience by referring to the mad character's disturbed mental condition. Once on stage, the mad character gesticulates wildly.

The text supports these dramatic devices. The conventions of operatic discourse are violated. Instead of expressing complete ideas in sequences of more or less complete sentences, the mad character rapidly shifts between various emotional states, subject matters, and rhymes, further punctuating these fragmentary utterances with exclamations, sighs, laughs, cries, and senseless repetitions. In addition, the mad character suffers delusions about imaginary illnesses or dangers. The inversion of gender stereotypes enhances the impression of madness. Mad female characters, for example, are given the warlike words traditionally associated with men.

The music confirms and heightens the image of the character's madness. Monteverdi always tied his music closely to his texts. In the context of mad scenes, the rapid shifts and fragmented utterances of mad characters are accompanied by wild melodic leaps and quickly changing tones, rhythms, tempos, and harmonies. By the late seventeenth century, operatic mad scenes were a predictable convention rather than an innovation, and the frequency of their use gradually diminished.

Mad scenes continued in the classical operas of the eighteenth century, but they are subdued by Enlightenment concerns about reasonableness and aesthetic form. In the first act of Mozart's *Don Giovanni*, the Don repeatedly characterizes the accusations of the spurned Donna Elvira as the outpourings of a madwoman. But in the hands of a composer who believed that "passions, whether violent or not, must never be expressed to the point of exciting disgust" and that "music, even in the most terrible situations, must never offend the ear," the depiction of madness, real or alleged, is tempered by the observance of decorum.[4] Little wonder that Donna Anna and Don Ottavio remain skeptical about the Don's charges, for Elvira's allegedly mad accusations are made during the course of an exquisitely balanced quartet. Here as elsewhere, classical form contains and constrains the representation of even mad behavior.

Nineteenth-century romantic opera, with its renewed emphasis on the irrational and nonrational, reinvigorates the convention of the mad scene.[5] From the scorned Elvira (Vincenzo Bellini, *I Puritani*) to the demented czar Boris (Mussorgsky, *Boris Godunov*), romantic opera is replete with scenes of acute psychic distress. The early romantic archetype of these scenes occurs in the third act of Gaetano Donizetti's *Lucia di Lammermoor*. The scene climaxes with Lucia's flight into an extended reverie about her imagined marriage to Edgar. Despite its treacherous leaps and swoops, Lucia's gymnastic coloratura remains firmly within the bounds of classical tonality.[6]

It is only in the later romanticism of Wagner that the operatic representation of madness bursts the underlying bonds of tonal grammar. In his mature music dramas, Wagner established the orchestra as a kind of psychoanalyst *avant la lettre* of the characters' conscious motivations.[7] Through his use of leitmotifs, the orchestra sometimes confirms, sometimes amplifies, and sometimes contradicts the verbal text. In the third act of *Tristan und Isolde*, Wagner goes beyond words and gestures, and beyond mere orchestral commentary, to depict the madness of Tristan. Tristan's love for Isolde violates the conventions of society, and his delirious vision of Isolde violates the tonal conventions, the musical analogue of social conventionality, in an outpouring of chromaticism and dissonance.

In the first decade of the twentieth century, Vienna's deep psychological sensitivity pushed operatic madness beyond the isolated mad scene to an entire mad opera. The events of both *Elektra* and *Erwartung* take place at night, the time of dreams rather than consciousness, of passion rather than reason, of Dionysus rather than Apollo—and the time, according to the male anxieties of the era, of women.[8] Both operas represent their psychically distressed female central characters as alienated from their societies and political systems. Both operas present these women in the age-old, yet thoroughly contemporary, guise of hysterical murderesses. And finally, both operas, following the example of Wagner's *Tristan*, go beyond drama and text to represent these nocturnal realms of alienation and murder by manipulating and transforming the familiar tonal vocabulary of music.

ELEKTRA: FROM EPIC TRAGEDY TO FAMILY DRAMA

The title page of Hofmannsthal's libretto indicates that *Elektra* is a one-act tragedy that freely follows Sophocles ("Tragödie in einem Aufzug frei nach Sophokles"). With some exceptions, the main lines of the plot do follow the classical model. Where the following of Sophocles becomes "free" is when Hofmannsthal introduces the nuances and changes that transform the opera from a moral-political tale about the dynasty of Agamemnon into a "family drama" displaying the psychological imprint of early-twentieth-century Vienna. The fact that Hofmannsthal's adaptation does not slavishly follow Sophocles' original is not a problem in itself. The task here, rather, is to identify and interpret Hofmannsthal's changes.

Sophocles' *Electra* takes up a familiar episode in the tragic history of the house of Atreus. Upon his return from the Trojan War, Agamemnon, the king of Mycenae, has been murdered by his wife, Clytemnestra, and her lover, Aegisthus. In order to save her young brother Orestes, the heir to the throne, from a similar fate, the princess Electra has sent him into a protective exile abroad. The play is about the efforts of Orestes and Electra to take a moral-religious propitiation against the murderers of their father and thereby to restore the dynasty.

The classical play opens at dawn with a now adult Orestes, accompanied by a few companions, on the outskirts of Mycenae. Following the advice of the Pythian oracle, they devise a plot to penetrate the palace and carry out the necessary killings. They will gain entrance to the palace by posing as messengers bearing the news that Orestes has died in exile. Meanwhile, Electra emerges from the palace to yearn once again for the return of Orestes, when the murder of her father will be avenged by the blood of the murderers, the dynasty will be restored, and her material patrimony will be returned to her. No longer will the children of Clytemnestra and Aegisthus be favored at the expense of the progeny of Agamemnon. Electra's sister, Chrysotemis, agrees with the principles of Electra's hostility to Clytemnestra and Aegisthus but cautions her sister to be politically prudent: the weak should "bend before the strong."[9] Indeed, Chrysotemis reports that Clytemnestra and Aegisthus already have a plan to lock Electra away in a tower. Clytemnestra enters, disturbed by a horrible vision: Agamemnon, restored to life, once again sits on the throne of Mycenae. On her way to perform rites to dispel the vision, Clytemnestra reminds Electra that her killing of Agamemnon was a justified blood propitiation. Agamemnon sacrificed the life of their daughter, Iphigenia, in order to receive favorable winds for his fleet's campaign against Troy.

Convinced of the truth of the report of Orestes' death, Electra resolves to kill Clytemnestra and Aegisthus herself. But then Orestes and Electra are finally reunited, and Electra is apprised of the plan for the killings. With Electra standing guard at the palace door, Orestes and his companions, who pretend to bear the ashes of the dead Orestes, enter the palace and kill Clytemnestra. Aegisthus returns from a hunt. Deceived by Electra's reassurances about the death of Orestes, Aegisthus enters the palace and is also killed. The play closes with the chorus proclaiming the justice of the bloody events: "O house of Atreus, through how many sufferings hast thou come forth at last in freedom, crowned with good by this day's enterprise!"[10]

Originally written as a play, Hofmannsthal's libretto for *Elektra* strips the classical tragedy of its moral-religious and overtly political content and thereby transforms it into a drama about the psychosexual conflicts within a family. Gone are references to the Trojan War, Iphigenia, oracles, prophetic visions, an imperiled dynasty, and noble birthrights. Gone too is the conclusion of the classical play: the restoration of the dynastic house of Atreus. In their stead is a story about a daughter's inordinate attachment to the memory of her father and her implacable desire for bloody revenge against her mother, all set against a highly charged atmosphere of hysteria and its psychosexual foundation: irrational fear, fantasies of motherhood and sexual fulfillment, nightmares and dreams, psychic paralysis, and incestuous bisexuality. The opera concludes, not with the restoration of the rightful heirs to the patrimony of Atreus, but with Elektra launching into a frenzied dance of triumph, then falling dead to the ground.

At the time of the writing of *Elektra*, Hofmannsthal may or may not have read Josef Breuer and Freud's *Studies in Hysteria*.[11] But regardless of whether Hofmannsthal was directly influenced by Freud, it is clear that the deep psychological sensitivity of turn-of-the-century Vienna inclined Hofmannsthal to a psychoanalytic approach to the Greek classics. Indeed, Hofmannsthal's approach to *Electra* is remarkably similar to Freud's treatment of another classical play, *Oedipus Rex*. Both plays are transformed from tragedies concerned with morality and politics into examinations of the psychosexual relations in the drama of family life. The realization of the transformation of *Electra* lies in the details of Hofmannsthal's drama and text and in Strauss's score.

The mise-en-scène announces the transformation. Instead of

Sophocles' dawn, the action takes place at night. Instead of Elektra's being a disaffected resident of the palace, Elektra's alienation from her society is accentuated. She lives outside the palace in the courtyard. Utilizing an old technique dating back at least to baroque opera, Hofmannsthal has Elektra's unusual behavior and state of mind announced by maids who have gone to the courtyard in order to fetch water from the well. Much of Elektra's demeanor replicates the familiar iconography of operatic madness: her hair is dirty and disheveled; her eyes are ghastly; her cheeks are hollowed; her clothes are mere rags. Her behavior matches her appearance. Several times she is described as acting like a wild animal. She spits, she springs, she stares, she burrows, she eats from a "food-bowl down with the dogs."[12] On one occasion, her behavior suggests a symptom of hysteria. Immediately after the killing of Klytemnestra and Aegisth, she wants to lead a dance but finds herself paralyzed:

> The ocean
> grown twenty-fold more vast, engulfs
> all my limbs with its weight and I cannot
> lift myself! (22)

Although Elektra's single-minded devotion to the killing of her mother lends a greater degree of consistency than is usually found in the mad characters of opera, she still exhibits extreme swings of mood. From one scene to the next, she can be defensive, consumed by blood lust, sarcastic, ingratiating, defiant, incredulous, resolved, seductive, exultant, ashamed, and deceitful. According to the maids, Elektra's nightly lamentations for her father are interspersed with groans, screams, and cries. In the absence of her brother, Elektra accepts the traditional masculine task of exacting blood revenge.

Beyond these familiar representations of operatic madness, three episodes in the libretto suggest a distinct relation to the new psychological sensitivity. And all three show that Elektra is not the only psychologically disturbed woman in Hofmannsthal's

Mycenae. The first of these occurs early in the opera, immediately after Elektra's long soliloquy on blood revenge. Chrysotemis enters the courtyard and startles Elektra, "as if waking from a dream" (14). She has come to warn Elektra about the plan to lock Elektra in a tower and to tell her that Klytemnestra has had another of her recurring nightmares.

In Sophocles this meeting is an opportunity for the sisters to commiserate about their suffering, to agree in principle on the need for the punishment of Clytemnestra and Aegisthus, and to disagree on political tactics. Both sisters realize that their sexual deprivation has a political foundation. Clytemnestra and Aegisthus want to make sure that neither sister produces a child, who would have a legitimate claim to the throne of Mycenae. But in *Elektra* the discussion leaves the realm of politics in favor of psychosexuality. As in many of Hofmannsthal's works, the sisters are presented as antipodes, as contrasting psychological types,[13] and their differences revolve more around their responses to sexual frustration than around the advantages or disadvantages of political prudence.

Chrysotemis suffers the irrational fears of the hysteric:

> I cannot endure to stay in one room, I must
> go from one doorway to another, oh,
> upstairs, downstairs, it is as if something called me,
> and when I go in, an empty room
> stares at me. I am so frightened that
> my knees shake day and night, my throat
> is choked, I cannot even weep, it is as if
> everything were stone. Sister, have pity! (14)

And there is no indication that Chrysotemis's desire for children has any connection to dynastic succession:

> I want to have children
> before my body shrivels up, and even if it were a peasant
> to whom they gave me, I would bear him
> children and warm them with my body

on cold nights, when storms
shake the hut! (14)

But Elektra is unmoved. She refuses to make the accommodations
to the rulers that might ease her sister's fears and end her sister's
sexual frustration. Instead, she sarcastically suggests that Chrysotemis return to the palace, where there just might be a wedding
being prepared for her.

In the next scene Hofmannsthal reinterprets Sophocles' confrontation between Electra and Clytemnestra over the queen's
"vision." In Sophocles' *Electra* the vision is overtly political:
Agamemnon restored to his throne. And Clytemnestra intends
not only to follow the prescribed rites for ridding oneself of a
disturbing vision but to do so at Agamemnon's tomb. Electra
objects to this plan on religious-moral grounds. She claims that
Clytemnestra's rites would compound the crime of murder with
the sin of sacrilege.

But with its references to hysteria and dream interpretation,
Hofmannsthal's scene is psychologized. Klytemnestra has, not a
disturbing political vision, but simply another episode in her
ongoing series of nightmares. Neither the traditional sacrifices
nor her coterie of sycophants have been able to bring her any
relief. She describes a variety of hysterical symptoms—her
strength is paralyzed, her eyes are swollen, hallucinatory creatures crawl over her—but she knows that physically she is "not
even ill" (16). Desperate for help, she turns to the suddenly
ingratiating Elektra, who "speaks like a doctor" (15).

In the tradition of Joseph (the Bible) and Tiresias (Greek
myth), Elektra argues to interpret Klytemnestra's dream. During
the course of Klytemnestra's catalog of nightmarish horrors,
Klytemnestra reveals: "Every limb / in my body cries out for
death" (16). Elektra—as if aware of Freud's dictum that a "dream
is a *disguised* fulfillment of a *suppressed* wish"[14]—pronounces her
cure in the form of a prophecy: "When the appointed / victim

falls under the axe, then you will dream / no longer!" (16). Thinking that the "appointed victim" refers to some traditional blood sacrifice, Klytemnestra presses for details. Elektra finally reveals that it is Klytemnestra herself who is the victim and that it is Orest who, with the assistance of his vengeful sister, will effect the bloody cure that will surely free Klytemnestra from her dreams.

The final episode has no parallel in Sophocles' play, which supports the thesis that the psychology of *Elektra* has more to do with contemporary Vienna than it does with ancient Greece. Having been reluctantly persuaded of the truth of the news of Orest's death, Elektra is resolved to carry out the killings herself, with the assistance of Chrysotemis. Elektra starts to dig up the ax that was used to kill her father, and she tries to enlist Chrysotemis. Elektra plays on Chrysotemis's desire for sexual satisfaction not by abstract argument but by demonstration. Clutching and groping her horrified sister, Elektra extols Chrysotemis's slender feet, her slim and supple hips, the down on her cool and strong arms. Elektra entices Chrysotemis with promises of sexual ecstasy if only she will help with the killings.

Perhaps this lurid scene is nothing more than an attempt by Hofmannsthal to assure a good box office: *épater le bourgeois*. It does, however, seem likely that the particular form of this scene is not random, as it evokes the Freudian theory of primal bisexuality, particularly the bisexuality of women.[15]

If Hofmannsthal's drama and text internalize the politics of Sophocles' *Electra* and give the story instead a highly charged psychological atmosphere, Strauss's score intensifies the transformation. His leitmotifs, chromatic tonality, and waltz rhythms heighten and clarify the psychology of the opera.

Strauss uses just a few leitmotifs. The principal one is the thunderous Agamemnon motif. Repeated at the beginning of the opera and again at the end, the motif frames the action of the opera. The motif also punctuates Elektra's soliloquy on blood revenge, the longest and deepest account of the character's psychological motives. Like Wotan in Wagner's *Götterdämmerung*, the musical evocation of the absent Agamemnon allows him to dominate a work in which he does not appear.

Neither before nor after *Elektra* did Strauss display any profound dissatisfaction with the constraints of Western tonality. But his efforts to capture the psychological motivations and conflicts of *Elektra* prompted him to his most extensive use of chromaticism and dissonance.[16] Indeed, Adorno, who had little respect for Strauss and usually categorized him among the tonally reactionary German neoromantic composers, had high praise for the score of both the maids' scene and the confrontation between Elektra and Klytemnestra.[17]

The most intriguing and revealing element of Strauss's score is his use of waltz tunes and rhythms. If Hofmannsthal's drama and text reveal a modern Viennese psychological sensitivity transposed to ancient Greece, the score cements this connection through the musical emblems of late-nineteenth- and early-twentieth-century Vienna. Snippets of waltzes are scattered throughout the score, becoming longer and more pronounced as it heads for the finale. As the suddenly cooperative Elektra lights Aegisth's way into the palace and to his death, he cannot help noticing that Elektra has broken into a little dance: "Why are you staggering about like that with your torch? . . . Why are you dancing?" (22). But like the waltz elements in Maurice Ravel's *La valse*, those in *Elektra* provide an ironic commentary on the spirit of the age.[18] To the frenzied rhythms of an ever-quickening waltz, Elektra, the central figure in this aesthetic representation of Viennese psychological sensitivity, dances herself to death.

ERWARTUNG: UNCOMPROMISED ESTRANGEMENT

Elektra exemplifies one tendency of early-twentieth-century aesthetic modernism. It transforms familiar dramatic, textual, and musical materials in the direction of the new psychological sensitivity. But *Erwartung* (Expectation) goes much further. Here the new sensitivity is portrayed through new materials and the most advanced artistic techniques. Pappenheim's text, written to Schoenberg's specifications, is no adaptation of familiar content but something completely new. Schoenberg's music is no mere extension of late romanticism but one of the first scores in the thoroughly modernist style of musical expressionism.[19] Although both operas manifest the psychological sensitivity of prewar Vienna, *Erwartung* goes beyond *Elektra*'s evocation of Freud and psychoanalysis by representing fragments of familiar psychoanalytic ideas. Like the later *Ulysses* and *Finnegans Wake* of James Joyce, *Erwartung* attempts the aesthetic replication of the stream of consciousness. Only the physical appearance of the dramatis persona recalls some of the conventions of operatic madness.

The story, if such a traditional term can be used in this case, is simple. The distraught character, identified only as the Woman, walks in a forest at night. The odyssey of the walk appears to be a metaphor for the course of psychoanalytic treatment, with moments of clarity and revelation mixed with the Woman's often hysterical responses to her surroundings. Shards of a repressed memory, of repressed guilt—of him, of a lover, of another woman, of death—keep breaking through her reverie. Outside the other woman's house in the forest, she finds the corpse of her lover. The Woman has probably murdered him. The sight of the corpse evokes a flood of still-disjointed memories of their affair and of her lover's infidelity. There is no resolution to the story. The last line of the opera is indeterminate: "I was looking . . . "[20]

The mise-en-scène establishes the atmosphere of uncompromising estrangement. The action, of course, takes place at night. The locale is a forest. But this forest is no refuge from society à la Wagner and nineteenth-century romanticism, but rather a haunted realm of unexplained rustlings and terrifying shadows. If *Elektra* anachronistically invested ancient Greece with the psychology of modern Vienna, there is no politics, no society, no historical specificity in *Erwartung* whatsoever. Reference is made to a city in the distance, but the Woman, deeply involved

with her lover, has been alienated from it for quite some time: "I
knew nothing but you . . . / all this year" (27). The only character even lacks a personal name. In a fashion common to expressionism and existential philosophy as well as psychoanalysis, her
generic designation as the Woman indicates the purported univer-
sality of her inner world of psychic pain and suffering. There is no
communication. Except for a futile cry of "Help" when she discovers the corpse, the text is to be understood as an interior
monologue. And, of course, there are no police agencies. There is
not a hint that the murder of an unfaithful lover is of the slightest
concern to the state. In the spirit of Viennese psychological sensitivity, the criminality of murder is subordinated to the examination of its psychosexual motives and effects.

If one of the indications of Elektra's psychic disturbance is her
extreme shifts of mood between scenes, the Woman makes Elektra
seem like a paragon of stability. The Woman's moods—from relatively tame observations of her surroundings through hallucina-
tions, hysterical fears, and expressions of love, jealousy, and hatred
to moments of clarity and recall—are as fleeting as thought itself,
shifting from one disjointed word or phrase to the next. Ever-
changing verb tenses indicate the psychological simultaneity of
past memories, present circumstances, and hopes for the future.
The fragmented world of disturbed psychic life is represented in
the physical appearance of the printed page. Pappenheim's text is
full of ellipses, with very few periods or other terminal marks of
punctuation.

And yet, despite its novelty, the text does contain echoes of
earlier operas. In a macabre scene—which evokes not so much the
incestuous bisexuality of *Elektra* but the necrophilic climax to
another Strauss opera, *Salome*—the Woman showers the mouth of
the bloody corpse with kisses: "Now I shall kiss you until I die
of it" (27). The opera then concludes with the day-night imagery
of *Tristan und Isolde*. The daylight of society separated the nocturnal lovers of Wagner's music drama. The approaching dawn will
separate the Woman from the corpse of her lover, just as mornings

used to separate them when he was alive: "Morning separates us
. . . always morning . . . / How heavy your parting kiss . . .
/ Another interminable day of waiting" (28).

The tempos and tonal structure of Schoenberg's score replicate the shifts in the Woman's interior monologue. In the brief
score, which lasts approximately twenty-seven minutes in performance, one analyst has counted no fewer than 111 metronome
indications, with an additional sixty-five tempo controls.[21]

But the most innovative aspect of Schoenberg's thoroughly
modernist score is its tonal structure. If the tonality of *Tristan*
became the musical model for the most adventurous aspects of
Strauss's *Elektra*, *Tristan* is the harbinger, the point of departure for
the musical expressionism of Schoenberg's *Erwartung*. Poised between the Wagnerian neoromanticism of Schoenberg's early works
and the twelve-tone serialism of his compositions in the twenties
and thirties, the chromaticism and freed dissonance of musical
expressionism provide Schoenberg with the musical means of realizing the depth and range of the Woman's emotions as well as the
rapid shifts between her moods.

The text and music of *Erwartung* are paragons of modernism,
but the Woman's appearance provides a point of familiarity. By the
end of the opera, she, like many of her mad operatic sisters, has
disheveled hair, a torn dress, and hands stained with blood. The
once popular tours of Bedlam are long gone, as are the well-
attended examinations of hysterics conducted by the neurologist
Jean-Martin Charcot. But sights like these are now the fare of
Saturday night at the opera.

In the late nineteenth and very early twentieth centuries, the
political setbacks of Austrian liberalism turned the gaze of Austrian artists and intellectuals inward. In works like *Elektra* and
Erwartung, opera described psychological distress and suffering in
unprecedented depth and nuance. This model of modernist psychological opera would endure in works like Béla Bartók's *Bluebeard*, Alban Berg's *Wozzeck* and *Lulu*, Benjamin Britten's *Peter
Grimes*, and Krzysztof Penderecki's *Devils*. But if politics could turn

composers inward, it could also have the opposite effect. In retrospect, the political travails of late-nineteenth-century Austrian liberalism pale before the political crises of the early twentieth century. The life of the mind provided little refuge from the traumas of world war, socialism, fascism, and the development of consumer mass culture. In this context, opera composers, often against their will, were once again forced to redefine their positions vis-à-vis political events, movements, and institutions.

SIX

The Aesthetic Politics of the German Artist-Opera Pfitzner's *Palestrina*, Hindemith's *Mathis*, and Schoenberg's *Moses*

A composer is always a *zoon politikon* as well, the more so the more emphatic his purely musical claim.

—THEODOR W. ADORNO

RTIST-operas—operas that take the roles of art and the artist as their themes—pervaded musical theater in the early twentieth century. The commercially successful works of Richard Strauss were full of musical references and characters as well as characters drawn from the other arts. Among Strauss's works, *Der Rosenkavalier* and *Die Frau ohne Schatten* alluded to Mozart's *Le nozze di Figaro* and *Die Zauberflöte; Capriccio* revived the old debate about whether text or music is primary in opera; *Ariadne auf Naxos* contained an opera within the opera; and *Intermezzo* depicted incidents from Strauss's own life.[1] Puccini cast his operas with not only writers, painters, and poets but also a musician (Schaunard in *La Bohème*), a traveling minstrel (Jake Wallace in *La Fanciulla del West*), and, of course, the world's most celebrated fictional diva (Floria Tosca in *Tosca*). In spite of the frequency with which art and the artist occurred in the operas of these two composers, neither composer used his artist-operas as a means of exploring the real and unique problems

of art and the artist. The artists and musicians of Strauss and Puccini transported, diverted, and entertained opera audiences but never troubled them with the current aesthetic and political problems of art.

There were, however, alternatives to Strauss and Puccini. In three German-Austrian works, the artist-opera engaged contemporary dilemmas of art and the artist. Hans Pfitzner's (1869– 1949) *Palestrina* premiered in Munich in 1917. Paul Hindemith's (1895–1963) *Mathis der Maler* opened in Zurich in 1938. With Schoenberg's *Moses und Aron*, as with many of this composer's operas, there was a considerable delay between the writing and the performance of the work: the music for the first two acts was finished in 1932, but the opera did not receive its first concert performance until 1954, in Hamburg. Conceived during World War I and the interwar period, each of these works maintains a precarious existence on the periphery of the contemporary opera repertory.

In spite of their many differences, these three artist-operas bear some striking similarities. All three composers followed the lead of Hector Berlioz, Mussorgsky, and Wagner in serving as their own librettists. All three artist-operas were infused with an atmosphere of aesthetic and political crises. The modernist challenge to romanticism was the core of the aesthetic crisis. What was a twentieth-century composer to do with the romantic style and sensibility which had dominated opera for at least eighty years? The political crisis cannot be stated so concisely. In the most general of terms, *Palestrina*, *Mathis*, and *Moses* reflected the traumatic transitions of early-twentieth-century Germany: from the militaristic empire through the liberal Weimar Republic to the rise of the Third Reich. Eschewing the flight into inwardness of psychological operas, all three composers used their works as vehicles for expressing their mature views on the dilemmas of art and the artist.

The crises were not depicted in contemporary garb. Rather, the composers couched contemporary conditions in religious-historical allegories about art in periods of crisis and transition. As temporal settings for their artist-operas, Pfitzner and Hindemith followed the models of Berlioz's *Benvenuto Cellini* and Wagner's *Die Meistersinger* by choosing the Renaissance, Reformation, and Counter Reformation, the periods of transition from medieval to early modern Europe. Pfitzner set *Palestrina* in the Rome and Trent of 1563. Hindemith's *Mathis* was situated in and around Mainz during 1524 and 1525. Schoenberg's *Moses* drew on a much earlier period of transition, depicting some of the events of the Exodus from Egypt.[2]

Whether dramatizing sixteenth-century composers and painters or biblical prophets, the new works by Pfitzner, Hindemith, and Schoenberg treated many of the traditional themes of the artist-opera: the redemptive powers of art, the artist's relation to his patron, the estrangement of the artist from society. But these traditional themes were subsumed within a distinctly twentieth-century cluster of problems: the tension between aesthetic traditionalism and progressivism, the role of art in an era of political change, and the transformation of art from a means of communication and enlightenment to a means of manipulation and social control.

PALESTRINA: RESIGNATION AND THE LATE ROMANTIC ARTIST-OPERA

Both before and after *Palestrina*, the themes of art and the artist permeated Pfitzner's musical and prose works. He based an early opera, *Die Rose vom Liebesgarten*, on a painting by Hans Thoma. In later years, his cantata *Von deutscher Seele* set poems by Joseph von Eichendorff, and his choral fantasy *Das dunkle Reich* interpreted works by Michelangelo, Goethe, Conrad Ferdinand Meyer, and Richard Dehmel. But it was the works of Pfitzner's middle age, written during the crisis of World War I, that politicized the romanticism of his early works and that determined his enduring reputation as a German nationalist. The essays "Futuristengefahr: Bei Gelegenheit von Busonis Aesthetik" (1917) and "Die neue Aesthetik der musikalischen Impotenz" (1920) and the opera *Palestrina* revealed Pfitzner as a thoroughgoing romantic conservative on both aesthetic and political issues.

In *Palestrina*, the suffering Palestrina endures for his artistic creation and his conflict with a brutish society are familiar romantic themes, consonant with the standard image of the artist as sensitive soul, separate from and perhaps ahead of his contemporaries. But *Palestrina* introduces a new element into romantic self-consciousness, an element that gives this opera a programmatic, manifesto-like character which Pfitzner abhorred in principle. Where the earlier romantic artist struggled against hidebound artistic traditions and an insensitive society, the late romantic artist now struggles against the postromantic forces of aesthetic modernism. Once among the aesthetic avant-garde, the romantic artist now finds himself fighting a rearguard action.

Although the composer Palestrina was greatly renowned even in his own lifetime, we know little about him other than the general outlines of his birth and death, family life, and patrons and commissions. It is within this paucity of hard biographical evidence that the legend of Palestrina arose. The legend holds that a work by Palestrina, *Missa Papae Marcelli*, was instrumental in saving polyphonic music from being banned by the Council of Trent during the Counter Reformation. The ecclesiastical opponents of polyphony maintained that liturgical texts set to this style of music were unintelligible, and they demanded that polyphonic church music be replaced by the old Gregorian chant. Palestrina's *Missa Papae Marcelli*, according to the legend, was able to combine polyphony with the necessary textual clarity. This apocryphal legend is not supported by contemporary research: "That Palestrina's life and music was influenced by the Counter-Reformation is beyond doubt, but it is equally beyond doubt that the legends surrounding his role in these developments, particularly those concerning the *Missa Papae Marcelli*, have distorted the known reliable evidence beyond the limits of credibility."[3]

Pfitzner's *Palestrina* retells the legend of how the composer saved liturgical polyphony, but it has other aims as well. Pfitzner depicts Palestrina as a man and artist caught between the familiar sociopolitical traditions of the late Middle Ages and early Renaissance and the new values of the late Renaissance and Counter Reformation. At the same time, Pfitzner's Palestrina is faced with an aesthetic dilemma. Not only is he charged with the task of rescuing polyphonic style from reactionaries who want to restore Gregorian chant, but he is also faced with the challenge of the new music being developed in Florence. Although there is no evidence that the historical Palestrina felt threatened by the innovations of the Florentines, Pfitzner uses this new Palestrina legend of his own creation as a platform for criticizing the modernist works of his own contemporaries.

Palestrina is set in three acts. The first takes place in the composer's house. Silla, Palestrina's pupil, is playing one of his own compositions in the new Florentine style. Ighino, Palestrina's son, expresses concern about his father's sadness since the death of Palestrina's wife, Lucrezia. When Palestrina and Cardinal Borromeo, the composer's friend and patron, enter the room, the two boys leave. Borromeo explains the need for a Mass that combines polyphony with textual clarity, and he is enraged by Palestrina's unwillingness to take on the task. After Borromeo leaves, the ghosts of nine dead composers appear and urge Palestrina to write the Mass. As he takes up his pen, he hears the voices of angels, who dictate the Mass to him. He also sees the ghost of Lucrezia. Exhausted by his efforts, he falls asleep in his chair. Entering the room for their morning lesson, Silla and Ighino gather up the manuscript pages of the completed work.

The second act, which is set in the great hall of Cardinal Madruscht's palace in Trent, depicts the personal pettiness and national rivalries of the church hierarchs and their delegations. When the discussion turns to music, Borromeo informs the conference that the model Mass will be composed by Palestrina but that it is not yet ready. The cardinal has had the composer imprisoned for his disobedience. At the end of the session, a fight breaks out among the servants of the delegations. Madruscht's soldiers suppress the belligerents.

The third act finds the spiritless Palestrina back in his room. Ighino and a group of singers from Palestrina's choir remind the composer that the council has acquired the Mass manuscript and inform him that the Mass is being performed for the pope. From the street, a crowd acclaims Palestrina as the savior of music. Accompanied by the hierarchs, the pope himself comes to Palestrina's house to congratulate him on his achievement. After the others leave, Borromeo and Palestrina embrace and are reconciled. When Palestrina asks about Silla, Ighino confirms Palestrina's suspicion that the absent student has gone to Florence. The composer urges his son to join the ongoing celebration. Once again alone in his room, with the crowd outside still shouting his name in praise, Palestrina stares at a portrait of Lucrezia, then walks over to his organ and begins to play softly.

Pfitzner's aesthetic conservatism is readily apparent in both the music and the text of *Palestrina*. Like all his works, *Palestrina* reflects his individual compositional style within the Wagnerian idiom. Pfitzner's use of the leitmotif technique is limited but important. In addition, Pfitzner infuses *Palestrina* with a deliberately archaic tonal appearance, thus aurally evoking the world of the historical Palestrina. This archaism is apparent not only in Pfitzner's quotations from the *Missa Papae Marcelli* but also in the "archaic fifths and fourths, these organ sounds and liturgical finales," that imbue *Palestrina*, in Thomas Mann's words, "with a pious ancestral style."[4]

As Mann was well aware, the tonal appearance of *Palestrina* is more than historical atmosphere. It is also a reflection of Pfitzner's views on composition and the relation of composition to the history of music. For Pfitzner, composition is not the product of aesthetic experimentation involving abstract theoretical principles; this misguided procedure he attributes both to the musical innovators of the early baroque period and to the modernists of the twentieth century. Rather, composition is the product of artisan-like craft infused by inspiration. Both craft and inspiration, in turn, depend upon a knowledge and appropriation of the achievements of the musical past.

The character of musical composition as craft is readily apparent in the first act of *Palestrina*. Pfitzner's Palestrina is not a wealthy Renaissance artist-hero. He lives and works in a modest Roman house quite like that of a late-medieval artisan. In these humble surroundings, with the portrait of his recently deceased wife on the wall, the aging master instructs Ighino and Silla in the polyphonic technique of Renaissance composition. Silla feels shackled by polyphony and longs for the individualism and emotional expressivity of the Florentine musical progressives. Palestrina, however, finds aesthetic value not in individualism and emotionalism but in self-transcending, self-abnegating union with the great achievements of traditional music composed for religious purposes. Palestrina views the Florentine progressives as merely a "clique of amateurs" who "have taken antique, heathen writings / and worked out artificial theories, / according to which music will be made."[5]

Music is not just a medieval craft, however, and Palestrina is not just a medieval artisan. He is urged, then ordered, by Borromeo to compose the model Mass. But Palestrina—weary, saddened by the loss of his wife, lacking inspiration—refuses: "He can command, but only me— / he can't command my genius" (43). Borromeo is taken aback. Palestrina as a man remains subject to the cardinal's power and is resigned to whatever measures Borromeo chooses to take. His art is another matter. A work like the one Borromeo needs cannot be churned out with craftsmanlike efficiency. Palestrina needs inspiration: that is, his genius. And Borromeo's explanations about the crucial role of this exemplary Mass in the political-aesthetic deliberations of the Council of Trent do not provide this inspiration. Inspiration comes from within, from Palestrina's spirit and its communion with transcendent forces: the history of music, his dead wife, and divine grace.

The fifth, sixth, and seventh scenes of the first act are the crux of the opera. In despair about the futility of life and work, the exhausted Palestrina falls into a reverie. In his dream, the master composers of late-medieval and early-Renaissance polyphony enjoin him to write the Mass: "Your earthly mission, Palestrina, / fulfill your earthly mission" (51). The call of the history of music succeeds where the cardinal's threats had failed. First one and then a chorus of angels inspire him. During the angelic chorus, Lucrezia appears by his side to give him the necessary strength to see the task through. Prompted by musical tradition, inspired by divine grace, sustained by love, Palestrina completes the Mass, then falls into a deep sleep. In the dawn's light, Ighino and Silla slip into the room and gather up the pages of the work that will save not only liturgical polyphony but also Palestrina himself from the wrath of Borromeo.

The scenes of Palestrina's musical inspiration provide the clearest examples of Pfitzner's aesthetic romanticism and conservatism. Inspiration through love or divine grace, both of which are beyond the pale of rational analysis, is a traditional romantic notion.[6] Lucrezia's role typifies the pessimistic romantic association of love with death. Unlike the Orphic figures of baroque and classical artist-operas, who restore the beloved to life with the power of music, Pfitzner's romantic Palestrina-Orpheus has his musical powers restored by the dead beloved. Moreover, inspiration through the history of music exemplifies Pfitzner's aesthetic conservatism. The tradition of great music is Pfitzner's version of Edmund Burke's English garden. Music embodies in its history an inner logic, an inherent reason, and it should therefore be preserved and cultivated; music can be modified within limits, but it should never be overturned by new, abstract, rational compositional principles. Pfitzner's Palestrina, evoking Tristan-like associations of the danger of light and day, views these new compositional principles, not as harbingers of musical progress, but as threats to the very foundation of musical inspiration:

> But consciousness, the light that's deathly glaring,
> that rises, troubling like a new-born day,
> is enemy to art,
> to fantasy. (48)

In addition to differentiating between traditional and theoretical composition, *Palestrina* contrasts the private, dark, creative world of the artist with the public, bright, manipulative world of politics. The second act depicts a late session of the Council of Trent. In portraying this gathering of berobed bishops, archbishops, patriarchs, and cardinals, Pfitzner lampoons the world of politics, particularly parliamentary politics. This is not a world of spirituality, justice, or reconciliation. Rather, politics is associated with self-interest, pomp, and deceit; not far in the background lurk force and violence. Art intrudes in the form of Borromeo's promise to deliver the model Mass, but neither the spiritual nor the aesthetic qualities of the Mass have intrinsic significance for the council. The Mass itself is just another pawn in the brutal game of factional power politics and ultimately in the political combat against Protestantism.

Examples of the brutality of politics appear in all three acts. In the first act, Palestrina bemoans Silla's attraction to the Florentine modernists, but Palestrina permits Silla to follow his own aesthetic inclinations. Borromeo, however, expresses surprise that the master composer does not even threaten his rebellious pupil. In the second act, Borromeo shows himself ready to move beyond mere threats with his own subordinates. Because Palestrina refuses to accept Borromeo's commission, Borromeo throws him in prison, declaring, "And daily I wait to hear / if prison's breaking his resistance" (66). At the end of this act, after the close of the council session, the sublimated political conflict between the national-ecclesiastical factions breaks out into open fighting between their servants and retainers. In the name of the Holy Council, Madruscht orders soldiers to fire on the combatants and has the survivors bound over for torture on the rack. We learn in the third act that Palestrina's own incarceration ends only when Ighino, acting independently, delivers the manuscript of the dream-inspired Mass to Borromeo.

The world of the council and Palestrina's response to Borromeo illustrate two analytically distinct, yet practically compatible, types of conservative politics. The unromantic, realpolitik conservatism of Borromeo and the Council is set against the romantic, resigned conservatism of Palestrina.[7] To the extent that anything overrides the personal and factional conflicts of the council, it is the desire to preserve and restore the power of the church in the face of the Protestant Reformation. The disparate religious ideals of Catholicism and Protestantism are seldom mentioned in the opera, and when they are mentioned, Pfitzner depicts these ideals as mere ideological window dressing. In Pfitzner's account of the council session, Protestantism is not so much a spiritual challenge as a material threat to the power and prestige of vain men working in a this-worldly institution. It is clear that these men are willing to use any means for achieving their political objectives.

Palestrina, however, is gripped by a Schopenhauerian sense of the futility of direct action. He reveres the music of the past, but he resigns himself to the idea that the musical future may belong to the Florentines. He understands that the model Mass is necessary for the preservation of polyphony and would be useful in the struggle against Protestantism, but he feels that he is not up to the task. In only two instances is Palestrina roused to action, and neither of these lends much support to the notion that purposeful action proves efficacious in the real world. He writes the Mass, but he can do so only in a dream-induced state of ecstatic fervor. Afterward, he defies the cardinal and withholds the Mass, only to have his courageous gesture nullified by the well-intentioned action of Ighino. At the end of the opera, when the Mass has been triumphantly performed and has won the accolades of Borromeo, the papal choir, the people of Rome, and the pope, Palestrina is as impervious to the world's honors as he was to its threats. Honors, too, will pass away. Pfitzner imputes to Palestrina a tragic, resigned romanticism, which longs for the past but which is powerless to check the mounting forces of modernity.

Even as Pfitzner fits his opera with the trappings of historical accuracy, he projects a twentieth-century psychology of resignation onto the sixteenth-century figure of Palestrina. The artist is severed from his society. Even his apprentice-pupil Silla succumbs to the blandishments of the new compositional style and leaves for Florence. Back in Rome, Palestrina is able to achieve at best a mystical self-transcendence through his relation to the history of his art, through romantic love, and through his spiritual life. To be sure, this romantic psychology of resignation can provide a critical, indeed cynical, perspective: it can cut through the lofty rhetoric of political ideals to reveal their base motivations. But ultimately even cynicism leaves both art and the artist in the service of their political masters. In the hands of those engineering the Counter Reformation, the highest achievements of Renaissance music become effective instruments of propaganda.[8] This passivity and resignation are not unique to Pfitzner. Writing about romanticism and the decline of the historical novel, Georg Lukács observes that the "culmination of a desire for great deeds with a personal and social inability to accomplish them in reality is projected into the past, in the hope that this social impotence may lose its modern pettiness in the ostentatious attire of the Renaissance."[9]

Palestrina retains the idea of the power of music, but even this power is vitiated by the pessimism of late romanticism. Like the Orphic operas of the baroque and early classical periods, Palestrina's music has the power to redeem reality, in this case the reality of polyphony. Like the artist-operas of the classical period, Palestrina's music can reconcile the seemingly irreconcilable, in this case the breach between Palestrina and Borromeo. This idea of music's power of reconciliation persists even into the romanticism of Wagner. But Pfitzner himself pointed to the difference between the life-affirming optimism of *Die Meistersinger* and the morbid pessimism of his own *Palestrina*.[10] The final scene of the opera is one of tremendous pathos. The weary old composer gazes at the portrait of his wife, calls for the blessing of God, and then "allows his fingers to wander over the keys" of his organ (100). In the last great German artist-opera of the romantic period, the power of music resigns the artist to whatever misfortunes or turns of events that fate has in store.

With its critique of the council, deference to authority, and concern for loyalty, *Palestrina* is infused with the political spirit of Germany during World War I. The fact that Pfitzner chose parliamentary politics as the subject of his second-act satire was not simply fortuitous. In the military struggle of the German Empire against the parliamentary democracies, the deflation of the pretensions of parliamentary politics takes on ideological significance.

Although Pfitzner's cynicism about politics is so thoroughgoing that the opera can hardly be construed as a paean to German authoritarianism, Palestrina's relationship with Borromeo shows the ultimate futility of attempting to resist authority. The romantic conservatism of resignation inevitably defers to the unromantic conservatism of force.

In the context of the war, even Palestrina's objections to the Florentines take on added political significance. During this period, German romantic music was understood as the last stage in the development of a musical tradition dating from Heinrich Schütz and Johann Sebastian Bach through Mozart and Beethoven to Johannes Brahms and Wagner. Contemporary composers who worked within the tonal parameters that Wagner had both preserved and expanded—Richard Strauss, Max Reger, Paul Graener, and Pfitzner—were viewed as the legitimate successors to this German musical tradition.[11] German music was the precious cultural legacy of the German nation. It should therefore be defended against the assaults of foreign musics as well as the wrongheaded and possibly traitorous experimentation of some German composers. In the plot of *Palestrina*, Florence symbolizes the threat of alien musics, and Silla stands for the aesthetic-national treachery of some Germans. In postwar racist circles, Pfitzner's romantic conservatism was pushed one step further. Both German and non-German musics were understood as having a racial foundation, and ostensibly German modernist composers were not only suspect politically but racially as well.[12]

MATHIS DER MALER: RETREAT AND THE NEOCLASSICAL ARTIST-OPERA

Like Pfitzner's *Palestrina*, Hindemith's *Mathis der Maler* strikes a note of aesthetic conservatism and political resignation. But here the resemblance ends. Whereas *Palestrina* is the programmatic statement of a lifelong romantic conservative, *Mathis* is the aesthetic confession of a composer who once experimented with postromantic modernism but who is now committed to the musical models of the baroque and classical eras. Whereas *Palestrina* portrays the tragic political resignation of the romantic conservative, *Mathis* is the political statement of a composer who once attempted to commit his art to social and political causes but who has now retreated to an apolitical aestheticism.

The two artist-operas also differ in form and in the nuances of their aesthetic and political conservatisms. In *Palestrina* these doctrines are depicted in the circumstances surrounding a single event, the legendary saving of polyphony. The seven scenes of *Mathis*, on the other hand, trace the development of the aesthetic-political character of the artist against the historical backdrop of the Reformation, the Peasants' War, and the Renaissance. The Mathis who opens the opera is an aesthetic conservative and apolitical aesthete, but one who is plagued by doubts about the value of his art and life. The Mathis who closes the opera is once again an aesthetic conservative and apolitical aesthete, but now one whose life and art have lost their naive, uncertain, and haphazard character. Mathis thus attains full self-consciousness. The "problematic" Mathis moves, in Lukács's phrase, "from the accidental to the necessary."[13]

The major works of Hindemith's composing career date from after World War I.[14] In the romantic conservative circles of the German musical establishment, Hindemith was viewed as the most promising of the young composers, a potential champion of German music against non-German modernism, particularly the modernism of Schoenberg and his students. Although Hindemith dutifully served in the military during the war, his early compositions did not show a slavish reverence for the nationalist musical line. He experimented with jazz, popular dance forms, and musical expressionism. His early operas in particular were characterized musically by the modernist subjectivity of expressionism and theoretically by scandalous sexual themes designed to shock the audience. *Mörder, Hoffnung der Frauen, Das Nusch-Nuschi*, and *Sancta Susanna* are the clearest examples of Hindemith's expressionist period in opera.

By the time of the song cycle *Das Marienleben* (1923), Hindemith's experimental period was over. Like many other expressionists, he abandoned the hypersensitivity and egocentricity of expressionism for the New Objectivity. Stylistically, Hindemith's New Objectivity did not mean an accommodation with romantic conservatism; rather, he reached back beyond romanticism to the classical period and its emphasis on key-centered tonality and formal clarity. In addition, Hindemith's turn from expressionism was marked by the search for renewed ties between the artist and his community. This practical search for social reintegration is the motive for Hindemith's *Gebrauchsmusik*, or "music for use" (that is, music composed for performance by amateur players), as well as his academic activities in music. The end of Hindemith's career as a socially committed composer was reached in 1929, when he collaborated with Bertolt Brecht on the cantata *Lehrstück*. Hindemith wanted a piece whose performance would involve the audience. Brecht gave him a text that went beyond mere audience participation to political provocation. Hindemith's desire to be socially involved did not extend to collaborating on works designed to raise socialist revolutionary consciousness. Outraged, Hindemith refused to cooperate with Brecht on a revised version of this work. Hindemith later collaborated with the seemingly apolitical poet Gottfried Benn on the oratorio *Das Unaufhörliche*. Benn's subsequent membership in the Nazi Party was both a surprise and a disappointment to Hindemith.

In spite of Hindemith's embrace of New Objectivity and neoclassicism, the themes of his operas in the late twenties—*Hin und Zurück* and *Neues vom Tage*—recall the scandalous provocativeness of his early works. Hitler was offended by the scene in *Neues vom Tage* that includes a nude soprano singing from her bath. Hindemith's first artist-opera, *Cardillac* (1926), also dates from this period. The music is neoclassical, but the libretto, by Ferdinand Lion, is expressionistic. In typical expressionist fashion, only the lead character—the psychopathic artist-goldsmith, Cardillac— has a personal name. Cardillac is so enamored with his own creations that he is indifferent to all social relationships, including his relationship with his daughter. Indeed, he kills his customers in order to recover his works from them.

In the life and work of the sixteenth-century painter Mathis, or Matthias, Grünewald, Hindemith found an opportunity for the operatic statement of his mature aesthetic and political views. The life of Grünewald provided ample opportunity for poetic invention, since even less was known about him than was known about Palestrina. And unlike Palestrina's, Grünewald's fame was of recent vintage, for only in the late nineteenth and early twentieth centuries had scholarly and critical attention been paid to this great contemporary of Albrecht Dürer. On two points— Grünewald's lifelong reputation as a contemplative man and, after his death, the discovery that his personal effects contained several sermons by Martin Luther and documents pertaining to the Peasants' War—Hindemith constructs a picture of art and the artist buffeted by the historical currents of the early modern era.[15]

Like many former expressionists, Hindemith turned from the frequently esoteric forms of expressionist drama to the more accessible form of historical allegory, and *Mathis* represents this shift.[16] In *Mathis* and in his much later historical allegory about art and the artist, *Die Harmonie der Welt* (1957) (also with a libretto by the composer), Hindemith presented many of the ideas of his prose works, especially *Unterweisung im Tonsatz* (1937), *A Composer's World* (1950), and *Johann Sebastian Bach: Heritage and Obligation* (1950). Aesthetically, Mathis moves from a conception of art as personal expression to one of art governed by the two poles of mystical inspiration and natural law. Politically, Mathis comes to understand the world of historical institutions and movements as antithetical to artistic creation. There is a connection between the artist and his society, but it is not one forged by the actions of the artist.

The first scene of the opera finds Mathis near the end of a year's sabbatical granted by his generous patron, Cardinal Albrecht, the prince-archbishop of Mainz. In the idyllic setting of a monastery courtyard under a noonday sun in late May, Mathis pauses from his painting and reflects on the basis of his art. He is interrupted by the arrival of Hans Schwalb, the leader of the rebellious peasants, and Regina, Schwalb's young daughter, who are being pursued by government soldiers. Mathis not only shelters the two fugitives and gives them his horse, but he also resolves to take an active part in the peasants' cause.

The second scene takes place in the cardinal's palace in Mainz. A dispute rages between two rival factions, the Papists and the Lutherans, and among the latter are Riedinger, a rich citizen, and Ursula, his beautiful daughter. The cardinal enters, and all leave except for the leaders of the factions. Albrecht reluctantly agrees to comply with the papal order to burn Lutheran books. When Mathis returns from his sabbatical, he is greeted enthusiastically by Ursula, who is in love with him. An officer reports Mathis's aid to Schwalb, but Albrecht does not punish the painter. Instead, he allows Mathis to leave his service to join the peasant cause.

Riedinger's house is the setting for the third scene. Riedinger and his friends are about to hide their threatened books when Capito, an advisor to the cardinal but a man sympathetic to the Lutheran cause, enters the room. He has a letter from Luther to Albrecht that urges the cardinal to marry and thus secularize his principality. Since Albrecht is deeply in debt because of his extravagant expenditures on art, a marriage to Ursula would solve his financial problems. Meanwhile, Mathis enters to say good-bye to Ursula before he leaves to join the peasants. In order to serve the Lutheran cause, Ursula agrees to the proposed marriage with Albrecht.

The fourth scene finds Mathis and some rebellious peasants in a war-ravaged village. Mathis tries to stop the peasants from murdering a captured count and raping the countess, but he is rebuffed. Only the entry of Schwalb saves the countess. Government troops attack the village, rout the peasants, and kill Schwalb. The intercession of the countess saves Mathis's life, and he takes Regina along to seek shelter.

The fifth scene takes place in the cardinal's study. Capito tries to persuade Albrecht to follow Luther's advice. Impressed by Ursula's willingness to sacrifice herself for her religious cause, Albrecht recommits himself to his own ideals. He dismisses the wily Capito but permits the Lutherans to practice their faith openly. He also resolves to give up his excessive spending on art.

The sixth scene is crucial. Mathis and Regina stop to rest in a forest. Just before Regina falls asleep, they sing a duet about Mathis's vision of the *Incarnation*, the first panel of the *Isenheim* altar triptych. Then Mathis sings about the other two panels, *The Temptation of Saint Anthony* and *Saint Anthony in the Hermitage of Saint Paul*. At this point Mathis realizes the folly of his abandonment of art and commitment to the peasants.

The last scene is set in Mathis's studio and is in two parts. In the first part, Mathis is asleep, while Ursula attends the dying Regina. Ursula remarks about Mathis's amazing productivity since he returned to art. Regina has a vision of her father, then dies with Mathis by her side. After an interlude, the curtain opens on Mathis's nearly empty studio. The cardinal enters and gives Mathis a farewell embrace. The opera ends as Mathis packs up the few objects that represent the significant events in his life.

Like Pfitzner's aesthetic conservatism in *Palestrina*, Hindemith's aesthetic conservatism extends to the tonal appearance of *Mathis*. Hindemith evokes the sixteenth century by using the music of the era, including medieval chant, Protestant chorale, and several folk songs. Even so, the primary medium for the articulation of Hindemith's aesthetic views is the text of the opera.

In the sixteenth century, art was the product of patronage. Palestrina's patron, Borromeo, combined a measure of genuine aesthetic sensibility with the political realism necessary for the performance of his practical tasks. With Albrecht, however, the balance between aesthetics and politics is shifted toward aesthetics. Personally, Albrecht uses art as a welcome refuge from the worldly cares of his office. Politically, in the fashion of an absolute prince, he justifies his expensive acquisitions as expressions of the glory of his city and its citizens. Divided into religious factions, these citizens are in turn only too willing to indulge Albrecht in his artistic whims. Their financial contributions ensure their access to Albrecht and render him dependent upon their continued support.

If Albrecht's patronage is of questionable value, his favorite artist is also engaged in some artistic soul-searching. In Mathis's first-scene reflections, there are no romantic images of death and darkness. He extols nature and the spring sun as his sources of artistic energy. But at the same time Mathis is plagued by doubts about his art: "Have you fulfilled the task God laid on you? Is what you paint enough? Are you intent only on your own advantage?"[17] These doubts are echoed by Schwalb, who finds it incredible that apolitical painting is going on amid the turmoil of the Peasants' War. Mathis agrees with Schwalb's criticisms.

Upon his return to Mainz, Mathis presents himself to Albrecht. Against the counsel of his advisors, Albrecht refuses to punish him, ordering him back to work instead. Like Palestrina, Mathis refuses the order of his patron: "No one can compel me! I demand my discharge!" (23). But unlike Borromeo, a hurt but compliant Albrecht lets Mathis go his own way. Mathis's commitment to the peasant cause forces him to renounce not only his art but also the love of Ursula.

Toward the end of the opera, in the sixth scene, art returns as Mathis and Regina rest in the forest. In the first part of the scene, Mathis and the drowsing Regina conjure the celestial choir that will appear in the *Incarnation* panel. Mathis evokes the Orphic powers of music: "Are those who compose prayers making music, or do you hear the prayers of the musicians? When music has thus become prayer, nature listens intently" (28). This part closes with Mathis and Regina tying the Orphic vision of music to the mystical Pythagorean notion of the harmony of the spheres. Mathis states, "A mere vestige of the gleam of such spheres could transfigure our dark doings," and Regina responds, "The world is full of divine sound, it echoes in the hearts of men" (28).

The second part interprets the panel *The Temptation of Saint Anthony*. Before depicting the evil spirits and monstrous demons of the painting, Hindemith has various disguised characters beckon Mathis, in the persona of Saint Anthony, to follow false paths to art. Luxury urges Anthony-Mathis to pursue financial profit. The Merchant recommends that profit be used as a means to power. Ursula appears in the forms of the Beggar, Harlot, and Martyr. The Scholar encourages him to cultivate useless knowledge, and the Warlord recommends the manly virtues of combat. Anthony-Mathis recognizes all of these as inimical to the true end of art. Finally, the chorus, declaring that "your worst enemy is yourself" (29), descends on him in the form of the demons of the panel.

In the third part, Hindemith recreates the panel *Saint Anthony in the Hermitage of Saint Paul*. Mathis remains in the guise of Saint Anthony; Albrecht appears as Saint Paul. Paul-Albrecht helps

Anthony-Mathis come to a full understanding of his trials and describes the disconcerting effect that the Reformation and the Peasants' War has had on the heretofore sheltered artist. One last time, Anthony-Mathis defends his commitment to the peasants' cause: "Yes, to offer myself up to my God, to sacrifice blood and life to my people. And why was I not worthy of grace?" (29). Paul-Albrecht assures him that this, too, was an illusion, for by joining the peasant army as a mere soldier, Anthony-Mathis had betrayed art, the people, and his divine calling: "You have a superhuman gift for painting. It was ungrateful and disloyal of you, wantonly to throw away God-given talents. When you went to join the people, you betrayed them and renounced your calling" (29). Paul-Albrecht describes the people as a natural force which gives rise to the artist as one of its own emanations. The artist, in turn, is enjoined to offer his works to God. This part ends with the return of the natural and divine foundations of Mathis's art, which were hinted at in the first scene but now appear in the full light of consciousness. Paul-Albrecht and Anthony-Mathis close the scene in a grand duet: "We cannot get away from the sphere in which we were born, all of our paths keep us continually within it. Above us a broader sphere is to be seen: the power that keeps us upright. Whatever we set our hands to, if we are to prove ourselves, our deeds must be oriented to both poles. Let us be grateful to the earth! Let us praise heaven. Alleluia!" (29).

The formula works. In the seventh scene, we learn about Mathis's furious bout of creative activity. Now exhausted by his exertions, the weary Mathis gives up painting and awaits death with a clear conscience: "To the world and to God I have given what my poor powers could create" (31).

Mathis contains Hindemith's mature views on the role of the artist and the character of musical art. These views are consistent with those expressed in his prose works. In *A Composer's World,* Hindemith maintains that the musician, like the painter Mathis, works with the humility of a craftsman. But craftsmanlike humility is not enough to produce great art, for beyond the rational knowledge of the craftsman, "there is a region of visionary irrationality in which the veiled secrets of art dwell, sensed but not understood, implored but not commanded, imparting but not yielding."[18] The parallel between this assertion and Mathis's vision in the sixth scene of the opera is clear. Thus, like Pfitzner, Hindemith maintains that art is the product of craft *and* inspiration, with Hindemith insisting on the divine-irrational source of inspiration and avoiding Pfitzner's emphasis on the inspirational value of history or love. In *Johann Sebastian Bach: Heritage and Obligation*, Hindemith offers Bach, with one reservation, as the musical model of the humble, divinely inspired craftsman. Bach's only failing, says Hindemith, was his indifference "to the theoretical aspects of his art."[19] In *Mathis* this theoretical or scientific aspect of music is alluded to in the references to nature as a foundation of art and to the Pythagorean music of the spheres.

In *The Craft of Musical Composition*, Hindemith claims that there are three fundamental theories about the character of music. Some thinkers maintain that music is founded on the laws of nature; others, that music is based on the arbitrary instinct of the composer; and still others, that music is the product of the observed practice of music.[20] Hindemith, rejecting both the individualist and the historicist subjectivism of the second and third theories, identifies himself as a naturalist. From this perspective, the tonality of the Western baroque and classical periods is not the product of the genius of the composers or the accumulated practical knowledge of music. The properties of this music, rather, inhere in the natural properties of tones and the relationships between tones. And the composer is a scientist of tones, exercising his or her understanding of these pregiven, objective tonal relationships during the course of composition. Thus it is Hindemith, the scientific naturalist of music, who portrays Anthony-Mathis and Paul-Albrecht giving thanks to nature (as well as to heaven) in their duet at the end of the sixth scene.

But in spite of all its pretensions to lawfulness, science, and naturalness and all its excursions into mathematics, astronomy, and physics, Hindemith's naturalistic conception is a revival of medieval and indeed Pythagorean myths about the inherent harmony of the universe; the scientific jargon only thinly conceals the ancient roots of his conception.[21] It is a flight from the essential subjectivity of music—that is, a flight from the basic insight that music is made by people for other people. If Pfitzner's romantic conservative aesthetic wanted to preserve the grand tradition of great music from the possibly fatal attack of twentieth-century modernism, he at least recognized that music was a historical product. The great works were the products of individual and collective human effort. Because Pfitzner saw the human, historical subjectivity of music, he believed that music was vulnerable to the malicious subjectivity of the modernists. But Hindemith flies from subjectivity. He wants to secure the tonal structure of Western music—essentially the tonal structure of the baroque and classical periods—by reifying it. He misunderstands the human, historical, and subjective character of this music as natural, eternal, and objective. Twenty-one years after the first performance of *Mathis*, in *Die Harmonie der Welt*, Hindemith gave full rein to his aesthetic blend of science and myth, nature and mysticism. *Harmonie* depicts scenes from the life of Johannes Kepler (1571–1630), the German astronomer who combined mathematics, music, astronomy, and philosophy with an obsessive belief in the Pythagorean music of the spheres and the essential harmony of the universe.[22]

If close scrutiny of Hindemith's scientific-natural conception of music hints of the archaic and mythical, the reappearance of this conception in the first third of the twentieth century is indicative of its contemporary character. In *Literature and the Image of Man*, Leo Lowenthal discusses the changing function of nature in Western literature. In the Renaissance, nature is the "scene of man's activities, a field of conquest, and an inspiration." Somewhat later, presumably during the romantic era, nature becomes an alternative to society, an escape from unfulfilling social reality. Finally, beginning in the late nineteenth century, nature is the place where man surrenders his individual subjectivity—now more the source of frustration rather than of satisfaction—to impersonal, natural forces. For Lowenthal, the artistic surrender to nature symbolizes the surrender of the individual to no longer controllable social and technological tendencies.[23]

If Hindemith retreats from the historical subjectivity of music, he also retreats from political activism. In general, Hindemith is hostile to politics. Politics is inimical to art and culture and is ridden with selfish factionalism. Even the peasants' cause, prompted by genuine suffering and oppression, is corrupted by the politics of resentment. Whereas visionary leaders like Schwalb and idealistic intellectuals like Mathis are motivated by a sincere commitment to utopian goals, the best the peasants can offer is the replacement of one set of exploiters and oppressors by another. In this endless cycle of repression-revolt-repression, nothing really changes. Ultimately, order—the tangible order of the government forces and the mystical order of the harmonious universe—is deemed preferable to the chaos of anarchy and revolt.

For both Mathis and Albrecht, the mixture of politics and aesthetics is lethal. Mathis must renounce art in order to participate in the peasants' revolt. Albrecht finds that he, too, must renounce his aestheticism in order to govern effectively. Albrecht's expenditures on art nearly force him into an opportunistic marriage arranged by the Protestants. With the sacrificial offer of Ursula as his bride, Albrecht recognizes his own fiscal responsibility for creating a situation where ideals are manipulated and emotions falsified. He submits himself to the discipline of his faith and office: "My life will be rather that of a hermit than of a bishop. The splendour that has surrounded me will give way to meagre simplicity" (26).

The hostility between art and politics is also confirmed by a few relatively minor details in the opera. Pommersfelden, a leader of the Papist faction of burghers, objects to the realism of Mathis's paintings: "He has represented our Savior as a sick beggar. To us, a saint is no peasant. And the Mother of God was no country milkmaid" (30). If the bourgeois Pommersfelden attacks his work, Mathis fares no better at the hands of the peasants. Schwalb, as we have seen, views art as an inexcusable luxury during a time of strife. Later, when Mathis tries to check the peasants' desire for revenge, they remind him that he is "no peasant" and thus has no right "to meddle" in their affairs (24). When a gang of peasants attempt to rape the countess, they contemptuously destroy a painting of the Virgin.

The seamy side of politics infects the rivalry between the Papist and Lutheran factions. Hindemith is not as cynical as Pfitzner about the religious politics of the Reformation and Counter Reformation. There is a sense that the Reformation is posing a genuine crisis of conscience for morally responsible people. But the loftiness of the religious ideals does not prevent the factions from using some rather base tactics. Both sides prey on Albrecht's insatiable hunger for art. The Papists are quick to invoke the authority and force of both the state and the pope in order to advance their cause. The nadir of Catholic authoritarianism is the papal order to burn Protestant books. The Lutherans are more apt to use the power of their purses and their political cunning. Capito oversees the gathering of the condemned Lutheran texts. Armed with the letter from Luther, he has a bigger objective than the saving of a few books. In the second scene, a group of humanist students points to the foibles of both factions. But the students' invocation of the classical values of Renaissance humanism falls on deaf ears.

The most striking political images occur in the fourth scene. Temporarily victorious peasants are eating and drinking in front of a village inn. They hold the count and countess as prisoners. Their victory is only an opportunity for revenge and role reversal. Striking and kicking, they lead the count away to execute him: "You have trampled on us for a long time, now we shall trample you in the dirt. The blows we suffered you will suffer now. You were brutal; you will die a brutal death." The countess cries, "Are you no longer human?" And the peasants reply, "He has turned us into beasts" (23). One of the count's court musicians vindictively plays his violin during the count's execution. Meanwhile, the peasants force the countess to work as a serving maid. When the peasants are about to rape her, Mathis pleads with them to comply with the stated ideals of their revolt. They reply, "We are the masters. We will organize the world the way we want it, the way it pleases us" (24). Ultimately, however, the government army overwhelms the resistance mounted by the debauched and terror-stricken peasants. At the close of the scene, the dazed Mathis repents his political folly:

> To have the will to dare what one's will could not make happen! To rise above the capacity of man! To one alone was it granted to bear the world's cross. With his death, the shortcomings of humanity perished for all time. And you, feeble creature! You wanted to be a redeemer. You wanted to free your brothers from their chains. You took it upon yourself to improve on the wise plan of Providence. And what do you amount to? A discontented painter, a misfit. Make amends for what you have done. Submit to the forces that have shattered you. Give up. Slink away from the scene of your disgrace like a thief in the night. Tormenting firebrands of conscience, crazy running in circles—enough of them! (25)

If *Mathis* demonstrates that direct political commitment is ruled out as a means for the artist to reenter a revitalized community, this does not mean that Gebrauchsmusik and teaching were Hindemith's only avenues of social integration. There was another alternative. Like many other former expressionists who turned to the New Objectivity, Hindemith adopted a mystical-religious conception of community.[24] From the time of *Das Marienleben* on, Hindemith wrote a number of vocal works to religious texts. Rejecting the radical individualism of expressionism, yet frustrated in his efforts to forge links with real human communities and social movements, the newly objective artist revives notions of the mystical-religious community of man. Mathis therefore repents his involvement in the Peasants' War as not only folly but hubris: "To one alone was it granted to bear the world's cross." Later in the opera, Regina and Mathis pray for understanding and harmony in the world, but these virtues are seen no longer as the outcomes of human effort but as products of the Pythagorean music of the spheres and the harmony of the universe. At this point, the mystical-natural aesthetics of retreat meets the mystical-religious politics of retreat.

The references to radical mass movements and political book burnings obviously mark *Mathis* as a product of its era, which saw the dissolution of the Weimar Republic and the rise of Nazism. But the true contemporaneity of *Mathis* lies beneath the superficial resemblances between historical and current events. Its true contemporaneity lies instead in the social psychology of anxiety that sustains both the aesthetic and the political themes of the opera. Aesthetically and politically, Hindemith's Mathis retreats from an unstable, sometimes chaotic world. He searches for a mystical world of eternal values. Musical art is secured not by the vigorous defense of an aesthetic tradition, à la Pfitzner, but by the manifestation of eternal tonal relationships. Social integration is achieved not by participation in revolutionary movements, Left or Right, but in a mystical-religious vision of the community of man. To be sure, this flight from aesthetic and political reality leaves these realities practically intact. Hindemith's tonal science confirms the tonal practices of the baroque and classical periods; his mystical community coexists with actual regimes and movements. The only thing that does change is the ideology. The aesthetic and political status quo is given the patina of the divine and the eternal. Thus Mathis, in his aria of repentance, reproves himself for attempting "to improve on the wise plan of Providence."

For Hindemith, the Nazi accession to power signaled, not the beginning of a new and distinctly ominous era, but yet another passing stage in the ongoing turmoil of the Weimar Republic. Hindemith shared the belief of many Germans that the Hitler regime would soon be overturned. In the meantime, he thought that he could continue his musical career in Germany and wait for the inevitable change in political fortunes. His youthful aesthetic experimentalism during the Weimar Republic, not to mention his collaboration with Brecht, marked him as a "cultural bolshevik" within some sections of the Nazi culture establishment. But he believed that *Mathis*, with its German subject matter and negative attitude toward revolutionary movements, would at least be tolerated by the new culture masters. His mistaken perception of the Nazi regime is symbolized by his unsuccessful efforts to stage the first performance of *Mathis* in Germany. In 1938, Hindemith's emigration resolved the ambivalence of the Nazi regime against him. The books and music of Hindemith joined those of Schoenberg and others in the Düsseldorf exhibit of degenerate music.[25]

MOSES UND ARON: IMPOTENCE AND THE MODERNIST ARTIST-OPERA

If Hindemith, the enfant terrible become neoclassicist, held a varying position in the eyes of the defenders of German romantic music, the case of Schoenberg was not so problematic. After his early works, which demonstrated his mastery of the romantic musical idiom, Schoenberg became the living symbol of musical modernism, the driving force behind *Neue Musik*. This modernism is evident in his operatic masterpiece, *Moses und Aron*. Aesthetically, *Moses* poses the problem of the appropriate relation between aesthetic means and ends in a thoroughly contemporary manner. Neither the late romantic nor the classical approaches to this problem are raised to the status of absolutely valid models. Schoenberg's aesthetic radicalism risks artistic impotence rather than compromise its principles. Politically, *Moses* examines the cognitive role of the artwork in society. Is the art image a means to human emancipation or deception? Schoenberg's *Moses* may not be able to solve this issue, but it refuses to effect a facile resolution. Posing the problem of the estrangement of the artist in the sharpest possible terms, *Moses* suggests that the reconciliation of the artist and society cannot be resolved in art.

Like *Palestrina* and *Mathis*, *Moses* presents its aesthetic and political problems in a religious-historical allegory about the crises of the creative personality in a time of social change. Here the time of change is not early modern Europe but another archetypal period of change in Western culture: the Exodus from Egypt. Adapting incidents from the biblical books of Exodus and Numbers, Schoenberg depicts this transition at two levels. Superficially, the opera describes some of the events of the Israelites' physical movement from Egyptian bondage toward their promised land. It is at this level that *Moses* can be understood as a commentary on the contemporary fate of the Jews under Nazi rule. But at a deeper level, *Moses* is not so much about a people's geographical transition from one place to another as it is about a people's spiritual growth from a lower stage of consciousness and civilization to a higher one. At this level, *Moses* transcends the Jewish-Nazi nexus. It becomes an allegory about the emancipatory potential of enlightened human beings.

In both its style and thematic content, *Moses* was the centerpiece of Schoenberg's lifework in dramatic music. Along with *Erwartung*, the opera *Die glückliche Hand*, the song cycle *Pierrot Lunaire*, and the unfinished oratorio *Die Jakobsleiter* were the products of Schoenberg's expressionist period in the first two decades of the twentieth century. Schoenberg also explored musical expressionism in a theoretical work of 1911, *Harmonielehre* (revised in 1922). During this time, Schoenberg even tried his hand at painting in the expressionist style. In the twenties and early thirties, when he was composing *Moses*, Schoenberg ordered the practices of his expressionist period in his new serial or twelve-tone system of composition. Like *Moses*, the serial opera *Von Heute auf Morgen* was based on the development of a twelve-tone chromatic scale. In his later works, dating from the late thirties until his death in 1951, Schoenberg used both tonal and serial techniques. The choral works *Kol nidre*, *A Survivor from Warsaw*, and *Modern Psalms* were composed in this period.

The aesthetic-political themes of *Moses* permeate Schoenberg's librettos. In *Die glückliche Hand*, for example, an artist betrays his capacity for the highest order of creative work by investing his energy in a mere trinket. In the unfinished *Die Jakobsleiter*, the "chosen one" is an unwilling prophet whose spiritual understanding is plagued by popular illusions and rejections. Between *Die Jakobsleiter* and *Moses*, Schoenberg wrote a play called *Der biblische Weg*. Still unpublished and hard to find, the play depicts the tragedy of a modern Zionist Moses who fails in his mission of founding a new Jewish homeland because he becomes entangled in base human emotions and petty intrigues.[26] A theme of *Moses* recurs in Schoenberg's last work, *Modern Psalms*. Here once again the problem of how to invoke an inconceivable and imageless God is explored.

Moses was first conceived as an oratorio around 1923. The libretto was completed in 1928, and the music of the first two acts was finished in 1932. From that point until the last years of his life, Schoenberg wavered between intending to compose the music for the third act, understanding the work as complete in the two-act version, and including the third act in performances as a spoken drama.

No matter which version is accepted, there can be little doubt that *Moses* was not only a piece of music theater but also a statement of the composer's ardent religious faith in his later years. Born to Jewish parents in Vienna in 1874, the young Schoenberg did not practice religion until he was baptized as a Lutheran in 1898. From that point on, and like many other expressionists and former expressionists, Schoenberg found that matters of faith became an increasing preoccupation in both his life and his art. In Paris on July 30, 1933, exactly six months after Hitler's accession to power in Germany, a formal ceremony marked Schoenberg's embrace of the Jewish faith.

Schoenberg wanted *Moses* to be understood in religious rather than aesthetic terms.[27] (The political interpretations that I explore here would have been even more removed from the composer's own conception of his work.) Still, one need not share the structuralists' disdain for the artist's intentions to believe that this religious work reverberates with aesthetic and political content. Schoenberg's religious concerns in *Moses* revolve around the second commandment's prohibition of graven images.[28] It is not very surprising, therefore, to find that Schoenberg's deity and prophets are absorbed in the aesthetic relation between truth and representation and in the social and political implications of this relation.

The first act finds Moses at prayer. He is answered by the voice in the burning bush, who commands him to lead the Israelites out of their Egyptian bondage. Moses declares his inability to perform such a task, but the voice promises him the assistance of his brother, the glib Aron. Aron meets Moses in the wasteland. Although he never fully grasps Moses' idea of the inconceivable God, Aron is enthusiastic and confident. Together they return to the Israelites and proclaim God's message. Initially the Israelites reject this notion, but Aron wins them over through a series of miracles. The act closes with the Israelites prepared to march into the wasteland.

The second act opens with the anger of first the elders and then all the Israelites at Moses' forty-day retreat to the Mountain of Revelation. In order to placate their demand for a comprehensible deity, Aron orders the casting of the golden calf. An orgy of drunkenness, dancing, blood sacrifice, suicide, and sex follows. Moses descends from the mountain, and the golden calf disappears at his command. As Aron defends his actions, an enraged Moses smashes the tablets of the law. Aron conjures two more images, a pillar of fire by night and a pillar of cloud by day, to prompt the Israelites back on their trek into the wasteland. This act, and the composed part of the opera, ends with Moses expressing his exasperation and despair.

In the brief third act, Aron is in chains. Before the elders,

Moses accuses Aron of misrepresenting his idea of the inconceivable God. After Moses has Aron's chains removed, his brother falls dead.

If the tonal appearances of *Palestrina* and *Mathis* reflect the aesthetic philosophies of their respective composers, so too does the tonal appearance of *Moses* express Schoenberg's modernist aesthetics. The milieu of *Moses* is not evoked by simulating the aural world of the ancient Israelites. Nor is there an apotheosis of late romanticism or a mystical-natural retreat to classical tonality. Instead, the varied music of *Moses* is constructed by the thematic and harmonic transformations of a single twelve-note series.[29]

Like all of Schoenberg's serial compositions, the score of *Moses* is the product of the systematization of the techniques of his expressionist period. This systematization is Schoenberg's version of the typical pattern of development from the subjective excesses of expressionism to the restraint of New Objectivity. According to Adorno, the serial system has a dual character. On one hand, serialism represents the complete triumph of human purposes over the natural tonal materials of music. Instead of following Hindemith's newly objective retreat to a naturalistic conception of music, Schoenberg subjects the sonic material of music to the rationality of the composer and his system. On the other hand, serialism represents the subjection of the composer to a new, second nature of his own creation. Compositional techniques that were developed, in the expressionist period, as a liberating expansion of the expressive means of the composer now become the source of a self-imposed limitation: "The subject dominates music through the rationality of the system, only in order to succumb to the rational system itself."[30]

If art is, as Hegel believed, the sensuous form of the Idea, then *Moses* takes as its subject nothing less than what Schoenberg held to be the ultimate Idea: the "only one, infinite, thou omnipresent one, / unperceived and inconceivable God!"[31] The production, reproduction, and reception of this Idea in sensual form preoccupies the four protagonists of the opera: the divine voice in the burning bush; Moses, the producer of the Idea in its abstract essence; Aron, the reproducer of the Idea as sensuous appearance; and the chorus of the Israelites, the recipients of the Idea.[32]

In his aesthetic aspect, Moses is the symbol of the heroic integrity—and the heroic impotence—of the modernist artist. His art is a type of cognitive epistemology, wherein he attempts to transmit the lofty idea of the unperceived and inconceivable God through the most thorough rationalization of his means of artistic expression. His worth as an artist-producer lies in his ability to use his artistic materials as a means of rational expression and clarification of his ideas, and not in his ability to please an audience. Indeed, although popular acceptance would be welcome, the modernist artist is unwilling to seek this acceptance by compromising either his ideas or his rational techniques. In most circumstances, the modernist artist-producer can expect to be understood and appreciated by only a select few. In *Moses* the rationalization of modernist art is exemplified by the near mathematical precision of Schoenberg's serial composition and by the fact that the character of Moses is a speaking role. Schoenberg used *Sprechstimme* as an effective device in some of his earlier works. But in this opera, where the speaking role of Moses is so deliberately juxtaposed to the bel canto tenor of Aron, Schoenberg appears to be contrasting the more literary, restrained, referential, and mimetic values of the spoken drama to the histrionic, extravagant, gestural, ceremonial, and performance values of traditional opera.[33]

Like Pfitzner and Hindemith, Schoenberg concedes that there is more to art than can be comprehended in terms of reason, craft, and technique. There is the irrational or nonrational element of faith or intuition. Yet Schoenberg never wraps this faith or intuition in a veil of romantic or natural mysticism. The divine source of Moses' lofty idea is external to the artist-producer and is inconceivable to all those who lack faith. In the first act, it is the voice who calls the unwilling and incapable Moses to his artistic duty: to communicate the idea of God to the chosen people. This voice is the ultimate patron in the history of the artist-opera. More authoritarian than any Borromeo, more willing to let his clients flounder in the morass of their weaknesses and free will than any Albrecht, the voice enjoins Moses to his inescapable but ultimately impossible duty.

Moses pleads his inability to transmit the idea of God in effective images: "But my tongue is not flexible: / thought is easy; / speech is laborious" (44). With his dependence on Aron, Moses is like an opera composer who is dependent on artistic reproducers to transmit his message as a sensuous appearance. Aron, in turn, is confident that his "love [of the chosen people] will surely not weary of image forming" (48). Much of the opera revolves around Aron's images. When the willing but spiritually immature Israelites fail to comprehend the prophets' message, Aron performs the miracles of transforming Moses' rod into a serpent, withering Moses' arm with leprosy, and changing the Nile water into blood. Here Schoenberg accentuates the division of labor between the brothers by attributing these biblical feats of Moses and the burning bush to Aron. Whatever reservations Moses may have had about transmitting the idea of God through these conjurer's tricks, Aron is certain that the "all-knowing one" will understand that these means are necessary for a "childlike folk" (80). Aron's miracles work. They ready the Israelites to leave their onerous but familiar bondage in Egypt and to set forth into the unknown perils of the wasteland. For Moses, the wandering in the wasteland is a welcome time of material deprivation and spiritual growth in which the people can overcome their spiritual bondage and prepare themselves for life in the promised land: "In the wasteland pureness of thought / will provide you nurture, sustain you / and advance you" (80).

In order to save himself and the elders from the wrath of the people, Aron orders the creation of the golden calf: "Revere yourselves in this gold symbol!" (96). During the ensuing orgy, a lone youth reminds the people of their higher calling, only to be killed by the tribal leaders. When Aron defends his actions, he points out that Moses had destroyed a calf that was but an image, as are the tables of the law that Moses carries. Moses smashes the tables, yet the idea of the inconceivable God still appears to be defeated by the images of the two pillars. Schoenberg's score concludes with Moses sinking to the ground in despair: "O word, thou word, that I lack!" (124).

Moses appears to regain the upper hand in the third act. Aron defends his actions as undertaken for the good of the people: "For their freedom— / so that they would become a nation" (128). But Moses replies that service to the divine idea is the true goal. Even nationhood is only a means to this service, not an end in itself. Aron's tricks have freed the Israelites from the physical domination of the Egyptians but have kept them in spiritual tutelage. Moses declares:

> Images lead and rule this folk
> that you have freed,
> and strange wishes are their gods,
> leading them back to the slavery
> of godlessness and earthly pleasures. (130)

When the soldiers ask if Aron is to be put to death, Moses orders him released from his chains. But Aron, faced with returning to the wasteland but now deprived of his customary dependence on images (his chains), falls dead.

In *Moses* the aesthetic estrangement of the modernist artist from society is exemplified not only by the serial score and by the thematic distrust of the familiar images of art as graven idols, which bind one to the past rather than emancipate one for the future, but also by its problematic conclusion. Adorno wrote that "every interruption in the creative process—every forgetfulness, every new beginning—designates a type of reaction to society."34 If *Moses* ends with the second act, then the modernist artist admits the inevitability of his defeat. Any artist who pursues the highest ideas with the most advanced techniques faces the prospect of a tragic alienation from society. At best, only a portion of his ideas can be communicated, and then only if he is willing to compromise his techniques. The golden age of Mozart and Beethoven, where artistic integrity and technical modernity combined with popular acceptance, is forever gone. But if *Moses* ends with the third act, then the modernist appears to triumph. What is left lifeless in the dust is the symbol of the conventional in art. This conclusion, however, strikes a note of hollow optimism about the fate of modernist art. Would Moses be any more effective, would his tongue be loosened and his message heeded, by the mere fact of Aron's death? Analogously, is the estrangement of the modern artist resolved because Schoenberg proclaimed it to be so in the third act of an opera? It must remain a conjecture, but I believe that it is the shallow pseudoresolution of act three—more than lack of time or health problems—that led Schoenberg to leave this act without a score. In the end he preferred heroic impotence over a false victory. After *Moses*, as before, progressive art remains closed to all but the small band of initiates. The solution to the estrangement of the artist from wider society, if such a solution exists, lies beyond the powers of art.

Schoenberg's sympathetic portrayal of Aron allows him to pose the alienation of the modernist artist in the sharpest possible terms. It is Aron who loves the Israelites, who has the love that Moses lacks. It is Aron who sets the people on their way from Egypt to the promised land. Schoenberg makes no attempt to cheapen Aron's actions by depicting them as basely or selfishly motivated. But by defending the integrity of Aron's motives, Schoenberg demonstrates the poverty of even the best-intentioned reliance on the traditional tricks of the artistic trade. Truly progressive art depends on the most advanced materials and techniques. Old techniques, techniques that were progressive in their own day, are now merely sources of distortion and mystification. Even the catchwords of the classical and romantic eras—love, freedom, nation—show their shopworn edges in the harsh and revealing light of Schoenberg's modernism.

The politics of *Moses* is equally uncompromising. Unlike the chorus of most operas, the chorus of the Israelites is no mere magnifying force, lending the action an epic appearance.[35] In *Moses*, the chorus is a principal character. It is the response of the chorus to the message of Moses and the images of Aron that determines the political implications of the aesthetic relation between ideas and images. The conversation between the voice and Moses in the first scene indicates that images are not inherently hostile to ideas. The burning bush gets Moses' attention; the voice then instructs Moses on the ethical implications of his monotheism. Presumably, Moses' interaction with the divine in image form on the Mountain of Revelation had this same rational and enlightening character, as did the tables of the law, which Moses destroyed in an irrational fury. But when Moses and Aron, in the fourth scene of the first act, attempt to bring the divine message to the people through the rational means of words, they are met with confusion, ridicule, and rejection. In other words, the attempt to communicate through the rationalized images of modernist art only "provokes the rage of the normal."[36] It is only when Aron manipulates the hopes and fears of the people through the traditional illusory images of art that they muster the courage for the journey into the wasteland. Here the images of art are not the means of enlightenment through rational communication but are a means of manipulation and control. Despite the purity of his motives, Schoenberg's Aron is the propaganda minister and advertising campaign manager of the Exodus.

In *Moses*, images can be emancipating or confining. Aron's images imprison others in the status quo. Despite their theatricality and their seeming to be a spur to action, these images revolve in a circle of ever-sameness. First, the images are based on the traditional techniques of illusory art. Second, the images can only hasten, retard, or release preexisting dispositions in the audience. They cannot induce spiritual growth. Like opera audiences who burst into self-congratulatory applause at the recognition of a familiar aria, the Israelites of *Moses* worship themselves in the form of the golden calf. Aron's images are incapable of inspiring a higher stage of consciousness because they bypass reason in favor of emotional manipulation. At the end of the second act, the people may have resumed the journey to the promised land, but they have not yet achieved a full consciousness of the spiritual meaning of their quest. They still depend on childish images to lead them.

Schoenberg's Moses is a symbol of emancipation from political irrationality and manipulation. At the same time, Moses displays all of the ascetic characteristics of reason in Western culture.[37] It is Aron, not the austere intellectual Moses, who is capable of loving and being loved. It is Aron who holds the real, material happiness and freedom of the people to be worthwhile values. It is Aron who consents to the emotional and sensual gratification of the golden calf. And it is Aron who sings. But for Moses, Aron's attributes are the lower human characteristics which should be subordinated to the higher calling of reason. Instead of offering emotional and sensual gratification, Moses exults in the material deprivation and spiritual discipline of the wasteland.

Schoenberg's aesthetics of heroic impotence clearly poses the dilemma of progressive art versus regressive mystification, even if it is not able to resolve the dilemma in favor of the forces of progress. The same pattern recurs in the politics of *Moses*. The choice lies between the politics of gratification and the politics of deprivation. The Arons of the world—in show business, advertising, and politics—can offer a semblance of emotional and sensual gratification, albeit gratification that imprisons the individual in the status quo and his or her own base nature. The modernist Moses, on the other hand, offers enlightenment and spiritual growth, but only at a cost of emotional and sensual deprivation. Once again the alternatives are posed in the sharpest possible terms. And once again Moses-Schoenberg guarantees his impotence by defending political reason and progress. The second act concludes with the Israelites following the reassuring Aronist pillars—not the ideal of the inconceivable God—into the wasteland. That the Israelites prefer sensuous images is not only an indication of their aesthetic philistinism and political immaturity. It also contains a genuine moment of protest against the rationalist political enlightenment of modernist art, which is purchased at the expense of sensual human happiness.

Unlike the artist-operas of Puccini and Richard Strauss, *Palestrina*, *Mathis*, and *Moses* attempt to probe the aesthetic and political problems of art and the artist in the early twentieth century. The fate of romantic art is the core of the aesthetic problem. Pfitzner's *Palestrina* accentuates the Germanness of the romantic tradition and at the same time emphasizes the vulnerability of romanticism to modernist tendencies in art. For Pfitzner, progress in art should be frozen at the late romantic stage of development. Repelled by the hidebound character of late German romanticism, the young Hindemith experimented with modernist tendencies. As his compositional style matured in *Mathis*, however, he retreated from modernism into an absolute, ahistorical, mystical-natural neoclassicism. For Hindemith, the romantic-modernist debate is not so much resolved as mystically transcended. Schoenberg takes late romanticism as the point of departure for his thoroughly modernist art. In *Moses*, he neither freezes musical progress at late romanticism nor retreats behind late romanticism to a neoclassical stance. For Schoenberg, authentic art is art that continues to rationalize and develop its materials and techniques, even at the risk of the disapproval of an uncomprehending public.

In the historical context of World War I, the Weimar Republic, and the Third Reich, the political views of *Palestrina*, *Mathis*, and *Moses* closely parallel their aesthetics. Pfitzner is a staunch German nationalist. But the mood of Schopenhauerian resignation which pervades *Palestrina* leads him not so much to bombast and flag waving as it does to a passive acceptance of whatever fate has in store. Instead of redeeming or reconciling reality, the late romantic conception reduces the vaunted power of music to providing solace to an essentially passive subject. The mature Hindemith is less concerned with German nationalism. Like Mathis, he finds himself swept up in the turmoil of historical change, and

he comes to value stability in a renewed community as the foundation of artistic creativity. But with no real stable community on
the horizon, Hindemith retreats to a mystical community of hu-
mankind secured by equally mystical universal laws of order and
harmony. Schoenberg faces the physical and spiritual threat of
Nazism. His Moses condemns the dangers of political emotionalism and irrationality. At the same time, Schoenberg's ascetic politics of extreme intellectualism lacks a popular foundation, and its
failure is therefore inevitable. In his operas, Hans Werner Henze,
with his eclectic compositional techniques and commitment to
the political causes of the New Left and counterculture, would try
to resolve the aesthetic and political impasses of Schoenberg's
modernism by linking music to a new kind of political movement.

SEVEN

Eros and Revolt
Henze's *Bassarids*

Bliss was it in that dawn to be alive,
But to be young was very heaven.
—WILLIAM WORDSWORTH

ANS Werner Henze's opera *The Bassarids* was a product of the 1960s and early 1970s. During that period of political and cultural reappraisal in the West, New Left dissidents condemned the complacency of the political Establishment. General prosperity, technological proficiency, and at least a modicum of political participation were the achievements of advanced industrial societies, yet the war in Vietnam epitomized the state violence, racism, nationalism, and militarism that also flourished. With disdain for the politics of moderation and reform, the New Left tried to create a new kind of politics, a radical politics that would make the world right and just.

The counterculture was entwined with New Left radicalism. While the New Left denounced the failures of Establishment politics, the counterculture scoffed at the Establishment personality, which was seen as dour, boring, sexually repressed, and male. These psychological characteristics were believed to have important political implications: the Establishment's support of warfare in Vietnam and police violence at home were symptoms of its sensual and sexual repression.

[167]

This diagnosis determined the general orientation of the radical cure. The slogan was "Make love, not war," and here lay the genius, the uniqueness, and the fallibility of this radical movement. Unlike the Establishment, with the lethal stodginess of its men, but also unlike earlier movements of political radicalism, with the moral earnestness and indeed prudery of their leaders, this campaign for a new and better world was going to be more sensuous, more feminine, and much more fun.

A new conception of liberated human life emerged. The radicals rejected the consumer society of the West. Even the traditional socialist and communist goals of the seizure of state power and the socialization of the economy did not go far enough. Instead, informed by the works of such radical thinkers as Herbert Marcuse, Norman O. Brown, and Erich Fromm, the new vision of sensual freedom and fulfillment regarded the wealth of advanced industrial societies as the means for increasing instinctual gratification.[1]

Far from prizing the order, security, and consumerist prosperity sought by denizens of the Establishment, the radicals demanded a most elusive political goal. They demanded happiness. They transformed hedonism from a personal credo to a collective mission. If the achievements of advanced industrial societies had any value, it was the laying of a material foundation that could support the contemplated fulfillment. According to Freud, repressed instincts and unhappiness were the prices to be paid for civilization and prosperity. The counterculture turned Freud upside down. According to the countercultural vision of liberation, emancipated instincts and happiness were to be the rewards of life in a civilized and prosperous society.

The seeds of the new order were already germinating. Rock music formed the keynote of the counterculture, its anthems and hymnody. The movement also developed alternative hairstyles, clothes, symbols, intoxicants, gender roles, and sexual values as well as an alternative understanding of the intrinsic value of biological nature. Rejecting the West's enslavement to a vapid cycle of production and consumption, the counterculture turned East for models. The New Left heroized the Vietnamese communists, whom the Western Establishment had demonized. The counterculture rediscovered the spiritual wisdom of the East, embracing Zen, meditation, Hinduism, and other practices once thought exotic.

With its state subsidies, corporate patronage, and elite clientele, opera was a bastion of cultural opposition to the new radicalism. To be sure, such hybrids as the rock operas *Jesus Christ Superstar* and *Tommy* were created, but in practice these new forms were confined to the media of commercial mass culture. The opera house itself remained a haven where proper people, properly behaved, groomed, and attired, could find respite in the enjoyment of hallowed and familiar works. Or so they thought. In the audience turned up women in blue jeans and men with long hair. And on the stage at least one work, *The Bassarids*, seemed to be a musical dramatization of their worst nightmare: a triumph of the new radicalism, particularly in its countercultural form.

The idea for *The Bassarids* dated to the early sixties. The librettists, W. H. Auden and his lover Chester Kallman, broached the idea with Henze in 1962 and delivered the completed libretto the following year. The opera premiered at the prestigious Salzburg Festival in 1966. The Salzburg audience was accustomed to the lavish and politically conservative productions of Mozart, Wagner, and Richard Strauss.[2] Predictably, they were outraged by the new work, with its unfamiliar, modernistic score and scurrilous ideas. But *The Bassarids* has overcome the flak surrounding its inauspicious premiere. Henze now considers it the most important of his operas.[3] A recent editorial in *Opera News* calls it a masterpiece.[4]

Auden and Kallman based the libretto on Euripides' tragedy *The Bacchae*. As the composer and librettists originally conceived their version, costumes from a variety of historical periods would suggest the timelessness of the opera's central conflict: the confrontation between Pentheus, the austere young king of Thebes, and Dionysus, the sensuous young Olympian god.

But now, nearly thirty years after its premiere, we can also see the historical connections of the work. *The Bassarids* is not only an artistic disquisition on the perennial conflict between asceticism and sensual gratification. It is also an expression of a specific conflict in a specific age. In the 1960s and 1970s, the repression and expression of sensuality became a bitterly disputed political issue, and *The Bassarids* poses the promise and the limits of the era's sensual-sexual revolt. Poised between Henze's early operas, with their themes of alienation, and his later works, with their overt commitment to socialism and communism, *The Bassarids* captures the new radical spirit with Dionysian images of political, psychic, and natural emancipation.

The Bassarids is part of a new, post-scarcity conception of radical politics. The opera is not concerned with poverty and exploitation, the socioeconomic foundations of revolution in classical Marxist theory. Like the advanced industrial societies of the sixties, the Thebes of *The Bassarids* is prosperous; the economic dimension of its slave system is peripheral to the story. Also absent is a class-based conception of revolution; in the opera, the royal family, common citizens, and slaves all heed the subversive call of the new god from the East. For socioeconomic and class orientations toward political radicalism, one does better to turn to musical works like Marc Blitzstein's *Cradle Will Rock*, the Chinese ballet-opera *The Red Detachment of Women*, or Aram Khatchaturian's ballet *Spartacus*.

Like the modern governments of industrial societies, the Theban state under Pentheus is not a blatant tyranny in the traditional senses of the term. Pentheus is not the tool of an economically rapacious ruling class, nor is he prone to that personal self-interest that has characterized so many tyrannical rulers, both in history and in opera. Indeed, Pentheus's rule has transcended economic interest and personal indulgence in the

interest of the good of the state as a whole. But the virtues of
Pentheus's state only heighten the critical power of the opera, as it
reveals the latent violence and intolerance of even the most rational of states. Similarly, Pentheus's suppression of self-interest and
personal desire emphasizes the terrible cost of this transcendence:
the denial of sensuousness, both his own and that of his subjects,
and the refusal to recognize the inextinguishable power of nature
in all its forms.

Dionysus represents the sensuous alternative to the rule of
Pentheus. The opera retains the interest that Euripides' play had
in the divinity of Dionysus, but Henze's Dionysus is also distinctly modern and profane: a figure of the imagination and a
symbol of the repressed dimensions of the human psyche.[5] In
contrast to the civilized and orderly austerity of Pentheus, Dionysus represents the liberating possibilities of intoxication, sensuousness and sexuality, feminism and femininity, and reunion
with nature. Whereas the conflicts of the sixties were frequently
generational, age is not a factor in the opera. Both Pentheus and
Dionysus are young. But as was often seen in the confrontational
politics of the sixties, the important differences between Pentheus and Dionysus are embodied in seemingly trivial but emotionally charged matters of personal appearance. Pentheus, the
chaste king with the monkish demeanor, is enraged by the very
sight of Dionysus, with his long and perfumed hair, his sexually
ambiguous maenadic garb, and his simultaneously gentle and
insolent smile.

In spite of its portrayal of Dionysus as a sensual, countercultural alternative to Pentheus, *The Bassarids* is far from a blind
celebration of the Age of Aquarius. The opera retains a dialectical
edge. The reign of Dionysus may be the antithesis of the reign of
Pentheus, but it, too, has its dire consequences, as the closing
scenes chillingly illustrate.[6] The opera thus anticipates the self-
destruction of the counterculture: the transition from the sensuous euphoria of the sixties to the hangovers, sexually transmitted diseases, and drug overdoses of the seventies and eighties.

Hans Werner Henze was born in Gütersloh, Germany, in 1926.[7] Controversy about Henze's politics dates to the years around 1967 and 1968, when there was a distinct change in his life and work. As early as 1965, Henze displayed a sympathy with the moderate Left in his support of Willy Brandt's campaign to become chancellor of West Germany. But in 1967–68, at a peak of his critical and financial success as a composer, Henze became committed to the New Left, socialism, and communism, thereby also becoming the pariah of the conservative international music establishment.

Politically, Henze supported the new student movement, particularly Berlin's Students for a Democratic Society and its anti–Vietnam War activities. He resigned from the West Berlin Academy of the Arts and instead became a corresponding member of the East German Academy of the Arts. In 1969 he made two visits to Cuba. In April he was the guest of the National Council for Culture. He returned to Havana for a longer stay from October 1969 until April 1970. In 1972 he issued an election appeal on behalf of the German Communist Party. He also joined the Italian Communist Party.

Henze's commitment to radical leftist politics had a profound impact on his musical career and on the themes of his compositions. His community-oriented and unconventional activities contradicted the bourgeois model of the isolated composer creating for an elite audience. He collaborated with other composers on a stage cantata, *Streik bei Mannesmann*, and an opera, *Der Ofen*. He edited a series of books on music that reflected his favored themes: semiotics, music education, and mediating between elite and popular culture.[8] Between 1976 and 1980, he became the artistic director of the Cantiere Internationale d'Arte, held each summer in Montepulciano, Italy. Instead of following the example of other summer music festivals, with their expensive performances for affluent audiences, Henze attempted to involve musicians and nonmusicians, visiting artists and town residents, adults and children in various aspects of musical production and spectatorship.

His participation in the festivals in Deutschlandsberg, Austria (1984–86), and in his hometown of Gütersloh (1986–present) retained many of the populist and pedagogical aspects of Montepulciano. In the late 1980s, Henze accepted the artistic directorship of Die Münchener Biennale, a festival that provides a venue for performances of new operas by young composers.[9]

The subjects of his compositions also underwent a profound change. In his early works, Henze drew on classic texts by Heinrich von Kleist, Arthur Rimbaud, Torquato Tasso, Friedrich Hölderlin, and Virgil. His newer works set contemporary, politically radical works by Hans Magnus Enzensberger, Ernst Schnabel, Miguel Barnet, Gastón Salvatore, and Edward Bond.[10] The oratorio *Der Floss der "Medusa"* was a requiem for Che Guevara and set a text by Schnabel; the 1968 Hamburg premiere was aborted when police entered the concert hall to arrest students who had draped the stage with a red flag. The 1976 opera *We Come to the River*, using a libretto by Bond, was a scathing attack on militarism and imperialism. *The English Cat*, a 1983 opera on another text by Bond, satirized monetary greed as well as the pretensions of upper-class liberalism. Political radicalism also pervaded Henze's purely instrumental works. Premiering in Havana in 1969, the *Sixth Symphony* included fragments of the anthem of the Vietnamese Liberation Front and a song by a Greek freedom fighter. Henze's identification as the composer of late sixties' and early seventies' radicalism is epitomized by another instrumental work: he composed *Madrigal for Herbert Marcuse* for flute, clarinet, and bassoon.

Henze's turn to radicalism represented a new stage in his political development. The roots of this change, however, lay deep in his experience. Long before he knew that he was politically *for* socialism, he knew what he was politically *against*. His father was a committed Nazi who died during the war on the eastern front. The father's Nazism confirmed the antifascism of the son, as he once acknowledged: "My hatred of my father became entwined with my hatred of fascism."[11] For Henze the defeat of Nazism elicited little enthusiasm for postwar West Germany. His belief in the persistent authoritarianism of the Federal Republic of Germany and his homosexuality combined to estrange him from society.

Henze's music education at the Brunswick State School of Music was interrupted by an unwelcomed stint in the German army. After the war, he resumed his studies at the Heidelberg Church Music Institute and with Wolfgang Fortner. From Fortner he received his first instruction on the compositional problems and techniques of contemporary music. In 1949 Henze began his study of serialism under René Leibowitz in Darmstadt. Schoenberg's tonal serialism had been suppressed as degenerate by the Nazis, and at first the anti-Nazi Henze was enthusiastic. He was recognized as one of the budding young star composers of the serialist Darmstadt School. Then the orientation of Darmstadt turned from the tonal serialism of Schoenberg to the total serialism of Anton von Webern. Henze was willing to use serialism as one compositional technique among others, but a strict serialism seemed cold, abstract, mechanical, and overly technological. Most discouraging of all, extreme serialism sounded harsh and ugly to listeners. Without listeners, composition became a solipsistic enterprise: an exercise for the edification of the composer and perhaps a few of his colleagues.

Henze moved to Italy in 1953. Socially and politically, Italy represented a refuge from German authoritarianism. Aesthetically, Italy represented an alternative to the serialism that was dominating postwar German music. For Henze, melody was the primary attribute of Italian music. And melody was a component of music that offered a way out of the increasing isolation of the contemporary composer. In addition to musical form and verbal texts, melody is a means by which a composer communicates with listeners.

If the young Henze rejected the calculated musical elitism and isolation of Darmstadt, his early operas still retained socially imposed isolation and estrangement as dramatic themes. As he admitted, "There are always 'loners' at the centre of my operas."[12] *Boulevard Solitude* (1952) was the third operatic treatment of the fate of Manon Lescaut, the ill-starred courtesan. And in spite of the more congenial atmosphere that Henze found in Italy, the theme of loneliness and isolation persisted in his works. *König Hirsch* (1956), later shortened and revised as *Il Re Cervo* (1962), set the travails of the mythical King Leandro: parted from his beloved forest animals, surrounded by perfidious courtiers and scheming candidates for marriage, treacherously separated from his true beloved. *Der Prinz von Homburg* (1960) told the tale of the dreamy and artistic prince within the milieu of the Prussian military. Ostensibly a comic opera, *Der junge Lord* (1965) concluded with no happy marriage for Luise, the central character.

Between Henze's early operas of alienation, isolation, and estrangement and his later socialist works lay the two crucial operas to librettos by Auden and Kallman: *Elegy for Young Lovers* (1961) and *The Bassarids*. *Elegy* and *Bassarids* were products of Henze's move to Italy. Henze met Auden and Kallman at the Italian island resort of Ischia. Auden and Kallman had provided the libretto for Igor Stravinsky's successful 1951 opera *The Rake's Progress*, and Henze wanted an opera text from the two writers. *Elegy* continued the theme of alienation, but this time with important implications for the role of the contemporary artist. In *Elegy* Auden and Kallman wrote an original story about a fictional early-twentieth-century poet, Gregor Mittenhofer.[13]

Henze has called Mittenhofer a "bourgeois hero."[14] The description has several layers of meaning. It refers to Mittenhofer's isolated work habits: every year he retreats to a remote Alpine resort to write his poetry. It also refers to the basis of Mittenhofer's fame as a poet: he is known for the greatness of his works, not his odious personality. But most of all Henze's characterization is sardonic, a reflection of his deep antipathy to capitalism. Mittenhofer extracts his poetry, his artistic capital, from an essentially exploitative and parasitic relation to common people. During his annual visits to the resort, Mittenhofer bases his poetry on the visionary ravings of Hilda Mack. Hilda lost her husband, and her sanity, on her wedding night forty years earlier, when he was trapped in a blizzard on a trip to pick edelweiss for his bride. During this year's visit, Mittenhofer withholds knowledge about an approaching snowstorm from the young lovers Toni and Elisabeth, as they journey in the mountains to bring him edelweiss. Toni and Elisabeth die in the storm, but all is not lost. Their deaths inspire Mittenhofer to his finest work. The closing scene shows Mittenhofer receiving accolades in Vienna, as he gives a reading of his just completed poem, "Elegy for Young Lovers."[15]

Performances of *Elegy* achieved only moderate success. Years later, Auden would refer to the work as *Allergy for Young Lovers*.[16] But Henze was upset by the message of *Elegy*. Unlike Mittenhofer, he probably did not have psychological cruelty or tragic deaths on his conscience. It did seem, however, that he was an isolated artist producing self-contained works for his own fame and profit. Henze's later turn to cooperative and populist artistic activities can be attributed as much to *Elegy*'s critique of the bourgeois artist as to any explicitly socialist conception of the artist.

Henze's next collaboration with Auden and Kallman was *The Bassarids*. Henze wanted another libretto, and Auden and Kallman were eager to try their hands at an operatic tragedy. Composer and librettists agreed upon *The Bassarids*. Following Egon Wellesz's *Bacchantinnen* (1931) and Federico Ghedini's *Le Bacchanti* (1948), *The Bassarids* is the third operatic adaptation of Euripides' *Bacchae*.[17]

The opera is divided into four symphonic movements rather than the usual operatic acts. At Auden and Kallman's insistence, only the intermezzo conforms to Henze's deliberately anti-Wagnerian practice of composing operas with discrete musical set pieces. Arias, duets, and so on remain in the opera, but the score is more continuously composed than any of Henze's previous operas. At Henze's insistence, his continuous composing was modeled on a Mahlerian symphony rather than a Wagnerian music drama.

The sonata form of the first movement juxtaposes the themes of Pentheus and Dionysus. The movement depicts the arrival of Dionysus in Thebes and the effect of his arrival on the population and the royal household. After the chorus of citizens sings a hymn of praise to Pentheus, the new king, the offstage voice of Dionysus is heard. The citizens heed the summons of the voice and join Dionysus's cult on Mount Cytheron. Pentheus's grandfather, Cadmus, the former king of Thebes, is perplexed by the possibility that he might also be the grandfather of a god, for Dionysus is alleged to be the offspring of the conjugal union between Zeus and Cadmus's dead daughter, Semele. Cadmus's friend, the old prophet Tiresias, is enthusiastic about the new cult. Pentheus's mother, Agave, and her sister, Autonoe, ridicule the notion that their dead sister was the lover of a god. Both women are sexually attracted to the captain of the guards, who reads Pentheus's proclamation banning the new cult. Pentheus finally emerges from the palace and extinguishes the flame at the tomb of Semele. The voice is heard once again. This time it bewitches Agave and Autonoe, who dance their way to Cytheron.

Particularly appropriate in an opera about Dionysus, a series of bacchanalian dances compose the second-movement scherzo. This movement portrays Pentheus's confrontation with Dionysus and his followers. To the consternation of his fearful grandfather, Pentheus orders the captain to Cytheron, instructing him to arrest the members of the cult and to kill any resistors. Pentheus confides in the old servant Beroe, his nurse, and also the nurse of Semele. The captain returns with his prisoners: Tiresias, Agave, Autonoe, two of Agave's female slaves, a stranger, and a few others. Pentheus orders the torture of the slaves, and then he questions his mother. After finding her trancelike description of the rites on Cytheron to be incomprehensible, he sends her and Autonoe home under guard. He orders the destruction of Tiresias's house. Ignoring the warnings of Beroe, who has somehow intuited that the stranger is Dionysus, Pentheus assumes that the stranger is a priest in the new cult. The movement closes with the stranger describing the terrible vengeance wreaked upon a ship's crew when it tried to kidnap him on a trip to Naxos.

The third movement is in two parts, divided by the intermezzo. The initial adagio sets Dionysus's enchantment of Pentheus. In a rage against the impertinently smiling stranger, Pentheus orders his imprisonment. The stranger puts up no resistance. An earthquake frees the stranger and the other imprisoned Bassarids. The flame at Semele's tomb is miraculously relit. The stranger now casts his spell over Pentheus, using a magic mirror to offer Pentheus a vision of the rites on Cytheron.

The intermezzo, "The Judgment of Calliope," is in a deliberately anachronistic eighteenth-century style. It represents Pentheus's vision in the mirror. Dressed in eighteenth-century costumes, characters from *The Bassarids* take on the parts in the mythological scene. Tiresias becomes Calliope, sitting in judgment over the competing claims of Agave as Venus and Autonoe as Proserpine for the affection of the captain as Adonis. The judgment, which calls for dividing the body of the unlucky captain-Adonis among the women, foretells the fate of Pentheus in the main part of the opera.

The last part of the movement, a fugue, sets the deepening enchantment and death of Pentheus. Dionysus persuades Pentheus to go to Cytheron disguised as a maenad. Filled with foreboding, Beroe pleads for mercy on Pentheus, while Cadmus awaits the impending destruction of his dynasty. At Cytheron, the voice of Dionysus warns his worshipers about the presence of an interloper. The maenads capture Pentheus. Oblivious, in her trancelike state, to her son's pleas for recognition, Agave leads the maenads in tearing him to pieces.

The thematic variations of the fourth movement form a passacaglia. This last movement presents the vengeance and apotheosis of Dionysus. Gradually emerging from her trance, Agave is grief stricken by the enormity of her deed, and Autonoe places the blame for her role in the murder on Agave. Meanwhile, Dionysus orders the captain to set fire to the palace and exiles Cadmus,

Agave, and Autonoe from Thebes. Agave threatens that some day Dionysus will be punished. In the closing scene, a resplendent Dionysus summons his mother, Semele, from Hades. Semele, who is renamed Thyone, and Dionysus ascend into heaven. As the prostrate population adores the enormous idols of Thyone and Dionysus that have appeared at Semele's tomb, vines descend and sprout everywhere.

The Bassarids is no mere musical setting of an ancient play. The opera is faithful to the substance of the Euripides' tragedy, which is the confrontation between Pentheus and Dionysus, but it also introduces a number of structural and thematic changes.[18] Most obvious is the change in title, from *The Bacchae*, or the female followers of Dionysus, to *The Bassarids*, or the female *and* male followers of the god.[19] In order to keep the opera from degenerating into a dramatically static oratorio, Auden and Kallman redistribute some of the plot material that Euripides had assigned to the chorus, giving different elements to the individual characters, a few of whom are new additions to the play: Beroe, Autonoe, and the captain. Euripides' messengers are eliminated.

In addition, the ancient tragedy is overlaid with four new thematic dimensions: Christianity, psychoanalysis, Platonism, and Nazism. Auden and Kallman endow the interrogation of the unrecognized god, Dionysus, with hints of Pilate's interrogation of the unrecognized Christ. They also intended that the concluding apotheosis show the affinity between the Greek and the Christian divinities. In Henze's score, four quotes from Bach strengthen the Christian allusions.

Although never denying the religious nature of the conflict between Pentheus and Dionysus, the opera reflects a twentieth-century awareness of the psychoanalytic implications of this conflict. The chorus and orchestra provide a subconscious, Dionysian commentary on the characters' conscious words and actions.

The libretto attributes Pentheus's psychological austerity, religious monotheism, and style of rulership to an adherence to a repressive conception of Platonic philosophy. In *The Bassarids*, reason has none of the erotic associations that it sometimes has in Plato. In the opera, reason is a mechanism for the repression of sensuousness and sexuality. In contrast to the lyricism of Dionysus's music, the plainness and clarity of Pentheus's musical themes manifest his rational character.

As a product of the early 1960s, fewer than twenty years after the end of World War II, the opera is haunted by the specter of Nazism. The closing scene, where Dionysus reigns over the prostrate population of Thebes, is intended as a critique of life in a totalitarian state. An anti-Nazi message may also be implied in the portrayal of the captain. *The Bassarids* was written at the time of the capture and trial of the banal Nazi functionary, Adolf Eichmann,[20] and the captain's unhesitating acquiescence to his successive masters—first Pentheus, then Cadmus, then Dionysus—may parody the ready obedience of Eichmann-like Nazis.

During the course of their conflict, both Pentheus and Dionysus experience reciprocal cycles of rulership, tyranny, and victimhood. In the beginning, Pentheus is a rational and civilized ruler. After the capture of Dionysus and members of his cult, the rule of Pentheus reveals the tyrannical underside of reason and civilization. By the third movement, Pentheus's reason and civilization can provide no defense against the unleashed Dionysian powers of nature and instinct. Dionysus goes through a complementary cycle. He is first seen as the enigmatic prisoner of Pentheus. Later his natural and instinctual powers triumph over the fragile tissue of Pentheus's reason and civilization. The fourth movement ends with a vision of the mindless tyranny of nature triumphant. Although the trajectories of Pentheus and Dionysus move in opposite directions, they are nevertheless intimately related.

PENTHEUS: THE TRAGEDY OF REASON

In her appeal for Pentheus's life, Beroe tells Dionysus, "He is a good man" (42). Indeed, by familiar Western standards, past and present, Pentheus exhibits many admired qualities. In *The Bacchae*, Euripides portrays Pentheus as a staunch defender of his dynasty. In Auden and Kallman's libretto for *The Bassarids*, Pentheus's patriotism is overlaid and enhanced by a religious and intellectual Platonism. Pentheus is pious and morally upright. Like most late-twentieth-century conservatives, the legendary king of Thebes is an avowed enemy of all that is unpatriotic, impious, and sexually immoral.

Pentheus's religiosity embodies the Platonic reforms of ancient Greek polytheism. Cadmus and Tiresias worship many gods, but Pentheus is monotheistic. He is a pious worshiper of Zeus, the god of the heavens. Like Judeo-Christian monotheism, Pentheus's Platonic monotheism carries moral implications. Zeus is worthy of devotion not only because of his power and immortality but also because he is a paragon of moral righteousness. The righteousness of the god, in turn, sets the moral standard for his devotees. Pentheus is sexually continent and also abstemious with regard to the other pleasures of the flesh.

Pentheus's philosophy affects the central intellectual issue in the opera: Is Dionysus truly a god? As a Platonist, Pentheus seeks the truth according to the standards of reason.

In his search for the truth about Dionysus, Pentheus is a man of words. He is thoroughly logocentric. Truth resides in the right words; falsehood lies in the wrong words, the wrong kind of words, or, worst, no words at all. In the opera, Pentheus's first utterance—his ban on the new cult—is a carefully prepared written text. Pentheus's dialogues with the other characters are all searches for the truth, for true words about Dionysus. Rumors, opinions, lies, and ecstatic visions all fail Pentheus's logocentric standards for truth.

From the beginning of the opera, Pentheus is associated with daylight and the sun, the traditional visual imagery of Platonic reason. The citizens of Thebes sing their hymn acclaiming his accession to the throne in the brilliant, hard light of midday. With the help of the gods, Pentheus represents their hope for continued prosperity. Pentheus's Platonism is confirmed in his proclamation against the cult of Dionysus. The cult is condemned for its insult to Zeus and also for its irrational error and immorality. Pentheus is offended by the very notion that Dionysus, a god, could have been the offspring of an extramarital tryst between Zeus and Semele (the subject of *Semele*, Handel's 1744 opera). Such a notion contradicts his Platonic understanding of both divine goodness and the hierarchical orderliness of the universe. For Pentheus, this blasphemy may have infected the vast majority of the citizens of Thebes, but it can only be the invention of "idlers and babblers" (13).

As a good Platonist, Pentheus is contemptuous of popular opinion. In calculated defiance of the popularity of the new cult, he uses his cloak to extinguish the eternal flame at the nearby tomb of Semele. He proclaims the devotion to Semele to be a mere superstition, a product of "weak, ignorant women . . . [and] relic-mad credulous pilgrims" (14–15). Appeals to Pentheus for toleration or acceptance fare no better than the evidence of popular opinion. He refuses the advice of Cadmus and Beroe, and dismisses Agave's aria recounting the activities on Cytheron. He even rejects a supernatural interpretation of the evidence of his own senses. He denies the miraculous character of the earthquake that frees the imprisoned Dionysus and his followers: "My guards were bribed. / An earthquake is no miracle" (35).

Until his fatal bewitchment by Dionysus, Pentheus clings to reason. His interrogations of the captain, Agave, Cadmus, and the stranger-Dionysus are all intended to cut through what he believes to be a web of lies and misguided beliefs. In the second movement, when he confides in the faithful Beroe, his aria is laced with Platonic symbolism. The cult of Dionysus is the "worship [of] shadows / Of the True Good," and Dionysus himself

> Is but a name
> For the nameless Nothing
> That hates the light. (22)

If Pentheus has many of the Platonic attributes of the good Western man, he also has the accompanying liabilities. At both the psychological and political levels of analysis, Pentheus's Platonic reason displays its kinship with repression and hierarchy.

For Pentheus, reason is more than the epistemological foundation of truth. It is also an important mechanism in the political economy of the psyche. Psychologically, Pentheus uses his "higher" reason to repress the "lower" sensuous and passionate aspects of his character; indeed, his identity is predicated on this repression. His first appearance in the opera is delayed until the end of the first movement by an exercise in abstinence. Fasting and alone, he has spent a week in prayer and reflection, seeking the guidance of Zeus about the threat posed by the cult of Dionysus. Steeling himself for the coming struggle, Pentheus resolves to go beyond this limited period of abstinence and make sensual and sexual repression the governing principle of his life. He takes a vow against wine, the divine gift of Dionysus, and against the temptations of his lower appetites:

> Henceforth [I] will abstain
> From wine, from meats,
> And from woman's bed,
> Live sober and chaste
> Till the day I die! (23)

Pentheus may try to suppress his sensuality and sexuality, but he clings to his political authority. He understands the political order of his kingship, his dynasty, his morality, his religious convictions to be the equivalent of political order in general; in other words, without Pentheus as king, there are only chaos and anarchy. His proclamation against the cult of Dionysus begins with an imperial "we." The opera has many references to the name of Pentheus, almost invariably accompanied by his title as king. There is a sense, at once paranoid and prescient, that if Pentheus cannot be referred to according to the refrain "Pentheus the King," then there will be no Pentheus at all.

Politically, Pentheus's suppression of the cult of Dionysus represents his attempt to repress the sensuous and passionate character of the Theban population. Here Pentheus is a mistaken Platonist. Plato's own ideal Republic provided family life and private property as realms of satisfaction for the incorrigibly sensuous and passionate majority of the population. Pentheus, however, makes ineffectual attempts to impose the rigors of his austere rationality on the population as a whole.

Indeed, lacking controlled and limited modes of expression, Pentheus is ultimately unsuccessful in controlling his own instinctual nature. It breaks through his rational veneer in destructive and obsessive forms. Confronted by a movement advocating ideas that he does not understand, he lashes out in violence. Having repressed the broad range of his own sensuousness, he is obsessed with a narrow and prurient sexual curiosity.

In his search for the truth about Dionysus and his cult, Pentheus turns the Platonic dialogue as a mode of inquiry into brutal interrogation. His speech reveals his intensifying frustration at his inability to understand a cult that contradicts everything he holds dear. He commands answers to his questions, silences unwanted responses, and demands respect for his person and position. His authoritarian treatment of his family, subordinates, subjects, slaves, and foreigners includes hubris against a god. To the stranger-Dionysus he says, "Slave, bow to Pentheus, / Son of Echion, King of Thebes" (32). Enraged to a breaking point by the appearance and demeanor of the sexually ambiguous Dionysus, Pentheus, the would-be Platonic king, loses the last remnants of rationality. He raves like a frustrated street thug, threatening to "root out his [Dionysus's] perfumed hair" and to "break that smiling mouth" (34).

But Pentheus himself commits no violent acts. He leaves these to the captain and guards, those eminently flexible representatives of both the military and the police powers of the Theban state. By linking the use of the captain and guards to Pentheus's incomprehension, frustration, and rage, the opera strips all legitimacy from the exercise of state force. Despite Pentheus's rationalizations, the attempt to eradicate the cult of Dionysus by violence is not justified by reason. Rather, like the foreign and domestic crusades of some advanced Western governments in the fifties and sixties, the violence of the Theban state reflects the psychological pathologies of the political leadership.

Against the westward movement of the cult into Thebes, the captain and guards are an unrestrained but curiously ineffective military force. Pentheus orders the captain to wage a fierce counterinsurgency campaign: "Return with all you can find, / Kill all who resist" (21). Legendary precursors of twentieth-century anticolonial, anti-imperial guerrillas, the Bassarids seem to blend into the landscape around Cytheron. "Though [he] could hear more, many more," of the unarmed cultists lurking nearby, the captain returns with but a handful of captives (24).

Against the members of the cult in Thebes, Pentheus uses the captain and guards as a political police, ordering a counterintelligence operation against the captives and their sympathizers. Despite the fact that Semele and her son Dionysus are Theban, Pentheus views the new cult as an alien, inferior, but dangerous infection of the Theban state. This operation is revealing not only because of its violence but also because of the distinctions that Pentheus introduces into it. By police force and violence, Pentheus hopes to restore the traditional social and political order of Thebes.

With the unseen but increasingly threatening chorus of the Bassarids singing in the background, Pentheus directs the operation against the new cult. He exhibits the typical political and social chauvinism of classical Greece. Noncitizen Bassarids, both foreigners and Theban slaves, are aliens who threaten the established order. They have no legal protections. They are imprisoned, questioned, and tortured without restraint. (One Bassarid dies during the interrogation, causing the captain to wonder at the physical courage of these ostensible inferiors, at their willingness to endure pain without betraying their cause.) Pentheus also punishes Theban citizens who are soft on Dionysianism. He orders the destruction of Tiresias's house because of his adherence to the new cult. Protected by royal blood from harsher treatment, Pentheus's mother and aunt are locked in their house. By this act Pentheus tries to reinforce traditional Greek patriarchy. Until this Dionysian disturbance, even royal Greek women were largely confined to household domesticity.

Pentheus's attempt to imprison Dionysus, the "oriental conjurer" (16), is both ineffective and unwise. During the earthquake, Dionysus and his followers simply walk out of the prison. But with or without an earthquake, the attempt to imprison Dionysus is a crucial mistake. It represents Pentheus's futile rejection of aspects of his own nature. According to the legend, Pentheus is the son of Echion, a man who grew out of the earth. Yet in his rational and spiritual conception of his own nature, Pentheus, the Platonist and the devotee of celestial Zeus, is denying the earthy, passionate, and sensuous aspects of his character. Pentheus denies the divinity of the Dionysus who stands before him, just as he denies the Dionysus who lives within his psyche. Pentheus attempts to imprison the captured Dionysus, just as he attempts to imprison the Dionysus who lives within him.

If Pentheus's use of force and violence betrays his self-conception as a rational king, so too does his irrepressible sexuality. Even before the capture of Dionysus, he exhibits a compulsive curiosity about the real and imagined sexual behavior of others. Pentheus does not conceive of sexuality as an essential part of human life. Having relegated his own sexuality to the status of a sinful passion, he understands others' sexual activities as lewd and lascivious violations of proper human behavior. Falling under the spell of Dionysus, Pentheus finds that at first his sexual curiosity is heightened. Later, when the spell intensifies, Pentheus's full sexuality is released, revealing a propensity for some of the more exotic sexual predilections.

According to the reports filtering back to Thebes, the actual cult activities on Cytheron are rather tame: some nature rites, music, lots of dancing. But Pentheus cannot help but interpret the reports in terms of his own sexual obsessions. For him, any nocturnal gathering of a large number of women released from their normal social duties and constraints suggests rampant "whoring" (26). In the intermezzo, Pentheus is under the hypnotic spell of Dionysus. Accompanied by the ominous, mocking laughter of the Bassarids, Dionysus uses a magic mirror to give Pentheus a glimpse of the rites on Cytheron. All Pentheus can see are transgressions of the conventional moral order and gender roles: the sexual aggression of two tipsy women, Agave and Autonoe, who attempt to seduce the captain. In contrast to the more continuous, symphonic construction of the main part of the opera's score, the intermezzo's division into set pieces and use of old-fashioned instruments (mandolins) emphasize the still traditional and constrained character of Pentheus's vision. The bemused Dionysus remarks, "They saw what they would see" (40).

Throughout the opera, Pentheus is depicted as a model of heterosexual masculinity. Before Agave's conversion to the new cult, she praises the masculine strength of Pentheus's opposition to Dionysus. Later, when Pentheus prepares for his surreptitious trip to Cytheron, Dionysus tells him that, as a disguise, only a woman's dress will do, for "in man's [garb] they know you" (41). Pentheus is confident of his strength in any forthcoming battle against the maenads, the most crazed of Dionysus's female followers. Pentheus's quintessential masculinity not only prescribes the struggle against the predominantly female Bassarids but is also manifested in his hostility to the sexual ambivalence and ambiguity of Tiresias and Dionysus. But the intensification of Dionysus's spell over Pentheus triggers the release of Pentheus's repressed sexuality, and the event reveals some surprises. Beneath Pentheus's apparently unassailable masculinity and heterosexuality lay several repressed dimensions: homosexuality or bisexuality (he notices the beauty of Dionysus); transvestism (after his initial hesitation, he delights in his feminine attire and ability to dance like his mother); and exhibitionism (he wants all of Thebes to see him in his new dress).

Throughout his defense of *the* true religion of Zeus and *the* true order of Thebes, Pentheus rejects the possibility that there may instead be multiple truths. As he departs on his fatal journey to Cytheron, Pentheus experiences a brief moment of symbolic revelation. As the opera progresses, the musical themes associated with Dionysus gradually overwhelm the musical themes associated with Pentheus. Now the contest is over. Singing the music of Dionysus, Pentheus sees "two suns": two truths rather than one. He sees "two Thebes": the Thebes of Pentheus and the Thebes of Dionysus (44). And he finally intuits the identity of the beautiful stranger: he sees the stranger as a bull, one of the animal forms of divine Dionysus.

Pentheus's moment of recognition comes too late. The inexorable power of Dionysus unravels Pentheus's logocentric universe of reasonable truth. At Cytheron, the hidden Pentheus finally sees the rites firsthand, but his reason and his words fail him. Trying to achieve his investigative purpose, yet transfixed by Dionysus, Pentheus, the once proud master of true words, babbles incoherently:

> Waiting. For what? Go to it! Go!
> Your shadow watches, waits, knows and sees . . .
> Nothing, nothing, lights, warm
> Nothingness. King and God are not needed:
> Shall we descend to comfort oblivion?
> O dance, dance the due praise.
> And waiting? Loveliness. Nothing?
> Pentheus, is Agave near and peace made? (47)

Alas, Agave is very near. When Pentheus is captured by crazed maenads led by Agave, who is hallucinating, he makes a desperate effort to save his life. He vainly tries to bring Agave to her senses by reminding her of their respective identities, by using the words that truly describe their beings in a logocentric world. His entreaties are met by monosyllabic "No's," then by the maenads' nonverbal cry, "Ayayalya." The *sparagmos*, or ritual dismemberment, begins. As the maenads begin to tear him apart with their bare hands, Pentheus utters a final scream, and the words, the reign, the reason, and the life of Pentheus are plunged into darkness.

DIONYSUS: THE TRIUMPH OF INSTINCT

The outcome of the conflict between Pentheus and Dionysus is never in doubt. However powerful, however much in command of captains and guards, no mere king can defeat a god. And Pentheus takes on not just any god. Within a contemporary opera seria, a *Musiktragödie*,[21] Pentheus challenges the deity who is both the god of music as passionate expression and the patron god of the Dionysia, the ancient festival observances held in Athens and the origin of Western drama. The music and action of the opening scene foretell the outcome. The hymn of the citizens of Thebes is a ceremonial acclamation of Pentheus's accession to the throne. With just an "Ayayalya" sung by the unseen Dionysus, erstwhile orderly and loyal Thebans dance off to Cytheron to become Bassarids. Later in the first movement, the sound of a distant guitar—the lyre of sixties' countercultural Dionysians—overcomes the hostility of Agave and Autonoe to the young god and sends them off dancing to Cytheron as well.

The dramatic tension in the opera lies in the unfolding of the character of Dionysus. Throughout, Dionysus is the antithesis of Pentheus, but the meaning of this antithesis changes with the shifting relations of power. In the early movements, when the enigmatic character of Dionysus is defined by his opposition to the rule of Pentheus, the god is benign: a victim of Pentheus's repression-induced persecution, the hope for a sensuous alternative. Here the character of Dionysus is an "irrefutable indictment" of the repressiveness of Western civilization. In the later movements, when the more developed character of Dionysus has displaced Pentheus as the ruler of Thebes, the sinister aspects of the god are apparent. The horrors of the reign of Dionysus now become the most "unshakable defense" of Western civilization.[22]

From the outset, Dionysus represents the antithesis of Pentheus's intellectual Platonism, the alternative to all that Platonism denounces and ignores. If Pentheus is associated with daylight and the sun, Dionysus—like the *Zauberflöte* queen, Don Giovanni, and Tristan and Isolde—is an operatic creature of the night. If Pentheus seeks the truth through prolonged rational reflection, the truth of Dionysus is immediately intuited through the senses. If Pentheus is a logocentric man of words, the verbally reticent Dionysus is associated with musical themes and instruments, a nonverbal religious exclamation, laughter, even humming.

The starkest contrasts between Pentheus and Dionysus are seen in their differing relations to nature, understood as both the inner force guiding human beings and the external world in its entirety. Pentheus is indelibly associated with Thebes, the capital city of his kingdom, a symbol of urbanity and civilization. In order for Pentheus to travel to the environs of Cytheron, a rural region of his own kingdom, he must go through an elaborate preparation. At Cytheron, he is an alien intruder. Dionysus even calls him a trespasser (49).

Dionysus, however, is at home in nature. Consonant with the renewed nature romanticism of the sixties' counterculture, his song extols the delights of life in the "pleasant hermitage" of the country (18). All kinds of people flock to Cytheron, the Woodstock of the ancient world, to enjoy wine, music, dancing, and perhaps sex amid the beauties of nature. Pentheus does not engage in economic or military depredations of nature; the opera contains no analogues to polluting factories, napalm, Agent Orange, or saturation bombing. Still, Dionysus accuses Pentheus of being the enemy of nature, because the king tries to obstruct those who seek communion with external nature (18).

Pentheus's morality and piety are predicated on the repression of his instinctual nature. As a divine patron of instinct, Dionysus is indifferent to Pentheus's morality and religiosity, and hostile to the repression that sustains them. When Pentheus, ever curious, questions Dionysus about his sexual chastity, Dionysus is evasive: "I? I am I" (37). Posed in the repressive moral language of chastity, this approach to the sexuality of Dionysus is completely irrelevant. When Beroe lauds Pentheus's goodness in her plea for his life, Dionysus is unconcerned: "What is his goodness to me? / I have no need of his worship" (43). In his rejection of Pentheus's morality and religiosity, Dionysus is not beyond good and evil in the Nietzschean sense. He is not a being who has seen through the fiction of existing morality and now sets his own moral standards. Rather, the whole issue of morality is immaterial to him. As a divinity associated with nature and instinct, Dionysus is beneath good and evil. He is a primal force interested only in securing obedience to his divine commands—the satisfaction of the urges of the instincts.

As an instinctual force, Dionysus disdains the familiar designations of civilized life. Socially and politically, the Thebes of Pentheus is constituted by a series of hierarchical statuses: foreigner and citizen, slave and free, woman and man, commoner and aristocrat. But none of these matters to the god of instinct. In the ancient world, the popularity of Dionysus lay in his antiaristocratic disregard for the traditional social and political hierarchies.[23] Likewise, in the opera, the voice of Dionysus makes no distinctions. All human beings, from the lowest to the highest, feel the urges of the instincts. All human beings are invited to join the "glad unanimity" of the Bassarids (18). What matters to Dionysus is not their status but their compliance with his commands.

Dionysus's indifference to hierarchies goes beyond society and politics. He also disrupts nothing less than the ontological order of the universe. As the son of a god and a mortal woman, he is the offspring of different levels of being. Unlike Dionysus, Pentheus fears a cult that will bring new disorders among the species, a cult wherein "men are beasts and beasts are men" (22). Indeed, the

Bassarids sing of their new Dionysian mixtures between human, animate, and vegetative beings:

> Day. Hide. Robed in the bark of pine,
> Wait. Wear mien of the beast. Be still.
> And with night we shall rouse with you.
> Dionysus, the new moon. (23)

There are hints that the Dionysian mixture of types of beings has perilous aspects, but these are not fully apparent until Dionysus overthrows the power of Pentheus. Early in the first movement, the seer Tiresias observes that "Dionysus kills and renews," but the reference to killing is vague (6). At this point in the opera, Dionysus is remote and obscure, and his cult is innocent and playful. Later, just before he begins his enchantment of the king, Dionysus sings an ominous aria, part of which recounts the fate of sailors who tried to kidnap him—an earlier set of opponents. The aria anticipates the conclusion of the opera:

> Vines clambered up the mast
> And roped the oars.
> A leopard pawed the deck.
> The maddened crew leapt to the sea,
> Dolphins, not men.
> The God was everywhere. (33)

Failing to comprehend the implied warning, Pentheus responds to the aria with a diatribe against Dionysus. But even the Bassarids know that Tiresias was right: following Dionysus means death as well as wine, dancing, and song. They sing of a different aspect of Dionysian nature, of "the smooth / Maggot hatch hungry, who waits us" (47).

The dismemberment of Pentheus is only the beginning of the revenge of Dionysus. Having deposed Pentheus, Dionysus reveals the intolerance and authoritarianism of the instincts. Pentheus banned the cult of Dionysus, and now Dionysus bans the opponents of his cult. The surviving members of the house of Cadmus are exiled from Thebes. The rational authoritarianism of Pentheus culminated in hubris against a god, and now the instinctual authoritarianism of Dionysus demands abject worship: "Down slaves, / Kneel and adore" (61).

Awakened from her murderous trance, only Agave has the courage to condemn the dangers of Dionysus: "The strong Gods are not good" (59). As she leaves Thebes to begin her exile, she predicts that Dionysus, like Uranus and Chronos before him, will one day meet an unhappy fate. But there is nothing in *The Bassarids* to suggest that fate. (The downfall of Dionysus would have to occur in a very different opera from a very different decade.) Instead, this opera ends with the apotheosis of Dionysus. Calling to mind Orfeo and Christian images of the Ascension and the Assumption, Dionysus and Semele-Thyone rise into heaven.

THE AMBIVALENCE OF DIONYSUS

The instinct-reason conflict clearly ties *The Bassarids* to an old operatic theme, one traceable from *La favola d'Orfeo* through *Don Giovanni* and *Tristan und Isolde* to *Lady Macbeth of Mtsensk*. But what is most distinctive about Henze's opera, and what links it most firmly to its sixties' countercultural context, are the ways in which it departs from its operatic predecessors. The relative prosperity of advanced industrial societies gave rise to a demand for reducing instinctual repression, for creating a new, erotic, and hedonistic ethos of instinctual gratification and happiness. In the earlier operas, Dionysianism was individualistic and suppressed. In the 1960s opera *The Bassarids*, Dionysianism is collective and victorious.

As it was in the sixties' counterculture, in *The Bassarids* the advocacy of Dionysianism is collective rather than individual. The conflict between instinct and reason may be epitomized by the struggle between two individual characters in the opera, but it has a profound impact on society as a whole. Would operatic Thebes follow Pentheus or Dionysus? Would it repress or indulge the instinctual desire for happiness? Indeed, the instinct-reason controversy has already begun before the belated appearances of Pentheus at the end of the first movement and Dionysus in the second movement. In this collective conception of the theme, *The Bassarids* does not merely repeat the familiar operatic contest between the nonconformist morality of an instinctual individual or individuals and a repressive society. Instead, in the manner of the sixties, *The Bassarids* offers sensuousness and sexuality as a universal vision of how life might be enhanced, might be happier, for everyone. In the history of opera, perhaps only the golden calf scene in Schoenberg's *Moses und Aron* anticipates the collective Dionysianism of *The Bassarids*.

And not only is the Dionysianism of *The Bassarids* collective. It is also triumphant. In earlier operas, the champions of the instincts—from Don Giovanni through Katerina Ismailova—were also the martyred saints of the Dionysian cause. Political reason demanded that these characters either join Orpheus in renouncing the error of their instinctual ways or die. In these works, opera was cathartic: it recalled the repressed life of the instincts, only to repress it again.[24] But *The Bassarids* is a product of the sixties, where prosperity raised the possibility of a qualitatively new standard of life. Unlike the instinct-reason operas of earlier eras, *The Bassarids* does not portray the defeat of Dionysus. Pentheus, the defender of repression, is killed because of his moral beliefs. But Dionysus, the defender of the pleasures of the senses, experiences apotheosis.

The Bassarids envisions both the promise and the horror of a victorious Dionysianism. The counterculture's vision of a more sensuous life available to all may have altered human behavior and relations in many ways, but it did not succeed in becoming the new standard for social life. But in Henze's opera, which was realized at the time of the counterculture's most utopian expectations,[25] we find an image of what an instinctually liberated form of life might be like for both individuals and society as a whole.

The New Left condemned the nationalism, racism, and sexism of advanced industrial societies. These politically invidious distinctions among nations, races, and genders perpetuated need-less social and political conflicts and thereby obstructed the possible emergence of a qualitatively new and liberated form of human life. Like the countercultural protesters, the Dionysus of *The Bassarids* assaults the traditional political and social distinctions of Thebes. Pentheus is killed, and the surviving members of the house of Cadmus are exiled. Having stripped the state of its apparent necessity and inevitability, Dionysus disrupts the entire status hierarchy of Thebes. Ancient and seemingly permanent status distinctions are dissolved, or at least reduced to political insignificance. And by the opera's end, neither instinctual renunciation nor the martyrdom of the sensuous have come to the rescue of the old political and social order. All people are united in their new, egalitarian identity. All are devotees of Dionysus.

In place of the austere, rational, and hierarchical order of Pentheus, Dionysus brings the emancipation of sensuousness and sexuality: the alternative consciousness of wine and intoxication, the pleasures of music and dancing, the celebration of both carnal gratification and external nature. To be sure, the opera also portrays the horrors of an untrammeled Dionysianism. But in opposition to an anti-instinctual status quo, the erotic hedonism of Dionysus—like the erotic hedonism of the sixties' countercul-ture—retains its indisputable moment of truth. It reveals the repressive, self-denying character of every moral, religious, political, or economic ideology of suffering and sacrifice.[26]

The Bassarids projects the countercultural ideals of the sixties onto the operatic stage. It also projects the disaster that would result if these ideals were realized in an extreme form. The closing scene—with Thebes in flames, the populace prostrate before the idols of Dionysus and Semele-Thyone—depicts the tragic consequences of the new order. The reign of Pentheus represented the dictatorship of civilization over nature, of repressive reason over the instincts. Having eliminated all restraining forces, the subsequent reign of Dionysus represents the dictatorship of nature over civilization, of the instincts over reason. In *The Bassarids*, the citizens of Thebes got what some sixties' radicals thought that they wanted: a society ruled by erotic instincts. In the opera, the results of this rule are not very encouraging.

With the removal of the Theban political and social hierarchy, Dionysus creates a new egalitarianism. Yet the closing scene portrays this egalitarianism as far from the democratic ideal of an equal and sovereign citizenry. Rather, the former citizens of Thebes are now passive, submissive, and anonymous followers of Dionysus. In their visual conception of the closing scene, composer and librettists wanted to suggest the egalitarian passivity, submissiveness, and anonymity of a population subjected to fascist or Nazi rule. But another interpretation is possible, one that is more consistent with the central theme of the opera. In this interpretation, the equality of Dionysus's cult is the equality of a population dominated by its need for instinctual gratification and dependent on those institutions or individuals who provide the means for that gratification.

In the new Dionysian order, all wear the same leopard skin, carry the same thrysus staff, sing the same song, dance the same dance, drink the same wine—and all are the slaves of the same god who provides for their pleasure and happiness. Pentheus's tyranny of reason over the instincts is replaced by Dionysus's tyranny of the instincts: the constant and insatiable need for gratification. The rational, civilized Thebes of Pentheus was repressive, violent, and hierarchical. But unlike the renaturalized cult of Dionysus, it also provided the political preconditions for the development of individual distinctiveness and a degree of personal autonomy.

Dionysus's assault on hierarchy is not confined to politics and society. Like the countercultural ideals of the sixties, the triumph of Dionysus also entails a leveling of the components of the human psyche and a transvaluation of the place of human life within nature. The lower instincts are freed from the censorious tyranny of higher reason. Human beings become once again primarily instinctual beings—that is, beings whose character and behavior are determined by their biological nature rather than by the artifices of reason and civilization. This view emphasizes the kinship between human beings and lower forms of natural life; the older hierarchical conception had emphasized the gulf that separates them.

Motivated by desire and reunited with the other forms of biological life, the followers of Dionysus are no longer protected by reason and civilization against the primal forces of nature. The opera reminds us that nature is not all sublime vistas and fuzzy bunnies. The dismemberment of Pentheus recalls the brutality of death in nature. In portraying the populace entangled in vines, the closing scene captures the vulnerability of renaturalized human beings to lower life forms even as it foreshadows the post-Dionysian hangover of the 1970s and 1980s. Wine—the gift of Dionysus, the fruit of the vine—once freed the Thebans from the tyranny of reason. But with the removal of repressive reason, they are now dependent upon, even addicted to, this product of vegetative nature. If *The Bassarids* were reset to the seventies or eighties or later, directors of the closing scene would not be limited to vines as a symbolic prop. They would be able to choose from an array of vegetative or viral masters from lower nature.

Postscript

When I get up in the morning, my daily prayer is, grant me today my illusion, my daily illusion.

—ERNST BLOCH

 N at least one important respect, the *fin de millénium* Right and Left are in complete agreement. With the defeat of the New Left, the self-immolation of the counterculture, and the collapse of communism, the historical trajectory of modern Western politics and culture seems to come to an impasse. From aristocratic absolutism through bourgeois republicanism and Marxist socialism to the New Left and the counterculture, there had been a sense of history as progress: the present age appeared better than the past, and the future held the possibility of boundless improvement.

But conservatives now proclaim the end of history, that is, the permanence of the existing liberal capitalist order. As Francis Fukuyama has articulated this new vision: "In terms of ideology and big institutions we can't really improve in a fundamental way. We are all going to be liberal democracies and part of the global capitalist order in some sense. You can make things worse but you can't make people's lives substantially better by changing those basic institutions."[1] Secure in politics and the economy, only academia and the arts are stubbornly, almost treasonably, recalcitrant. From the perspective of conservative culture warriors, the "post's" and their confederates in political and cultural theory—poststructuralism, postmodernism, postcolonialism, deconstruction, multiculturalism, feminism—deny the West the triumphal laurels of culture.

Against the traditional views of Western culture, the ostensible heirs of the Left mount an unrelenting relativism: there are no universal claims to truth or beauty. The very notion that Western history either progresses or comes to an end is nothing more than a metanarrative, a fictitious discourse that has been imposed upon historical phenomena by self-interested and self-deluded cultural chauvinists. As an element of New Left and countercultural criticism, Henze's *Bassarids* helped to lay the foundation for the new relativism's assault on Western reason, violence, domination, racism, sexism, and heterosexism.

But this relativism is also turned against the New Left and the counterculture. Like *The Bassarids* and its vision of the transition from the reign of Pentheus to the reign of Dionysus, the New Left's attempt to restructure and redirect the achievements of Western civilization was just the latest version of the metanarrative of abrupt and total transformation, another misguided venture in the "properly masculine business" of revolution.[2] According to Michel Foucault, a leading figure in the new theoretical tendencies, "There is no single locus of great Refusal, no soul of revolt, source of all rebelliousness, or pure law of the revolutionary." Without the grand but illusory politics of revolution, progressives are chastened. They should focus on the microlevel "points of resistance [that] are present everywhere in the power network."[3] These narrowly based political movements remain dedicated to political reform. But because they lack both a unifying symbol (like the war in Vietnam) and a new unifying ideology, the former components of the New Left are fragmented into an identity politics, wherein the separate interests of gender, race, ethnicity, and sexual orientation are pursued without any transcendent sense of historical development. Within the new relativism, the counterculture fares no better than the New Left. The countercultural attempt to reduce or eliminate psychological and sexual repression is now viewed as just another manifestation of Western culture's inherently dominating discourse of sexuality.[4]

In the realm of opera, the new postmodern relativism coincides with a period of crisis. According to an issue of *Daedalus* devoted to the future of opera, in the late twentieth century opera has a dual character. In terms of audience attendance, number of companies and performances, and dissemination through recordings, television, videos, and films, opera has never been healthier. Given the great expense of staging an opera, production costs are a historical and persistent problem, but this is not the core of the crisis. The crisis, rather, lies in the repertory. Out of the four-hundred-year history of opera, the standard performing repertory confines itself to works from the nineteenth century and early twentieth century. Within this ossified repertory, it is almost impossible for new works to gain a firm foothold.[5]

Stage directors are the self-appointed saviors of the late-twentieth-century repertory crisis. Critics who view opera as a strictly musical art form decry the directors' search for new "intellectual motivations" in the standard works as "directional arrogance" and a distraction to an audience eagerly waiting "to hear whether the soprano and tenor are able to cope with their high notes."[6] But these sometimes capricious interpretations can be seen in a better light: as the efforts of stage directors who are trying to restore a political edge to works that have become too familiar, comfortable, and noncontroversial through innumerable traditional stagings. For the most part respectful of the composer's score but eminently flexible with stage direction, setting, and text, postmodern directors often recover a sense of political meaning by transferring the action out of its intended historical era.

With regard to new operas, several American works have drawn critical attention. Anthony Davis's *X: The Death of Malcom X* (1985) and Stewart Wallace's *Harvey Milk* (1995) are operatic manifestations of the new postmodern identity politics of race and sexual orientation. Stage directors are a driving force behind a number of other postmodern operas. Using the avant-garde techniques of spoken theater, these operas exhibit many of the tendencies of postmodern art: a turning away from the Eurocentric art tradition; a mixing of art genres; a blurring of the distinctions between high art and popular culture and between history and fiction. Director Robert Wilson is the co-creator of *Einstein on the Beach* (1976), the first part of composer Philip Glass's trilogy that also includes *Satyagraha* (1980) and *Akhnaten* (1983); later they collaborated on *the CIVIL warS* (1984). Peter Sellars conceived John Adams's *Nixon in China* (1987) and *The Death of Klinghoffer* (1991). Colin Graham directed the acclaimed Metropolitan Opera world premiere of John Corigliano's *Ghosts of Versailles* (1991).

The sources for postmodern operas are familiar: history, contemporary affairs, and literature. Despite the postmodern reputation for playfulness, the dramatic values of these operas are intense, and the political issues that they pose are serious. Yet, with the possible exception of *Satyagraha*, these operas are separated from their political predecessors by their disconnection from a sense of historical direction and purpose. To adapt Wagner's famous remark about Meyerbeer, operatic postmodernism represents political effect without cause.

Along with Terry Riley and Steve Reich, Philip Glass (b. 1937) is one of the developers of postmodern musical minimalism. In Glass's case, the audience's revulsion toward Western musical modernism led him to seek a more popular and accessible model of "escape" in the musics of the East.[7] Avoiding the offending dissonances of modernism, the repetitive rhythmic patterns of Glass's orchestral scores confine themselves to the role of monotonous and inoffensive vocal background. Set to minimalist scores, Glass's trilogy presents musical and dramatic "portraits of powerful personalities": Einstein as a man of science, Akhnaten as a man of religion, and Gandhi as a man of politics.[8]

In *Einstein on the Beach*, Wilson and Glass make only glancing allusions to Einstein's great intellectual achievement, the theory of relativity, or to its implications for atomic energy and Einstein's troubled attitude toward nuclear weapons. Instead, through a steady accretion of Einstein trivia, they construct a plotless, visually striking, and ultimately pointless mélange of pop icons, genres, and counter-rationality. Wilson and Glass's Einstein is a 1940s pop superstar.[9] As if imitating the famous photograph of Einstein, all the characters in the opera emulate the physicist's attire—sneakers, white shirt, baggy pants, and suspenders. A female performer carries an Einsteinian pipe. Each element of Einstein's apparel is as iconographic as Davy Crockett's coonskin cap, Pat Boone's white bucks, or Elvis Presley's pompadour, and throughout the opera, the most enduring image of the title character refers to his avocation: Einstein as violinist. This media Einstein of baggy pants, pipes, and violins is reinforced by references to media figures from the 1960s and 1970s: the Beatles, Frankie Valli and the Four Seasons, Mr. Bojangles, Patty Hearst, David Cassidy, and Carole King. At a number of points, soloists or the chorus sing solfège and meaningless random numbers, with no discernible loss of intelligibility.

Set to a libretto by Glass and three associates, *Akhnaten* is a more conventional work than *Einstein*. It is not drowned in trivia about the title character, and it pays some attention to the ideas of a peculiar-looking pharaoh whose introduction of monotheism in Egypt may have provided the model for later Judeo-Christian monotheism. The opera also retains a conventional narrative structure as its three acts follow the rise, reign, and fall of the controversial and ultimately unpopular ruler. In spite of Glass's expression of unconcern about the "historical validity" of the work,[10] a semblance of historical authenticity is created by the libretto's heavy reliance on ancient texts. Still, in at least two respects, the opera bears the marks of the postmodern sensibility. An epitome of linguistic multiculturalism, the text is sung in Egyptian, Akkadian, Hebrew, and the vernacular of the audience. And the opera playfully juxtaposes ancient texts with the late-twentieth-century quotidian in the form of excerpts from Fodor's and Frommer's tourist guides to Egypt. Lacking the contemporary parallels of Schoenberg's *Moses*, Glass's operatic essay on the foundations of monotheism is strictly anecdotal.

Multicultural, postcolonial, anti-Eurocentric, and a blend of myth and history, *Satyagraha* is the most quintessentially postmodern work in Glass's trilogy, and it is also the only one that approaches political significance. Sung to Sanskrit texts that Constance DeLong selected from the Bhagavad Gita, the opera depicts six episodes in the young Mohandas Gandhi's nonviolent struggle against South African racism. The important role of the chorus gives the opera an epical quality. In the first act, the opposed armies described in the Bhagavad Gita are revealed to be the antagonistic Europeans and Indians of early-twentieth-century South Africa. In the third act, Gandhi's protesting Indians are reincarnated as sixties' civil rights activists. The nonsinging historical witness in each of the three acts—Leo Tolstoy, Indian poet Rabindranath Tagore, and Martin Luther King, Jr.—represent the past, present, and future of Gandhi's communal pacifism and civil disobedience. There can be no question that the problem of racism and the tactic of civil disobedience represent important aspects of twentieth-century politics, yet I have a gnawing reservation about the politics of this work. Condemning, in a late-twentieth-century opera, the racism of early- and mid-twentieth-century South Africa and the American South resembles that "safe fearlessness" that James Agee observed in Hollywood films about racism.[11] *Satyagraha* takes a courageous stand against an already discredited foe.

With the operas of John Adams (b. 1947), we move from twentieth-century history to current events. There are precedents for *Nixon* and *Klinghoffer*. The long-forgotten operas of the French Revolution portrayed current events, and the *Zeitoper* of Weimar Germany delighted in placing the accoutrements of contemporary life on the operatic stage. Like Glass's trilogy, Adams's operas are set to minimalist scores. Alice Goodman provided the librettos for both works.

Nixon revolves around five well-known scenes from the American president's trip to China in 1972. Sellars's realization of the landing of Nixon's plane, *Spirit of '76*, and the president's dramatic emergence from the aircraft is a coup de théâtre. The opera also depicts Nixon's meeting with Mao Tse-Tung, a state banquet, Pat Nixon's tour of a factory and a communal farm, and the Nixons' attendance at—and surprising participation in—a performance of *The Red Detachment of Women*. The opera closes with a fictional tableau showing the leading characters in their beds on the last night of the visit. Throughout the opera, the diplomatic and ideological significance of the event is acknowledged, but it is subordinated to Glass-like portraits of the characters' personalities. The tone is set in the first scene, when the excited president's conception of making history turns out to be little more than making news, providing photo opportunities, and gaining airtime with major television networks. In the meeting between Nixon and Mao, the chairman is more a poet of revolution than an ideologue. He declares his preference for "right wingers" like Nixon, who responds by expressing his solidarity with the downtrodden: "Like you I take my stand / Among poor people. We can talk."[12] In this postideological conception, Henry Kissinger provides a foil for the generally sympathetic figures of the other characters. A would-be Machiavelli, the skulking, womanizing, and besotted Kissinger is out of his depth in his conversations with Mao and Chou En-lai.

The subject of *Klinghoffer* is the 1985 Palestinian hijacking of the Italian cruise liner *Achille Lauro* and the killing of Leon Klinghoffer, a wheelchair-bound Jewish American passenger. Unlike *Nixon*, *Klinghoffer* does not depict the particulars of the event. It does not represent the takeover of the ship, the shooting of Klinghoffer, or the disposal of his body in the sea. Rather, the opera concentrates on the individual and choral reflections on the incident. *Klinghoffer* poses deep political questions: the biblical, historical, and contemporary claims of Arabs and Jews to the Palestinian-Israeli homeland; the legitimacy of terrorist tactics by the politically weak against the politically strong. Yet, in what is

an exercise of either truly Olympian detachment or political eva-
siveness, the opera takes no stand on these issues. In the prologue,
the chorus of exiled Palestinians and the chorus of exiled Jews are
of exactly equal duration. Each of the four Palestinians is a finely
etched, individually motivated character rather than the stock
Middle Eastern terrorist portrayed in the mass media, yet these
same Palestinians kill an innocent and helpless man. The
ship's captain commiserates with the Palestinians, then consoles
Klinghoffer's widow. The composite character of the Swiss grand-
mother–Austrian woman–British dancing girl reveals the banal
and uncomprehending responses of outsiders to the Palestinian-
Israeli conflict. In apparent deference to postmodern identity
politics, the opera seems to maintain that one must have an
existential connection to the conflict in order to understand it.

From its mixed genre designation as "grand opera buffa"[13]
through its ambiguous politics, The Ghosts of Versailles, by John
Corigliano (b. 1938), is a masterpiece of postmodern pastiche.
Corigliano's score achieves popular accessibility not through the
minimalism of Glass and Adams but through a resurrection of
classical and romantic style within the musical set pieces of pre-
Wagnerian opera. Co-creator William M. Hoffman's libretto is
based on Beaumarchais's third Figaro play, La Mère coupable, but
surrounds the familiar dramatic and operatic characters with a
figure drawn from literary history (Beaumarchais himself) and
personages from political history (Louis XVI, Marie Antoinette,
and other aristocratic denizens of Versailles, plus the Revolution-
ary-era populace of Paris). Colin Graham's star-studded Met production displayed enough stage magic to delight a baroque monarch—or a late-twentieth-century audience long accustomed to
Hollywood special effects.

In Ghosts, the core of Beaumarchais's play—the plight of the
countess's illegitimate son, Léon, and the count's illegitimate
daughter, Florestine—is intertwined with a story about the play-
wright's love for the ghost of Marie Antoinette. In an unsurpassed
display of the postmodern belief in history as discourse and narra-

tive, Beaumarchais vows to save his beloved from her fate by rewriting history, by constructing a new "history as it should have been."[14] In sections set from the actual court records, Marie Antoinette is once again tried, convicted, sentenced, and imprisoned. But this time Beaumarchais, aided by his own fictional creation, the wily Figaro, plots the escape of the queen.

With *Ghosts*, liberal capitalism repudiates a seminal event in its own political history. In a tradition that is as old as Edmund Burke and as new as the bicentennial critics of the French Revolution, the opera ignores the reactionary, exploitative, and obstructive character of the old regime in favor of a story about the needless cruelty inflicted on the royal family and aristocracy. Within the history of opera, *Ghosts* is the anti-*Fidelio* rescue opera. Instead of confining political fighters for justice, this opera's prison holds a queen and her court attendants. Instead of rehearsing the optimistic symbols and slogans of 1789, *Ghosts* is replete with the anti-Revolutionary symbols of the Terror: the tumbrel, the guillotine, severed heads mounted on poles, and "Liberty, Equality, Fraternity" as a graffito ominously scrawled on the wall of the Revolutionary tribunal when the judges (depicted as death's-heads) pronounce sentence on the helpless Marie Antoinette. Instead of an enlightened people proclaiming the virtue of *Fidelio*'s Leonore, the bloodthirsty Revolutionary mob of *Ghosts* cries for Marie Antoinette's head: "Join us, we'll butcher the bitch!" To be sure, the opera makes no case for restoring the monarchy. Louis XVI and the other Versailles ghosts are jaded and supercilious, and even the fanciful Marie Antoinette ultimately turns down Beaumarchais's offer to rewrite her fate. Late in the opera, Beaumarchais rhapsodizes about the future, when the monarchs live on and somehow "poverty is abolished" and "education is free," but the opera provides no indication about the nature of this alternative to reactionary monarchy and bourgeois revolution.

The political impasse of postmodern opera is hardly unique. In political and cultural theory, progressive thinkers retain the

desire to be critical, effectual, and radical. But because many of
them lack a unifying and transcendent historical vision, many of
their theories are little more than "rhetoric and posturing."[15]
From nuclear weapons, religious reform, and racism through ideological conflict, terrorism, and revolution, postmodern operas
pose many of the crucial issues of the age without taking a stand
on any of them. Unable to conceive an alternative to a self-perpetuating liberal capitalist status quo, progressive artists lose themselves in "intellectual meanderings."[16] Victims of closed political
horizons, postmodern operas commemorate more than the defeat
of a particular movement or movements. These works are re-
quiems for the lost political hopes of modern Western culture.

Notes

PREFACE

1. Some of the works reflecting the new political perspective on music and opera are Christopher Ballantine, *Music and Its Social Messages* (New York: Gordon and Breach, 1984); Catherine Clément, *Opera; or, The Undoing of Women*, trans. Betsy Wing (Minneapolis: University of Minnesota Press, 1988); Joseph Kerman, *Contemplating Music: Challenges to Musicology* (Cambridge: Harvard University Press, 1985); Richard Leppert and Susan McClary, eds., *Music and Society: The Politics of Composition, Performance, and Reception* (Cambridge: Cambridge University Press, 1987); Susan McClary, *Feminine Endings: Music, Gender, and Sexuality* (Minneapolis: University of Minnesota Press, 1991); Richard Norton, *Tonality in Western Culture: A Critical and Historical Perspective* (University Park: Pennsylvania State University Press, 1984); Henry Raynor, *A Social History of Music: From the Middle Ages to Beethoven* (New York: Taplinger, 1978); and Rose Rosengard Subotnik, *Developing Variations: Style and Ideology in Western Music* (Minneapolis: University of Minnesota Press, 1991).

2. Quentin Skinner, *The Foundations of Modern Political Thought*, vol. 1, *The Renaissance* (Cambridge: Cambridge University Press, 1978), xi. Skinner analyzes art as a vehicle for political ideas in "Ambrogio Lorenzetti: The Artist as Political Philosopher," in *Proceedings of the British Academy* 72 (1986): 10–56.

3. See Theodor W. Adorno, *Introduction to the Sociology of Music*, trans. E. B. Ashton (New York: Seabury Press, 1976); Theodor W. Adorno, *Philosophy of Modern Music*, trans. Anne G. Mitchell and Wesley V. Blomster (New York: Seabury Press, 1980); Plato, *Republic*, trans. Robin Waterfield (Oxford: Oxford

University Press, 1993); *The Laws of Plato,* trans. Thomas L. Pangle (New York: Basic Books, 1980); Augustine, "De Musica," in The *Writings of Saint Augustine,* vol. 2, trans. Robert Catesby Taliaferro (New York: Fathers of the Church, 1947), 324–72; Augustine, *Confessions,* in *The Writings of Saint Augustine,* vol. 5, trans. Vernon J. Bourke (Washington, D.C.: Catholic University of America Press, 1953), 306–8; Jean-Jacques Rousseau, *Le devin du village,* with Eva Kirchner et al., cond. René Clememcic, Alpe Adria Ensemble, "Coro Gottardo Tomat" di Spilimbergo, Nuova Era 7106/07; Max Weber, *The Rational and Social Foundations of Music,* trans. and ed. Don Martindale, Johannes Riedel, and Gertrude Neuwirth (Carbondale: Southern Illinois University Press, 1958); and Allan Bloom, *The Closing of the American Mind: How Higher Education Has Failed Democracy and Impoverished the Souls of Today's Students* (New York: Simon and Schuster, 1987). For contemporary historical, political, and social research on opera, see Anthony Arblaster, *Viva la Libertà! Politics in Opera* (London: Verso, 1992); J. M. Balkin, "Turandot's Victory," *Tale Journal of Law and the Humanities* 2 (1990): 299–341; Alessandra Lippucci, "Social Theorizing on the Operatic Stage: Jean-Pierre Ponnelle's Postmodern Humanist Production of Verdi's *La Traviata,*" *Text and Performance Quarterly* 12 (July 1992): 245–73; Rosanne Martorella, *The Sociology of Opera* (New York: Praeger, 1982); Paul Robinson, *Opera and Ideas: From Mozart to Strauss* (New York: Harper and Row, 1985); and John Zerzan, "Tonality and the Totality," *New Political Science* 20 (1991): 97–116.

INTRODUCTION

1. Carl J. Friedrich, *The Age of the Baroque, 1610–1660* (New York: Harper and Brothers, 1952), 80.

2. Herbert Lindenberger, *Opera: The Extravagant Art* (Ithaca: Cornell University Press, 1984), esp. 145–96.

3. See Robinson, *Opera and Ideas,* 155–209, and Arblaster, *Viva la Libertà!* 91–145.

4. Frankfurt Institute for Social Research, *Aspects of Sociology,* trans. John Viertel (Boston: Beacon Press, 1972), 101.

CHAPTER 1: THE PRINCE AS DEITY, BEAST, AND TYRANT

1. Leo Schrade, *Monteverdi: Creator of Modern Music* (New York: W. W. Norton, 1950), 208.

2. See Iain Fenlon, "The Mantuan Stage Works," and Jane Glover, "The Venetian Operas," both in *The New Monteverdi Companion,* ed. Denis Arnold and

Nigel Fortune (London: Faber and Faber, 1985), 251–87, 288–333; and Gary Tomlinson, *Monteverdi and the End of the Renaissance* (Berkeley: University of California Press, 1987).

3. Monteverdi's Mantuan letters are filled with complaints about overwork, hurried work, ill health, and especially the irregular payment of his very modest salary. See *The Letters of Claudio Monteverdi*, trans. Denis Stevens (Cambridge: Cambridge University Press, 1980).

4. Quentin Skinner, "Political Philosophy," in *The Cambridge History of Renaissance Philosophy*, ed. Charles B. Schmitt, Quentin Skinner, and Eckhard Kessler (Cambridge: Cambridge University Press, 1988), 429.

5. José Antonio Maravall, *Culture of the Baroque: Analysis of a Historical Structure*, trans. Terry Cochrane, Theory and History of Literature, vol. 25 (Minneapolis: University of Minnesota Press, 1986), 227.

6. Samuel Berner, "Florentine Society in the Late Sixteenth and Early Seventeenth Centuries," *Studies in the Renaissance* 18 (1971): 203–46. See also Ellen Rosand, *Opera in Seventeenth-Century Venice: The Creation of a Genre* (Berkeley: University of California Press, 1991), 10; Jacob Burckhardt, *The Civilization of the Renaissance in Italy*, vol. 2, *The Discovery of the World and of Man, Society and Festivals, Morality and Religion*, trans. S. G. C. Middlemore (New York: Harper and Row, 1958), 316; and Paolo Fabbri, *Monteverdi*, trans. Tim Carter (Cambridge: Cambridge University Press, 1994), 67.

7. This paragraph and the next are indebted to William J. Bouwsma, *Venice and the Defense of Republican Liberty: Renaissance Values in the Age of the Counter Reformation* (Berkeley: University of California Press, 1968).

8. Rosand, *Opera in Seventeenth-Century Venice*, 125–53.

9. See Richard Mackenney, *The City-State, 1500–1700* (Atlantic Highlands, N.J.: Humanities Press International, 1989), 15.

10. The evolution of the legend of Orpheus is traced in John Warden, ed., *Orpheus: The Metamorphoses of a Myth* (Toronto: University of Toronto Press, 1982).

11. Samuel Berner, "Florentine Political Thought in the Late Cinquecento," *Il pensiero politico* 2 (1970): 189. For the near divinity of the prince, see also Skinner, "Political Philosophy," 390.

12. Jacopo Peri, *Euridice*, ed. and trans. H. M. Brown (Madison: A-R Editions, 1981), xvi.

13. The quotation is from John Underwood's translation of the libretto included in the recording of Claudio Monteverdi, *L'Orfeo: Favola in musica*, with Eric Tappy et al., cond. Michel Corboz, Ensemble Vocal et Instrumental de Lausanne, Edward Tarr Brass Ensemble, Erato 2292–45445–2, p. 11. For all subsequent citations, page numbers appear in parentheses in the text.

14. Marvin Carlson, *Theories of the Theatre: A Historical and Critical Survey from the Greeks to the Present* (Ithaca: Cornell University Press, 1984), 42.

15. Nino Pirrotta, *Music and Culture in Italy from the Middle Ages to the Baroque: A Collection of Essays* (Cambridge: Harvard University Press, 1984), 355.

16. F. W. Sternfeld, "The Orpheus Myth and the Libretto of *Orfeo*," and John Whenham, "*Orfeo*, Act Five: Alessandro Striggio's Original Ending," both in *Claudio Monteverdi: "Orfeo,"* ed. John Whenham (Cambridge: Cambridge University Press, 1986), 20–34, 35–41.

17. Joseph Kerman, *Opera as Drama*, rev. ed. (Berkeley: University of California Press, 1988), 25, 28.

18. Maravall, *Culture of the Baroque*, 237–40.

19. Arnold Hauser, *The Social History of Art*, vol. 2, *Renaissance, Mannerism, Baroque*, trans. Stanley Godman and Arnold Hauser (New York: Vintage Books, 1957), 93.

20. There is some controversy as to whether enough of the aristocracy moved from the cities to the countryside to support a theory about economic refeudalization during the early baroque period. It is clear, however, that there was an ideological attempt to cloak the nobility in medieval garb. See Samuel Berner, "The Florentine Patriciate in the Transition from Republic to *Principato*, 1530–1609," *Studies in Medieval and Renaissance History* 9 (1972): 4–6; Maravall, *Culture of the Baroque*, 134; and J. G. A. Pocock, *The Machiavellian Moment: Florentine Political Thought and the Atlantic Republican Tradition* (Princeton: Princeton University Press, 1975).

21. Maravall, *Culture of the Baroque*, 89.

22. Henry Raynor, *A Social History of Music: From the Middle Ages to Beethoven* (New York: Taplinger, 1978), 170–71.

23. Wayne A. Rebhorn, *Foxes and Lions: Machiavelli's Confidence Men* (Ithaca: Cornell University Press, 1988), 183–89.

24. The quotation is from David G. Evans's translation of the libretto included in the recording of Claudio Monteverdi, *Il ritorno d'Ulisse in patria*, with Sven Olof Eliasson et al., cond. Nikolaus Harnoncourt, Concentus musicus Wien, Teldec 2292–42496–2, p. 45. For all subsequent citations, page numbers appear in parentheses in the text.

25. Hanna Fenichel Pitkin, *Fortune Is a Woman: Gender and Politics in the Thought of Niccolò Machiavelli* (Berkeley: University of California Press, 1984), 136, 200, 206, 249.

26. Niccolò Machiavelli, *The Chief Works and Others*, vol. 1, trans. Allan Gilbert (Durham: Duke University Press, 1965), 65.

27. Bouwsma, *Venice and the Defense of Republican Liberty*, 501.

28. Schrade, *Monteverdi*, 350–56.

29. Rebhorn, *Foxes and Lions*, 80–81.

30. Patrick J. Smith, *The Tenth Muse: A Historical Study of the Opera Libretto* (New York: Schirmer Books, 1970), 108.

31. Tomlinson, *Monteverdi and the End of the Renaissance*, and Franco Croce, "Baroque Poetry: New Tasks for the Criticism of Marino and Marinism," both in *The Late Italian Renaissance, 1525–1630*, ed. Eric Cochrane (London: Macmillan, 1970), 215–59, 377–400.

32. Gerard Walter, *Nero*, trans. Emma Craufurd (London: Allen and Unwin, 1957), 109–35, 175–98.

33. William Everdell, *The End of Kings: A History of Republics and Republicans* (New York: Free Press, 1983), 106.

34. The quotation is from the translation of the libretto included in the recording of Claudio Monteverdi, *L'incoronazione di Poppea*, with Helen Donath et al., cond. Nikolaus Harnoncourt, Concentus musicus Wien, Teldec 8.35247 ZC, p. 120. For all subsequent citations, page numbers appear in parentheses in the text.

35. *The Operas of Monteverdi*, English National Opera Guide, no. 45 (London: John Calder, 1992), 71.

36. Cf. Iain Fenlon and Peter N. Miller, *The Song of the Soul: Understanding "Poppea,"* Royal Musical Association Monographs, vol. 5 (London: Royal Musical Association, 1992), 90–93. Fenlon and Miller argue that Seneca's Stoicism represents the moral perspective of the opera.

37. Sebastian de Grazia, *Machiavelli in Hell* (New York: Vintage Books, 1994), 112.

38. Paolo Fabbri lists five possible composers of the duet, including Monteverdi (*Monteverdi*, 260–61).

39. Ronald G. Witt, Introduction to *The Earthly Republic: Italian Humanists on Government and Society*, ed. Benjamin G. Kohl and Ronald G. Witt (Philadelphia: University of Pennsylvania Press, 1978), 124–25.

40. Algernon Sidney, *Discourses Concerning Government* (New York: Arno Press, 1979), 205.

41. Leo Lowenthal, *Literature and the Image of Man: Studies of the European Drama and Novel, 1600–1900* (Boston: Beacon Press, 1957), 98.

CHAPTER 2: THE DIALECTIC OF OPERATIC CIVILIZATION

1. See Otto Erich Deutsch, *Mozart: A Documentary Biography*, trans. Eric Blom, Peter Branscombe, and Jeremy Noble (Stanford: Stanford University Press, 1965), 380.

2. Joseph Kerman, *Opera as Drama*, rev. ed. (Berkeley: University of California Press, 1988), 103.

3. Brigid Brophy, *Mozart the Dramatist: The Value of His Operas to Him, to His Age, and to Us*, rev. ed. (New York: Da Capo Press, 1988), 23.

4. See Norman Hampson, *The Enlightenment: An Evaluation of Its Assumptions and Values* (Harmondsworth: Penguin Books, 1968); and Maurice Cranston, *Philosophers and Pamphleteers: Political Theorists of the Enlightenment* (New York: Oxford University Press, 1986).

5. G. W. F. Hegel, *Philosophy of Right*, trans. T. M. Knox (Oxford: Oxford University Press, 1967), 108.

6. Alexis de Tocqueville, *Democracy in America*, trans. George Lawrence, ed. J. P. Mayer (New York: Anchor Books, 1969), 287. Exactly 150 years after the publication of *Democracy in America*, Tocqueville's phrase inspired another widely read book on American political values: see Robert Bellah et al., *Habits of the Heart: Individualism and Commitment in American Life* (New York: Harper and Row, 1985).

7. See Terry Eagleton, *The Ideology of the Aesthetic* (Oxford: Basil Blackwell, 1990), 20; and Nicholas Till, *Mozart and the Enlightenment: Truth, Virtue, and Beauty in Mozart's Operas* (New York: W. W. Norton, 1992), 21.

8. Eagleton, *Ideology of the Aesthetic*, 259.

9. Michel Foucault, *The History of Sexuality*, vol. 1, *An Introduction*, trans. Robert Hurley (New York: Pantheon Books, 1978), 116.

10. Jean Starobinski, *1789: The Emblems of Reason*, trans. Barbara Bray (Charlottesville: University Press of Virginia, 1982), 38.

11. Hampson, *Enlightenment*, 217.

12. For commentaries on the political implications of Kant's and Schiller's aesthetics, see Eagleton, *Ideology of the Aesthetic*; Herbert Marcuse, *Eros and Civilization: A Philosophical Inquiry into Freud* (New York: Vintage Books, 1962), 157–79; Herbert Marcuse, *An Essay on Liberation* (Boston: Beacon Press, 1969); Herbert Marcuse, *Counterrevolution and Revolt* (Boston: Beacon Press, 1972); and Josef Chytry, *The Aesthetic State: A Quest in Modern German Thought* (Berkeley: University of California Press, 1989), 70–105.

13. Michael F. Robinson, "The 'Comic' Element in *Don Giovanni*," in *Mozart: "Don Giovanni,"* English National Opera Guide, no. 18 (London: John Calder, 1983), 10. In addition, there were at least thirty-five Don Juan ballets between 1761 and the time of Mozart's *Don Giovanni*; see Charles C. Russell, *The Don Juan Legend Before Mozart: With a Collection of Eighteenth-Century Opera Librettos* (Ann Arbor: University of Michigan Press, 1993), 78.

14. See Søren Kierkegaard, *Either/Or*, vol. 1, trans. David F. Swenson and Lillian Marvin Swenson (New York: Anchor Books, 1959), 45–134.

15. Kerman, *Opera as Drama*, 58.

16. Andrew Steptoe, *The Mozart–Da Ponte Operas: The Cultural and Musical Background to "Le nozze di Figaro," "Don Giovanni," and "Così fan tutte"* (Oxford: Clarendon Press, 1988), 106.

17. Robinson, "The 'Comic' Element in *Don Giovanni*," 9.

18. Kerman, *Opera as Drama*, 58–108.

19. Georg Lukács, *The Historical Novel*, trans. Hannah Mitchell and Stanley Mitchell (Lincoln: University of Nebraska Press, 1983), 19–20.

20. On the historical reality of seventeeth-century Seville, see two works by Mary Elizabeth Perry: *Crime and Society in Early Modern Seville* (Hanover: University Press of New England, 1980) and *Gender and Disorder in Early Modern Seville* (Princeton: Princeton University Press, 1990).

21. John Locke, *Two Treatises of Government*, 2d ed. (Cambridge: Cambridge University Press, 1970), 369.

22. The seducers in Laclos's *Les liaisons dangereuses* similarly adapt their language to that of their intended victims. See Anne Deneys, "The Political Economy of the Body in the *Liaisons dangereuses* of Choderlos de Laclos," in *Eroticism and the Body Politic*, ed. Lynn Hunt (Baltimore: Johns Hopkins University Press, 1991), esp. 57–60.

23. G. W. F. Hegel, *Aesthetics: Lectures on Fine Art*, vol. 2, trans. T. M. Knox (Oxford: Clarendon Press, 1975), 902.

24. Cited in Peter Conrad, "The Libertine's Progress," in *Don Giovanni: Myths of Seduction and Betrayal*, ed. Jonathan Miller (Baltimore: Johns Hopkins University Press, 1990), 85.

25. Wayne A. Rebhorn, *Foxes and Lions: Machiavelli's Confidence Men* (Ithaca: Cornell University Press, 1988), 136–37.

26. Locke, *Two Treatises*, 271–72.

27. Cf. Brigid Brophy, who argues for the Roman Catholic assumptions of the opera (*Mozart the Dramatist*, 203).

28. The quotation is from Lionel Salter's translation of the libretto included in the recording of Wolfgang Amadeus Mozart, *Don Giovanni*, with Ruggero Raimondi et al., cond. Lorin Maazel, Chorus and Orchestra of the Paris Théâtre National de l'Opéra, CBS Masterworks M3K 35192, p. 260. For all subsequent citations, page numbers appear in parentheses in the text.

29. Leo Lowenthal, *Literature and the Image of Man: Studies of the European Drama and Novel, 1600–1900* (Boston: Beacon Press, 1957), 125.

30. Herbert Marcuse, *One-Dimensional Man: Studies in the Ideology of Advanced Industrial Society* (Boston: Beacon Press, 1964), 61.

31. Sheila Hodges, *Lorenzo Da Ponte: The Life and Times of Mozart's Librettist* (London: Grafton Books, 1985), 23, 25.

32. Quoted in ibid., 81.

33. Karl Marx, *Early Texts*, trans. and ed. David McLellan (Oxford: Basil Blackwell, 1971), 152, 154.

34. See Ivan Nagel, *Autonomy and Mercy: Reflections on Mozart's Operas*, trans. Marion Faber and Ivan Nagel (Cambridge: Harvard University Press, 1991), 36.

35. Lowenthal, *Literature and the Image of Man*, 119.

36. Marcuse, *One-Dimensional Man*, 61.

CHAPTER 3: OPERA AND REVOLUTIONARY VIRTUE

1. See Carol Blum, *Rousseau and the Republic of Virtue* (Ithaca: Cornell University Press, 1986); Maurice Cranston, *Philosophers and Pamphleteers: Political Theorists of the Enlightenment* (Oxford: Oxford University Press, 1986), 62–97; Bernadette Fort, ed., *Fictions of the French Revolution* (Evanston: Northwestern University Press, 1991); Norman Hampson, *A Cultural History of the Enlightenment* (New York: Pantheon Books, 1968), 165–283; Lynn Hunt, *Politics, Culture, and Class in the French Revolution* (Berkeley: University of California Press, 1984), 19–51; Joan B. Landes, *Women and the Public Sphere in the Age of the French Revolution* (Ithaca: Cornell University Press, 1988), 66–206; Candice E. Proctor, *Women, Equality, and the French Revolution*, Contributions in Women's Studies, no. 115 (Westport, Conn.: Greenwood Press, 1990); Simon Schama, *Citizens: A Chronicle of the French Revolution* (New York: Knopf, 1989), 171; and Joel Schwartz, *The Sexual Politics of Jean-Jacques Rousseau* (Chicago: University of Chicago Press, 1984).

2. Jean-Jacques Rousseau, *The Social Contract and Discourses*, trans. G. D. H. Cole (New York: E. P. Dutton, 1950), 69–75.

3. Robespierre, quoted in Blum, *Rousseau and the Republic of Virtue*, 242. See also Fort, *Fictions of the French Revolution*, 36–37.

4. The distinction between male virtue and female virtue is from Schwartz, *Sexual Politics of Rousseau*.

5. For a more in-depth comparison of the two great musicians, see Georgio Pestelli, *The Age of Mozart and Beethoven*, trans. Eve Cross (Cambridge: Cambridge University Press, 1984).

6. Quoted in Maynard Solomon, *Beethoven Essays* (Cambridge: Harvard University Press, 1988), 22.

7. Theodor W. Adorno, *Introduction to the Sociology of Music*, trans. E. B. Ashton (New York: Seabury Press, 1976), 56.

8. Elliot Forbes, ed., *Thayer's Life of Beethoven*, vol. 1 (Princeton: Princeton University Press, 1967), 441.

9. Emily Anderson, ed., *The Letters of Beethoven*, vol. 1 (New York: St. Martin's Press, 1961), 334, 355; and Michael Hamburger, ed., *Beethoven: Letters,*

Journals, and Conversations, trans. Michael Hamburger (New York: Thames and Hudson, 1951), 109, 230. For interpretations of Revolutionary ideas in *Die Zauberflöte,* see Jean Starobinski, *1789: The Emblems of Reason,* trans. Barbara Bray (Charlottesville: University Press of Virginia, 1982), 205–26; Landes, *Women and the Public Sphere,* 89; and H. C. Robbins-Landon, *Mozart: The Golden Years, 1781–1791* (New York: Schirmer Books, 1989), 259–60.

10. Arnold Hauser, *The Social History of Art,* vol. 3, *Rococo, Classicism, Romanticism,* trans. Stanley Godman and Arnold Hauser (New York: Vintage Books, 1958), 84–99; and Georg Lukács, *The Historical Novel,* trans. Hannah Mitchell and Stanley Mitchell (Lincoln: University of Nebraska Press, 1983).

11. Winton Dean, "Opera Under the French Revolution," *Proceedings of the Royal Musical Academy* 94 (1967–68): 77–96; and Edward J. Dent, *The Rise of Romantic Opera,* ed. Winton Dean (Cambridge: Cambridge University Press, 1976), 47–94.

12. Andrew Steptoe, *The Mozart–Da Ponte Operas: The Cultural and Musical Background to "Le nozze di Figaro," "Don Giovanni," and "Così fan tutte"* (Oxford: Clarendon Press, 1988), 129.

13. Paul Robinson comes to the same conclusion. See "*Fidelio* and the French Revolution," *Cambridge Opera Journal* 3 (March 1991): 23–48.

14. See Alan Rich's liner notes in Ludwig van Beethoven, *Leonore,* with Edda Moser et al., cond. Herbert Blomsted, Staatskapelle Dresden and Leipzig Radio Chorus, Arabesque, 8043–3L.

15. The quotation is from Avril Bardoni's translation of the libretto included in the recording of Ludwig van Beethoven, *Fidelio,* with Gabriele Schnaut et al., cond. Christoph von Dohnányi, Vienna Philharmonic Orchestra and Chorus, London 436 627–2, p. 93. For all subsequent citations, page numbers appear in parentheses in the text.

16. Karl Marx, *Critique of Hegel's "Philosophy of Right,"* trans. Annette Jolin and John O'Malley (Cambridge: Cambridge University Press, 1970), 113–16, 125.

17. Schama, *Citizens,* 393.

18. Hampson, *Cultural History of the Enlightenment,* 186.

19. Albert Soboul, *The French Revolution, 1787–1799: From the Storming of the Bastille to Napoleon,* trans. Alan Forrest and Colin Jones (New York: Vintage Books, 1975), 13.

20. Schama, *Citizens,* xv.

21. Soboul, *French Revolution,* 596.

22. See Landes, *Women and the Public Sphere,* 17–89.

23. Ibid., 89.

24. Galina Osipovna Sokolnikova, *Nine Women Drawn from the Epoch of the French Revolution,* trans. H. C. Stevens (Freeport, N.Y.: Books for Libraries Press, 1969), 20, cited in ibid., 110.

25. Crane Brinton, *Decade of Revolution: 1789–1799* (New York: Harper and Row, 1934), 200.

26. See Ernst Bloch, *Principle of Hope*, trans. Neville Plaice, Stephen Plaice, and Paul Knight, 3 vols. (Cambridge: MIT Press, 1986), 1:163, 3:1100, 3:1103; Adorno, *Sociology of Music*, 62; and Theodor W. Adorno, *Philosophy of Modern Music*, trans. Anne G. Mitchell and Wesley V. Blomster (New York: Seabury Press, 1980), 129–30.

27. See Louis Marin, *Portrait of the King*, trans. Martha M. Houle, Theory and History of Literature, vol. 57 (Minneapolis: University of Minnesota Press, 1988).

28. Starobinski, *1789*, 242n.1.

29. *Beethoven: "Fidelio,"* English National Opera Guide, no. 4 (London: John Calder, 1980), 27–28.

30. See Peter Conrad, *A Song of Love and Death: The Meaning of Opera* (New York: Poseidon Press, 1987), 297–98.

31. Romaine Rolland, *Beethoven the Creator: The Great Creative Epochs, from the "Eroica" to the "Appassionata,"* trans. Ernest Newman (New York: Dover Publications, 1964), 175–76.

CHAPTER 4: THE UTOPIAN VISION OF ROMANTIC
ANTICAPITALISM

1. For examples of genealogies of Nazi ideas, see Georg Lukács, *The Destruction of Reason*, trans. Peter Palmer (Atlantic Highlands, N.J.: Humanities Press, 1981); George L. Mosse, *The Nationalization of the Masses: Political Symbolism and Mass Movements in Germany from the Napoleonic Wars Through the Third Reich* (New York: New American Library, 1975); George L. Mosse, *The Crisis of German Ideology: Intellectual Origins of the Third Reich* (New York: H. Fertig, 1981); and Fritz R. Stern, *The Politics of Cultural Despair: A Study in the Rise of the Germanic Ideology* (Berkeley: University of California Press, 1961).

2. For an overview of the critical reception of *Parsifal*, see Lucy Beckett, *Richard Wagner: "Parsifal"* (Cambridge: Cambridge University Press, 1981), 103–28.

3. *Selected Letters of Friedrich Nietzsche*, trans. and ed. Christopher Middleton (Chicago: University of Chicago Press, 1969), 260.

4. Friedrich Nietzsche, *Human, All Too Human: A Book for Free Spirits*, trans. R. J. Hollingdale (Cambridge: Cambridge University Press, 1986), 210–11.

5. Theodor Adorno, *In Search of Wagner*, trans. Rodney Livingstone (London: NLB, 1981), 80, 67, 145, 93, 140, 146.

6. Karl Marx, quoted in Saul K. Padover, *Karl Marx: An Intimate Biography*

(New York: McGraw-Hill, 1978), 547. See also John Bokina, "Wagner and Marxist Aesthetics," in *Wagner in Retrospect: A Centennial Reappraisal*, ed. Leroy R. Shaw, Nancy R. Cirillo, and Marion S. Miller (Amsterdam: Rodopi, 1987), 138–51.

7. John Zerzan, "Tonality and the Totality," *New Political Science* 20 (1991): 108.

8. Robert W. Gutman, *Richard Wagner: The Man, His Mind, and His Music* (New York: Harcourt Brace Jovanovich, 1968), 431.

9. Paul Lawrence Rose, *Wagner: Race and Revolution* (New Haven: Yale University Press, 1992), 135, and *Revolutionary Anti-Semitism in Germany: From Kant to Wagner* (Princeton: Princeton University Press, 1990), 395.

10. Gutman, *Richard Wagner*, 439. Gutman's identification of *Parsifal* with Nazi religiosity was anticipated by an authoritative source: Hitler is said to have remarked, upon leaving a Bayreuth performance, "Out of *Parsifal* I make a religion" (quoted in Charles Bracelen Flood, *Hitler: The Path to Power* [Boston: Houghton Mifflin, 1989], 432).

11. For *Parsifal*'s ideology of sexual repression, see Peter Wapnewski, "The Operas as Literary Works," in *Wagner Handbook*, ed. Ulrich Müller and Peter Wapnewski (Cambridge: Harvard University Press, 1992), 91. The classic work on the distinction between ideology and utopia is Karl Mannheim, *Ideology and Utopia: An Introduction to the Sociology of Knowledge*, trans. Louis Wirth and Edward Shils (New York: Brace and World, 1936). See also Ernst Bloch, *The Utopian Function of Art and Literature: Selected Essays*, trans. Jack Zipes and Frank Mecklenburg (Cambridge: MIT Press, 1988).

12. Quoted in Ernest Newman, *The Life of Richard Wagner*, vol. 2, *1848–1860* (Cambridge: Cambridge University Press, 1976), 245n.6.

13. See Robert Sayre and Michael Löwy, "Figures of Romantic Anti-Capitalism," *New German Critique* 32 (1984): 42–92.

14. Georg Lukács, *The Theory of the Novel: A Historico-Philosophical Essay on the Forms of Great Epic Literature*, trans. Anna Bostock (Cambridge: MIT Press, 1971), 152.

15. See Ralf Dahrendorf, *Society and Democracy in Germany* (New York: Anchor Books, 1969).

16. For an overview of the evolution of Wagner's work, see Beckett, *Richard Wagner*, 1–23.

17. The fictionalized history of *Die Meistersinger* is relative. Paul Robinson argues that, compared to the fictionalized history of Richard Strauss's *Der Rosenkavalier*, *Die Meistersinger* is a model of social and political realism (*Opera and Ideas: From Mozart to Strauss* [New York: Harper and Row, 1985], 210–61).

18. See Jessie L. Weston, *From Ritual to Romance* (Garden City, N.Y.: Doubleday Anchor Books, 1957), and *The Legends of the Wagner Drama: Studies in Mythology and Romance* (Boston: Longwood Press, 1977), 155–217.

19. Walter Sokel, *The Writer in Extremis: Expressionism in Twentieth-Century German Literature* (Stanford: Stanford University Press, 1959), 154.

20. The quotation is from Lionel Salter's translation included in the recording of *Parsifal*, with René Kollo et al., cond. Georg Solti, Vienna Philharmonic Orchestra, London, 417 143–2, p. 14. For all subsequent citations of the libretto, page numbers appear in parentheses in the text.

21. I would use the term "state" here, except that, like "opera," it is a term of opprobrium for Wagner. Despite Wagner's anarchistic antipathy to the state, which he associates with bureaucratism, militarism, and the excessive restriction of individual freedom, his ideal order still retains a political hierarchy and the power of political decision-making.

22. The mastersingers' guild in *Die Meistersinger* is also an example of a Wagnerian republican council, albeit without the eucharistic element.

23. See Richard Wagner, "On State and Religion" and "What Relation Bear Republican Endeavors to the Kingship?" in *Richard Wagner's Prose Works*, 8 vols., trans. William Ashton Ellis (London: Kegan Paul, 1895–99; repr., St. Clair Shores, Mich.: Scholarly Press, 1972), 4:3–34, 136–45. See also Maurice Boucher, *The Political Concepts of Richard Wagner*, trans. Marcel Honoré (New York: M & M Publications, 1950), 25–28, 94.

24. Martin Gregor-Dellin and Dietrich Mack, eds., *Cosima Wagner's Diaries*, 2 vols., trans. Geoffrey Skelton (New York: Harcourt Brace Jovanovich, 1978–80), 2:525, 530.

25. *Correspondence of Wagner and Liszt*, trans. Francis Hueffer, rev. ed. (New York: Greenwood Press, 1969), 1:189.

26. See Jonathan Beecher, *Charles Fourier: The Visionary and His World* (Berkeley: University of California Press, 1986), 118.

27. Bloch, *Utopian Function of Art and Literature*, 10.

28. Richard Wagner, "The Revolution," in *Prose Works* 8:232.

29. Richard Wagner, "Against Vivisection," in *Prose Works* 6:197.

30. Max Horkheimer, "Schopenhauer Today," in *The Critical Spirit: Essays in Honor of Herbert Marcuse*, ed. Kurt H. Wolff and Barrington Moore, Jr. (Boston: Beacon Press, 1967), 64, 65.

31. Richard Wagner, "Religion and Art," in *Prose Works* 6:241.

32. Ibid., 6:213.

33. Boucher, *Political Concepts of Richard Wagner*, 155.

34. Wagner, "Religion and Art," 6:223, 224.

35. See Georg Lukács, *Soul and Form*, trans. Anna Bostock (Cambridge: Cambridge University Press, 1974), 39.

36. Martin Geck, "Parsifal: A Betrayed Childhood; Variations on a Leitmotif by Alice Miller," *Wagner* 9 (April 1988): 75–88.

CHAPTER 5: THE POLITICS OF PSYCHOLOGICAL INTERIORIZATION

1. Joan Peyser, *The New Music: The Sense Behind the Sound* (New York: Delacorte Press, 1971), 30.

2. William J. McGrath, *Dionysian Art and Populist Politics in Austria* (New Haven: Yale University Press, 1974), 247. This idea also underlies William J. McGrath, *Freud's Discovery of Psychoanalysis: The Politics of Hysteria* (Ithaca: Cornell University Press, 1986), and Carl E. Schorske, *Fin-de-Siècle Vienna: Politics and Culture* (New York: Knopf, 1980). The following paragraph on the travails of Austrian liberalism is based on these books.

3. My account of the treatment of madness in the operas of Monteverdi and his early baroque contemporaries is indebted to two works by Ellen Rosand: *Opera in Seventeenth-Century Venice: The Creation of a Genre* (Berkeley: University of California Press, 1991), 346–60, and "Operatic Madness: A Challenge to Convention," in *Music and Text: Critical Inquiries*, ed. Steven Paul Scher (Cambridge: Cambridge University Press, 1992), 241–87. For an analysis of the socially conventional behavioral expectations of royal and commoner characters in Monteverdi, see Chapter 1.

4. Emily Anderson, ed., *The Letters of Mozart and His Family* (New York: W. W. Norton, 1989), 769.

5. See Irving Kolodin, *The Opera Omnibus: Four Centuries of Give and Take* (New York: E. P. Dutton, 1976), 131–55.

6. For a discussion of the tonality of *Lucia*, *Tristan*, and *Erwartung*, see Richard Norton, *Tonality in Western Culture: A Critical and Historical Perspective* (University Park: Pennsylvania State University Press, 1984), 222–42.

7. Thomas Mann, *Essays*, trans. H. T. Lowe-Porter (New York: Vintage Books, 1957), 197–254.

8. Peter Gay, *The Bourgeois Experience: Victoria to Freud*, vol. 1, *Education of the Senses* (Oxford: Oxford University Press, 1984), 168–201.

9. Sophocles, *Electra*, in *Aeschylus, Sophocles, Euripides, Aristophanes*, trans. Edward P. Coleridge (Chicago: Encyclopaedia Britannica, 1952), 159.

10. Sophocles, *Electra*, 169.

11. See Karen Forsyth, "Hofmannsthal's *Elektra*: From Sophocles to Strauss," in *Richard Strauss: "Elektra,"* ed. Derrick Puffett, Cambridge Opera Handbooks (Cambridge: Cambridge University Press, 1989), 20.

12. All quotations from the text of the opera are taken from the translation of the libretto included in the recording of Richard Strauss, *Elektra*, with Birgit Nilsson et al., cond. Georg Solti, Vienna Philharmonic Orchestra, London OSA 1269/A 4269, p. 13. I have, however, retained the German versions of the

characters' names, in order to distinguish them from the corresponding characters in Sophocles' *Electra*. For all subsequent citations, page numbers appear in parentheses in the text.

13. See Michael P. Steinberg, *The Meaning of the Salzburg Festival: Austria as Theater and Ideology, 1890–1938* (Ithaca: Cornell University Press, 1990), 150.

14. Freud, quoted in Schorske, *Fin-de-Siècle Vienna*, 187.

15. Elizabeth Young-Breuhl, ed., *Freud on Women: A Reader* (New York: W. W. Norton, 1990), 12–26, 89–153, 166–81, 342–62.

16. For an analysis of Strauss's *Elektra* score, see the essays by Karen Forsyth, Derrick Puffett, Arnold Whitehall, Tethys Carpenter, Carolyn Abbate, and Robin Holloway in Puffett, *Richard Strauss*.

17. See Theodor W. Adorno, *Philosophy of Modern Music*, trans. Anne G. Mitchell and Wesley V. Blomster (New York: Seabury Press, 1980), 53, 149, 161; and Karen Forsyth, "Hofmannsthal's *Elektra*," and Derrick Puffett, "Synopsis," both in Puffett, *Richard Strauss*, 2, 45.

18. Schorske, *Fin-de-Siècle Vienna*, 3–4.

19. For an overview of the politics of expressionism, see Stephen Eric Bronner and Douglas Kellner, eds., *Passion and Rebellion: The Expressionist Heritage* (New York: J. F. Bergin, 1983).

20. The quotation is from the translation of the libretto included in the recording of Arnold Schoenberg, *Works*, with Janis Martin, cond. Pierre Boulez, BBC Symphony Orchestra and Chorus and Ensemble Contemporain, CBS Masterworks 79348/US–13M 378633, p. 28. For all subsequent citations, page numbers appear in parentheses in the text.

21. Robert Craft, "*Erwartung*: Notes on the Dramatic Structure," in Schoenberg, *Works*, 5.

CHAPTER 6: THE AESTHETIC POLITICS OF THE GERMAN ARTIST-OPERA

1. For Strauss's allusions to Mozart's operas, see Herbert Lindenberger, *Opera: The Extravagant Art* (Ithaca: Cornell University Press, 1984), 104.

2. Perhaps a fourth artist-opera should have been included in this chapter. Composer Ernst Krenek wrote his own libretto for *Jonny spielt auf*, a 1927 German-language work about art and the artist. Treating *Jonny* would have lengthened an already long chapter, and I had two other reasons for excluding the opera. First, the work does not represent Krenek's mature views on art. The jazzy *Zeitoper* style of *Jonny* proved to be but an early, passing phase in Krenek's long career as an opera composer. Second, the plot, which portrays contemporary events, is not a historical allegory, as are the three operas I examine here. For information about *Jonny*, see Ernst Krenek, *Exploring Music*, trans. Margaret

Shenfield and Geoffrey Skelton (New York: October House, 1966), 23–27, 54, 196; and Susan C. Cook, *Opera for a New Republic: The Zeitopern of Krenek, Weill, and Hindemith* (Ann Arbor: UMI Research Press, 1988), 75–108.

3. Lewis Lockwood, "Palestrina," in *The New Grove Dictionary of Music and Musicians*, vol. 13, ed. Stanley Sadie (London: Macmillan, 1980), 122.

4. Thomas Mann, *Reflections of a Nonpolitical Man*, trans. Walter D. Morris (New York: Frederick Ungar, 1983), 298.

5. The quotation is from Veronica Slater's translation of the libretto included in the recording of Hans Pfitzner, *Palestrina*, with Nicolai Gedda et al., cond. Rafael Kubelik, Bavarian Radio Symphony Orchestra and Chorus, Tölz Boys' Choir, Deutsche Grammaphone 427 417–2, p. 36. For all subsequent citations, page numbers appear in parentheses in the text.

6. Mosco Carner, "Pfitzner v. Berg, or Inspiration v. Analysis," *Musical Times* 118 (May 1977): 379–80.

7. For the distinction between romantic and unromantic conservatism, see Robert Sayre and Michael Löwy, "Figures of Romantic Anti-Capitalism," *New German Critique* 32 (Spring–Summer 1984): 42–92. Thomas Mann also distinguishes between the two conservatisms of *Palestrina*: Borromeo's conservatism is "robust" and "authoritarian," whereas Palestrina's is "ironical" and "tender" (*Reflections of a Nonpolitical Man*, 306).

8. Arnold Hauser, *The Social History of Art*, vol. 2, *Renaissance, Mannerism, Baroque*, trans. Stanley Godman and Arnold Hauser (New York: Vintage Books, 1957), 125.

9. Georg Lukács, *The Historical Novel*, trans. Hannah Mitchell and Stanley Mitchell (Lincoln: University of Nebraska Press, 1983), 224.

10. Mann, *Reflections of a Nonpolitical Man*, 311.

11. For an analysis of romantic tonality as both preservation and expansion of the tonality of the "common practice era," see Richard Norton, *Tonality in Western Culture: A Critical and Historical Perspective* (University Park: Pennsylvania State University Press, 1984), 212–30. For an account of the transformation of German Wagnerism from an aesthetically progressive to an aesthetically conservative tendency, see David C. Large and William Weber, eds., *Wagnerism in European Culture and Politics* (Ithaca: Cornell University Press, 1984).

12. Michael Meyer distinguishes between the nationalism of Pfitzner's romantic conservatism and the racism of musicologists associated with the Nazi movement and the Third Reich. See "A Reference in the Music Commentary of Theodor W. Adorno: The Musicology of *Volk* and Race," *Humanities in Society* 2 (Fall 1979): 401–16.

13. Georg Lukács, *Soul and Form*, trans. Anna Bostock (Cambridge: MIT Press, 1974), 23.

14. I have based the next few paragraphs about Hindemith's early career on

the following sources: Ian Kemp, *Hindemith* (London: Oxford University Press, 1970); Joel Sachs, "Some Aspects of Musical Politics in Pre-Nazi Germany," *Perspectives of New Music* 9 (Fall–Winter 1970): 74–95; and Geoffrey Skelton, *Paul Hindemith: The Man Behind the Music* (London: Victor Gollancz, 1975).

15. Elaine Padmore, "Hindemith and Grünewald," *Music Review* 33 (August 1972): 191.

16. See Walter Sokel, *The Writer in Extremis: Expressionism in Twentieth-Century German Literature* (Stanford: Stanford University Press, 1959), 161.

17. The quotation is from Bernard Jacobson's translation of the libretto included in the recording of Paul Hindemith, *Mathis der Maler*, with Dietrich Fischer-Dieskau et al., cond. Rafael Kubelik, Bavarian Radio Symphony Orchestra and Chorus, Angel SZCX–3869, p. 14. For all subsequent citations, page numbers appear in parentheses in the text.

18. Paul Hindemith, *A Composer's World* (Cambridge: Harvard University Press, 1952), 221.

19. Paul Hindemith, *Johann Sebastian Bach: Heritage and Obligation* (New Haven: Yale University Press, 1952), 20.

20. Norman Cazden, "Hindemith and Nature," *Music Review* 15 (November 1954): 288.

21. Ibid., 306.

22. Kemp, *Hindemith*, 51–52.

23. Leo Lowenthal, *Literature and the Image of Man: Studies of the European Drama and Novel* (Boston: Beacon Press, 1957), 190–220. A similar development characterizes the history of modern philosophy. In spite of Hindemith's conscious reservations about the Nazis, his natural mystification of music replicates the typical Nazi subordination of history and human subjectivity to natural myth. See Herbert Marcuse, "The Struggle Against Liberalism in the Totalitarian View of the State," in *Negations: Essays in Critical Theory*, trans. Jeremy J. Shapiro (Boston: Beacon Press, 1968), 23–31.

24. Sokel, *Writer in Extremis*, 141–63.

25. Skelton, *Paul Hindemith*, 159. The Nazi condemnation of Hindemith seemed to put him in the company of the anti-Nazi progressives. Theodor W. Adorno, however, upholds the reactionary implications of Hindemith's aesthetic and political retreat. According to Adorno, Hindemith's return to the antiquated tonality of the baroque and classical eras exemplifies his aesthetically reactionary character. Moreover, Adorno views Hindemith's Gebrauchsmusik as an uncritical affirmation of the status quo. From this perspective, Hindemith's problems with the Nazi regime were not those of a progressive struggling against the forces of reaction. Rather, Hindemith's difficulties arose from the fact that he was the wrong kind of reactionary. See Theodor W. Adorno, *Philosophy of Modern Music*, trans. Anne G. Mitchell and Wesley V. Blomster (New York: Seabury

Press, 1980), 33–34, and Martin Jay, *Adorno* (Cambridge: Harvard University Press, 1984), 42, 136–37.

26. Harry Halbreich, "Schoenberg and the Jewish People," in the recording of Arnold Schoenberg, *Moses und Aron*, with Gunter Reich et al., cond. Pierre Boulez, BBC Symphony Orchestra and Singers, Orpheus Boys' Choir, Columbia M2 33594, pp. 4–5.

27. See Karl H. Worner, *Schoenberg's "Moses und Aron,"* trans. Paul Hamburger (New York: St. Martin's Press, 1963), 42.

28. Bluma Goldstein, *Reinscribing Moses: Heine, Kafka, Freud, and Schoenberg in a European Wilderness* (Cambridge: Harvard University Press, 1992), 163.

29. Worner, *Schoenberg's "Moses und Aron,"* 92–101.

30. Adorno, *Philosophy of Modern Music*, 68. Adorno may have exaggerated the completeness of Schoenberg's triumph over nature. See Norton, *Tonality in Western Culture*, 231–60.

31. The quotation is from Allen Forte's translation of the libretto included in the recording of Arnold Schoenberg, *Moses und Aron*, with Franz Mazura et al., cond. Georg Solti, Chicago Symphony Orchestra and Chorus, London 414 264–2, p. 42. For all subsequent citations, page numbers appear in parentheses in the text.

32. This distinction between artistic production (Moses) and reproduction (Aron) is derived from Adorno. See Jay, *Adorno*, 139.

33. Lindenberger, *Opera*, 75–76.

34. Adorno, *Philosophy of Modern Music*, 132.

35. Lindenberger, *Opera*, 36.

36. Frankfurt Institute of Social Research, *Aspects of Sociology*, trans. John Viertel (Boston: Beacon Press, 1972), 105.

37. See Max Horkheimer and Theodor W. Adorno, *Dialectic of Enlightenment*, trans. John Cumming (New York: Seabury Press, 1972).

CHAPTER 7: EROS AND REVOLT

1. Herbert Marcuse, *Eros and Civilization: A Philosophical Inquiry into Freud* (New York: Vintage Books, 1962); Herbert Marcuse, *One-Dimensional Man: Studies in the Ideology of Advanced Industrial Society* (Boston: Beacon Press, 1964); Herbert Marcuse, *An Essay on Liberation* (Boston: Beacon Press, 1969); Herbert Marcuse, *Counterrevolution and Revolt* (Boston: Beacon Press, 1972); Norman O. Brown, *Life Against Death: The Psychoanalytical Meaning of History* (Middletown, Conn.: Wesleyan University Press, 1959); Norman O. Brown, *Love's Body* (New York: Random House, 1966); Erich Fromm, *Marx's Concept of Man* (New York: F. Ungar, 1961); and Erich Fromm, *The Art of Loving* (New York: Perennial Library, 1974).

2. For the political history of the Salzburg Festival in its earlier years, see

Michael P. Steinberg, *The Meaning of the Salzburg Festival: Austria as Theater and Ideology, 1890–1938* (Ithaca: Cornell University Press, 1990).

3. Hans Werner Henze, in the booklet accompanying the recording of *The Bassarids*, with Karan Armstrong et al., cond. Gerd Albrecht, RIAS Chamber Choir, South German Radio Choir, Berlin Radio Symphony Orchestra, Koch International, CD 314006 K3, 1991, p. 14. For all citations of the libretto of the opera, page numbers appear in parentheses in the text. Like several recent productions, this recording omits the intermezzo. The libretto for the intermezzo can be found in W. H. Auden and Chester Kallman, *Libretti and Other Dramatic Writings by W. H. Auden, 1939–1973*, ed. Edward Mendelson (Princeton: Princeton University Press, 1993), 283–93.

4. P[atrick] J. S[mith], "Viewpoint: Henze's *Bassarids*," *Opera News* 55 (January 1991): 6. Smith's praise of the opera represents a considerable change in his views, as he had earlier referred to the libretto as a patchwork of "half-assimilated ideas" (*The Tenth Muse: A Historical Study of the Opera Libretto* [New York: Schirmer Books, 1970], 386).

5. Cf. Albert Henrichs, " 'He Has a God in Him': Human and Divine in the Modern Perception of Dionysus," in *Masks of Dionysus*, ed. Thomas H. Carpenter and Christopher A. Faraone (Ithaca: Cornell University Press, 1993), 15.

6. This interpretation was inspired by Camille Paglia, *Sexual Personae: Art and Decadence from Nefertiti to Emily Dickinson* (New York: Vintage Books, 1991). Paglia argues that Euripides' *Bacchae* is the parable for the sexual revolution of the sixties' generation (102). She also points to the revolution's inherently ambiguous results (98, 227, 231, 269). See also Paglia's *Sex, Art, and American Culture: Essays* (New York: Vintage Books, 1992).

7. I based parts of this section on "Hans Werner Henze: Music and Mission," a paper that I presented with Richard Norton at the Annual Meeting of the Western Association of German Studies, Wichita, Kansas, October 3, 1980. I based the brief overview of Henze's life and work on the following sources: Peter Heyworth, "Henze and the Revolution," *Music and Musicians* 19 (September 1970): 36–40; Robert Henderson, "Hans Werner Henze," in *The New Grove Dictionary of Music and Musicians*, vol. 8, ed. Stanley Sadie (London: Macmillan, 1980), 489–96; Hans Werner Henze, *Music and Politics: Collected Writings, 1953–1981*, trans. Peter Labanyi (Ithaca: Cornell University Press, 1982); and Ian Strasfogel, "The Other Side of the Churchyard Wall," *Opera News* 51 (May 1987): 30–33.

8. Hans Werner Henze, ed., *Zwischen den Kulturen: Neue Aspekte der musikalischen Ästhetik I* (Frankfurt am Main: S. Fischer Verlag, 1979), Hans Werner Henze, ed., *Die Zeichen: Neue Aspekte der musikalischen Ästhetik II* (Frankfurt am Main: Fischer Taschenbuch Verlag, 1981); and Hans Werner Henze, ed., *Lehrgänge—Erziehung in Musik: Neue Aspekte der musikalischen Ästhetik III* (Frankfurt am Main: Fischer Taschenbuch Verlag, 1986).

9. See Hans Werner Henze, ed., *Neues Musik Theater: Almanach zur 1. Münchener Biennale* (Munich: Carl Hanser Verlag, 1988), 7–13, 181.

10. Henderson, "Henze," 494.

11. Henze, *Music and Politics*, 178.

12. Ibid., 138.

13. Among nineteenth- and twentieth-century operatic essays on the roles of art and the artist, *Elegy* thus joined Wagner's *Meistersinger*, Berlioz's *Benvenuto Cellini*, Pfitzner's *Palestrina*, Krenek's *Jonny spielt auf*, Hindemith's *Mathis der Maler*, and Schoenberg's *Moses und Aron*. See Chapter 6 for an analysis of *Palestrina*, *Mathis*, and *Moses*.

14. Henze, *Music and Politics*, 109–18.

15. Klaus Theweleit sees the theme of death and artistic creativity in Monteverdi's *Orfeo*, the first operatic masterpiece. In Theweleit's strained interpretation, Orpheus deliberately wills the second and fatal loss of Eurydice in order to gain inspiration for his music. See Klaus Theweleit, "Monteverdi's *L'Orfeo*: The Technology of Reconstruction," in *Opera Through Other Eyes*, ed. David J. Levin (Stanford: Stanford University Press, 1993), 147–76.

16. Charles Osborne, *W. H. Auden: The Life of a Poet* (New York: Harcourt Brace Jovanovich, 1979), 254.

17. Henze, *Music and Politics*, 143.

18. For the comments of the composer and librettists on this work, see Hans Werner Henze, "*The Bassarids:* Hans Werner Henze Talks to Paul Griffiths," *Musical Times* 115 (1974): 831–32; Henze, *Music and Politics*, 143–56; and Auden and Kallman, *Libretti*, 679–712.

19. Auden and Kallman deliberately chose an obscure title for the opera. In fact, shortly before the premiere of the opera, Henze had to ask Auden and Kallman "'what the fuck the "Bassarids" means'" (quoted in Robert Craft, "Words for Music, Perhaps," *New York Review of Books* 41, no. 18 [November 3, 1994]: 57n).

20. In referring to Eichmann as banal, I am using the characterization made famous by Hannah Arendt in *Eichmann in Jerusalem: A Report on the Banality of Evil*, rev. and enl. ed. (New York: Viking Press, 1964).

21. Auden and Kallman preferred the first formulation, Henze the second. See Henze, "*The Bassarids*," 831.

22. The quoted phrases are from Marcuse's characterization of Freudian psychoanalytic theory (*Eros and Civilization*, 11).

23. Henrichs, "'He Has a God in Him,'" 24; and E. R. Dodds, *The Greeks and the Irrational* (Berkeley: University of California Press, 1951), 76.

24. Marcuse, *Eros and Civilization*, 131.

25. For the earliness of the "moral climax" of revolution, see Michael Walzer, *Exodus and Revolution* (New York: Basic Books, 1985), 116. For the earliness of the

artistic representations of revolution, see Jean Starobinski, *1789: The Emblems of Reason*, trans. Barbara Bray (Charlottesville: University Press of Virginia, 1982).

26. See Herbert Marcuse, "On Hedonism," in *Negations: Essays in Critical Theory*, trans. Jeremy J. Shapiro (Boston: Beacon Press, 1968), 159–200.

POSTSCRIPT

1. Christian Göldenboog, "On Trust and Traditions: An Interview with Francis Fukuyama," *Deutschland* 2 (April 1996): 28. The quotation summarizes Fukuyama's thesis in *The End of History and the Last Man* (New York: Free Press, 1992).

2. Susan McClary, *Feminine Endings: Music, Gender, and Sexuality* (Minneapolis: University of Minnesota Press, 1991), 105.

3. Michel Foucault, *The History of Sexuality*, vol. 1, *An Introduction*, trans. Robert Hurley (New York: Pantheon Books, 1978), 95–96.

4. See Paul Breines, "Revisiting Marcuse with Foucault: *An Essay on Liberation* Meets *The History of Sexuality*," in *Marcuse: From the New Left to the Next Left*, ed. John Bokina and Timothy J. Lukes (Lawrence: University Press of Kansas, 1994), 41–56.

5. *Daedalus* 115, no. 4 (Fall 1986).

6. A. M. Nagler, *Misdirection: Opera Production in the Twentieth Century* (Hamden, Conn.: Archon Books, 1981), 10, 63. See also Henry Pleasants, *Opera in Crisis: Tradition, Present, Future* (New York: Thames and Hudson, 1989), 29–43.

7. Robert T. Jones, introduction to Philip Glass, *Music by Philip Glass* (New York: Harper and Row, 1987), xiii.

8. Glass, *Music*, 3.

9. Ibid., 29.

10. Ibid., 137.

11. Quoted in Otto Friedrich, *City of Nets: Hollywood in the 1940s* (New York: Harper and Row, 1986), 365.

12. The quotations are from the libretto included in the recording of John Adams, *Nixon in China*, cond. Edo de Waart, Orchestra of Saint Luke's, with Sanford Sylvan et al., Elektra-Nonesuch 9 791772–2, pp. 31, 32, 34, 37.

13. Michael C. Nott, "The Long Road to Versailles," *Opera News* 56 (January 1992): 10.

14. Quotations from the libretto of *Ghosts* are from the Public Broadcasting System telecast of September 14, 1992.

15. Michael Walzer, *The Company of Critics: Social Criticism and Political Commitment in the Twentieth Century* (New York: Basic Books, 1988), 206.

16. Leo Lowenthal, *An Unmastered Past: The Autobiographical Reflections of Leo Lowenthal*, ed. Martin Jay (Berkeley: University of California Press, 1987), 258.

Index

Absolutism, 21, 24, 26, 27, 55; in the baroque, 16, 17, 18, 19, 24, 36, 41; effect on opera, 20

Achille Lauro, The, 204

Adams, John, 11, 201, 203, 205; *The Death of Klinghoffer,* 201, 203, 204–5; *Nixon in China,* 201, 203–4

Adorno, Theodor W., 13, 67, 128, 161; criticism of *Parsifal* (Wagner), 88, 108; praise of *Elektra* (Strauss), 123; *In Search of Wagner,* 88; views of serialism, 158

Aesthetics, 53, 90, 153, 174; and aesthetic existence in *Don Giovanni* (Mozart), 62, 63, 64; in the eighteenth century, 44–45; and Monteverdi, 21, 22, 23; and Mozart, 59, 62; and Schoenberg, 10, 159, 161, 164–65; in the twentieth century, 123, 129, 130, 131

Agee, James, 203

Akhnaten (Glass), 11, 201, 202–3

Alienation: and estrangement, 130, 138; in the works of Schoenberg, 162; in the works of Henze, 174–76

Allegory: *Fidelio* (Beethoven) as, 75; in *Moses und Aron* (Schoenberg), 8, 9, 155; in the works of Hindemith, 8, 9, 143

Ancien régime, 81

Andrea Chénier (Giordano), 69

Anti-Semitism, 87, 110

Apollo, 2, 3, 21, 116

Ariadne auf Naxos (Strauss), 128

Arianna (Monteverdi), 14, 21, 31

Aristotle, 41

Artist-opera: in the classical period, 138–39; in the twentieth century, 2, 8, 128–30, 140

Auden, W. H., 169–70, 175, 176, 179, 181; *Elegy for Young Lovers,* 175; *The Rake's Progress,* 175

Bacchae (Euripides), 10, 169, 171, 179

Bach, Johann Sebastian, 139

Bacon, Francis, 43

Badaoro, Giacomo, 25

Bakunin, Mikhail, 107

Barnet, Miguel, 173

Baroque, 1, 3, 17, 19, 22, 133, 148, 149; period in opera, 21, 76, 138

Bartók, Béla, 126; *Bluebeard,* 126

Bassarids, The (Henze), 167, 169, 175, 176, 179–80, 193; Dionysianism in, 193–97; Dionysus contrasted with Pentheus, 190–93; echoes of psychoanalytic theory in, 113; interpreted as a conflict between Establishment and New Left, 10–11, 170, 171, 199; logocentrism of Pentheus in, 181, 188; Platonism in, 181–84, 190; plot of, 177–79; portrayal of countercultural ideal in, 194–97; role of Dionysus in, 12, 171, 183, 184, 185, 186, 187, 189–93, 195–97; role of Pentheus in, 170–71,

Bassarids, The (continued)
180–89, 195–97; sexual continence of Pentheus in, 181, 183,
186; sexuality of Dionysus in,
191, 195
Bastien und Bastienne (Mozart), 58
Bastille, 5, 64, 67, 83
Beatles, the, 202
Beaumarchais, Pierre Augustin
Caron, 205–6; *La Mère coupable*,
205–6
Beethoven, Ludwig van, 3, 65, 70,
72, 84, 85, 139, 162; *Cantata on the
Death of Joseph II*, 84; compared
with Mozart, 66–68, 69, 76, 78,
80; loyalty of, to republican spirit
79, 80; *Ninth Symphony*, 85. See
also *Fidelio*
Bellini, Vincenzo, 115; *I Puritani*,
115
Benn, Gottfried, 142
Benvenuto Cellini (Berlioz), 130
Berg, Alban, 126; *Lulu*, 126; *Woz
zeck*, 126
Berlioz, Hector, 129, 130; *Benvenuto
Cellini*, 130
Berner, Samuel, 18
Bhagavad Gita, 203
Biblische Weg, Der (Schoenberg),
156
Bildung, 19
Blitzstein, Marc, 170; *Cradle Will
Rock*, 170
Bloch, Ernst, 198
Bluebeard (Bartók), 126
Bohème, La (Puccini), 128
Boito, Arrigo, 3
Bond, Edward, 173; *The English Cat*,
173; *We Come to the River*, 173
Boone, Pat, 202
Boris Godunov (Mussorgsky), 115
Boucher, Maurice, 109
Boulevard Solitude (Henze), 175
Brahms, Johannes, 139
Brandt, Willy, 172

Brecht, Bertolt, 141–42, 154;
Lehrstück, 141
Breuer, Josef, 118
Breuning, Stephan von, 71
Britten, Benjamin, 126; *Peter Grimes*,
126
Brown, Norman O., 168
Bühnenweihfestspiel (consecration
stage play), 93, 110
Burke, Edmund, 135, 206
Burlador de Sevilla, El (Molina), 45
Busenello, Francesco, 32, 36
Byron. *See* Lord Byron

Caccini, Guilio, 14
Cantata on the Death of Joseph II (Bee-
thoven), 84
Capitalism, 11, 43, 91, 96, 106, 107,
108, 206, 207
Capriccio (Strauss), 128
Cardillac (Hindemith), 142
Cassidy, David, 202
120 journées de sodome, Les (Sade), 45
Charcot, Jean-Martin, 126
Cherubini, Luigi, 68
Chou En-lai, 204
Cicero, 5
Civilization and Its Discontents
(Freud), 113
CIVIL wars, the (Glass), 201
Class conflict, 2, 40, 107, 113, 198;
and aristocracy, 3, 4, 5, 12; and
aristocracy in *The Bassarids*
(Henze), 191; and aristocracy in
Don Giovanni (Mozart), 42, 47, 52,
54, 64; and aristocracy in *Fidelio*
(Beethoven), 66, 70, 79, 81; and
aristocracy in the works of Monteverdi, 24, 31, 32, 37, 38, 39, 40;
and bourgeoisie, 70, 73, 74, 81,
172, 175, 176, 198; and commoners, 20, 23, 24, 29, 30, 31, 32,
39, 46, 47, 52, 191; and middle
classes (popular classes), 4, 5, 12,
66, 81; and nobility, 20, 24, 29,

32, 40; and peasants, 9, 50, 150,
151; and slaves, 38, 170, 191, 196;
and working class, 6, 106, 113
Classical period (music), 148, 149,
154, 205
Class structure, 54, 61, 98, 106,
170; in the eighteenth century,
46, 50, 51, 52; in the works of
Mozart, 60, 62. *See also* Class con-
flict
Cold war, 11
Combattimento di Tancredi e Clorinda, Il
(Monteverdi), 29
Communism, 86, 89, 97, 101, 169,
198
Community and Society (Tönnies), 91–
92; theory of *Gemeinschaft* and *Ge-
sellschaft* in, 91–92, 97
Composer's World, A (Hindemith), 143
Concordet, Marquis de, 44
Conrad, Peter, 85
Corigliano, John, 11, 69, 201, 205;
The Ghosts of Versailles, 11, 69, 201,
205–6
Così fan tutte (Mozart), 41, 45, 68
Council of Trent, 130, 131, 134,
136, 137
Counterculture. *See* New Left
Counter Reformation, 8, 130, 131,
132, 137, 138, 151
Cradle Will Rock (Blitzstein), 170
Craft of Musical Composition, The
(Hindemith), 148
Critique of Judgment (Kant), 45
Crockett, Davy, 202

Daedalus (periodical), 200
Dante, 59; *Inferno*, 59
Dantons Tod (Einem), 69
Da Ponte, Lorenzo, 41, 42, 58–59,
64, 67, 68
Davis, Anthony, 200; *X: The Death of
Malcolm X*, 200
Death of Klinghoffer, The (Adams), 11,
201, 203, 204–5

Decline of the West, The (Spengler),
91–92; theory of *Kultur* and
Zivilisation in, 91–92
Dehmel, Richard, 130
De Long, Constance, 203
Deus ex machina, 26, 28, 42, 57, 69
Devils (Penderecki), 126
Devin du village, Le (Rousseau), 58
Dialogues des Carmélites (Poulenc),
69
Dionysus, 2, 116
Discourse on the Origin of Inequality
(Rousseau), 44
Discourses (Machiavelli), 65
Don Giovanni (Mozart), 4, 65, 68,
115, 190, 193, 194; alternative
endings of, 54; aspects of the
tragic hero in, 44; comic aspects
of, 53–58; contrasted with *Le
nozze di Figaro*, 54–55; crimi-
nality of title character in, 56–
57; Enlightenment thought in,
43–44, 53; notion of the prince
in, 55–56; plot of, 47–49; portrayal of social order and class
structure of Seville in, 49–52;
sensuousness in, 51, 60–62; sexuality in, 42, 48, 51, 54, 60; tragic
aspects of, 58–64
Don Giovanni Tenorio, ossia il dissoluto
(Goldoni), 45
Donizetti, Gaetano, 115; *Lucia di
Lammermoor*, 115
Don Juan (Lord Byron), 45
Don Juan (Strauss), 46
Don Juan, ou le festin de pierre (Molière), 45
Dramma per musica, 20
Dunkle Reich, Das (Pfitzner), 130
Dürer, Albrecht, 142

Eichendorff, Joseph von, 130
Eichmann, Adolf, 180
Einem, Gottfried von, 69; *Dantons
Tod*, 69

INDEX

Gender, 50, 54, 78, 114, 168, 195
199; politics in *Fidelio* (Bee-
thoven), 80; relationships in the
Enlightenment, 43; roles in the
works of Monteverdi, 29–30
Georgics (Virgil), 17
Gesamtkunstwerk (total work of art),
87, 109–10
Ghosts of Versailles, The (Corigliano),
11, 69, 201, 205–6
Giordano, Umberto, 69; *Andrea Ché-
nier*, 69
Glass, Philip, 11, 201–2, 204, 205;
Akhnaten, 11, 201, 202–3; CIVIL
wars, the, 201; *Einstein on the
Beach*, 11, 201, 201–2; *Satyagraha*,
11, 201, 203
Glückliche Hand, Die (Schoenberg),
155, 156
Gobineau, Arthur de, 108
Goethe, Johann Wolfgang von, 1,
130
Goldoni, Carlo, 45; *Don Giovanni
Tenorio, ossia il dissoluto*, 45
Gonzaga, Francesco, 1, 14, 15, 19,
21, 23
Goodman, Alice, 203; *The Death of
Klinghoffer*, 203, 204–5; *Nixon in
China*, 203–4
Götterdämmerung, Die (Wagner), 93, 123
Graener, Paul, 139
Graham, Colin, 201, 205
Grünewald, Matthias, 9, 142
Guevara, Che, 173
Guicciardini, Francesco, 16
Gutman, Robert, 88

Handel, George Frideric, 182; *Semele*,
182
Hapsburg, 56
Harmonie der Welt, Die (Hindemith),
143, 149
Harmonielehre (Schoenberg), 155
Harvey Milk (Wallace), 200
Hauser, Arnold, 22

Hearst, Patty, 202
Hegel, Georg Wilhelm Friedrich, 5,
42, 67, 107, 153, 158
Henze, Hans Werner, 3, 10, 12, 166,
167, 169, 170; *Boulevard Solitude*,
175; *Elegy for Young Lovers*, 175;
The English Cat, 173; *Der Floss der
"Medusa,"* 173; *Der junge Lord*,
175; *König Hirsch*, 175; *Madrigal
for Herbert Marcuse*, 173; *Der Ofen*,
172; politics of, 172; *Der Prinz
von Homburg*, 175; serialism in the
works of, 174; *Sixth Symphony*, 173;
Streik bei Mannesmann, 172;
themes of alienation, isolation,
and estrangement in the works
of, 174–76; turn to radicalism of,
173–74; *We Come to the River*, 173.
See also *Bassarids, The*
Hero, heroine: in *Don Giovanni*
(Mozart), 94; in *Fidelio* (Beethoven), 75, 78; in the works of
Wagner, 93
Hindemith, Paul, 3, 8, 9, 129, 130,
140, 146, 159, 165; aesthetic conservatism of, 145, 158, 165–66;
Cardillac, 142; *A Composer's World*,
143; *The Craft of Musical Composition*, 141; expressionist period of,
141; *Die Harmonie der Welt*, 143;
Hin und Zurück, 142; 152; idea of
Gebrauchsmusik of, 141, 152; *Johann
Sebastian Bach: Heritage and Obligation*, 143; *Lehrstück*, 141; *Das Marienleben*, 141, 152; *Mörder, Hoffnung
der Frauen*, 141; neoclassical period of, 142; *Neues vom Tage*, 142;
Das Nusch-Nuschi, 141; *Sancta Susanna*, 141; *Das Unaufhörliche*, 142;
Un terweisung im Tonsatz, 143;
views on hostility between art
and politics, 150–54; views on
role of artist and character of musical art, 147–49. See also *Mathis
der Maler*

INDEX

Weimar Republic, 8, 129, 153, 154,
165, 203
Wilson, Robert, 201; CIVIL wars, the,
201; *Einstein on the Beach*, 201–2
Wordsworth, William, 167
World War I, 8, 129, 130, 139, 141,
165
World War II, 80
Wozzeck (Berg), 126

X: The Death of Malcolm X (Davis),
200

Zauberflöte, Die (Mozart), 4, 68, 72,
73, 78, 128, 190
Zeitoper, 203
Zernan, John, 88